THERE IS NO AJAX

The Art of Blending DHTML, PHP and MySQL

Schien Dong

ISBN   1-4357-7481-0
EAN   978-1-4357-7481-0

Table of Content

Introduction

Software development is an art. Designing web sites and web-based applications that are instantly published and used by everybody on the Internet can be truly fulfilling and potentially profitable.

This book teaches you the techniques and design principles that allow you to build web products within the fraction of conventional timeframe. The process requires no special tools and the products work with nearly all types and all versions of browsers at substantially increased performance.

How is this possible? The Internet has changed drastically in the last decade, and the pace of change only seems to accelerate. New technologies, tools and books are introduced faster than one can count. How can one new to web development ever catch up?

It's true that much has changed in how the Internet is used. Components such as web browsers, networking devices and server software have also gone through major enhancements.

However, the building blocks of the web have not changed much since the dawn of the Internet. The HTTP protocol was first introduced in the late 80s, and went through one major revision in the early 90s, and has since stabilized. Since most Internet applications are HTTP-based, we can safely assume that the basic mechanism of HTTP will never change. If we stick to the timeless fundamentals, our way of building the web will also never expire.

You may find it hard to believe that modern techniques - especially ones illustrated in this book – even work with antique browsers such as Internet Explorer 5.0! Although our goal is not to bring Web 2.0 to a museum, it is important to know and appreciate the sophistication and readiness of Internet technologies that have served us for the past two decades.

Is this book for you?

If your goal is to master the essence of web programming, and build functional applications, you have picked the right book. However, this book will definitely not help you with any certification programs.

You need to be familiar with the syntax of a procedural programming language such as C. Although Java is an object oriented language, its syntax is similar to PHP and JavaScript. If you haven't done any sort of programming, make sure you learn about flow control statements such as conditional branching and loops. You could read the "Control Structures" section in the official PHP Manual:

http://www.php.net/manual/en/language.control-structures.php

If you can follow the above manual, you should have no problem following the rest of this book.

Organization of the Book

People tend to learn faster by following examples. You will see plenty of sample codes that guide you every step of the way. You will also see ample amount of encouragement to question what books teach you – this book included.

Too often I see developers blindly copy and paste broken code snippets, or apply superficial conventions simply because "everyone else does it".

Warning: That everyone else is doing it doesn't mean it is right.

A machine behaves in certain ways not because some book tells it to. There's a rhyme and reason to every component in a system. It is the nature of computing. To see that nature and build it as an integral part of your programming intuition, you first have to experience the outcome of different coding approaches.

Throughout this book, we will be building a few web sites and browser-based applications. There are times when you are presented with seemingly more than necessary information – do not be overwhelmed. The additional information helps you cut through the hypes of "Web 2.0" and "AJAX Applications". After all, they are just a blend of JavaScript, HTML, CSS, PHP[1] and MySQL[2].

Before you picked up this book, you have likely read a few other books in web development. Some teach you basic HTML, some focus on CSS and graphics, some talk about design patterns while others even attempt to

---

[1] Or server-side scripting in general. This book only covers PHP.
[2] Or other relational database systems such as PostgreSQL and MS SQL Server.

convince you that all questions can potentially be formulated as SQL queries. After having finished one of these books, were you at a point of building a fully functional web application? If not, would you consider reading the rest of them to figure out how all these technologies work together?

Let's take a different approach.

Instead of diving into the details of each topic, let's first explore just the essentials of every component and focus on how they are inter-connected. Then, we can work on the mastery of HTML, JavaScript, PHP, CSS and MySQL separately before discussing advanced development topics.

As a comprehensive curriculum for web development, this book starts with the building blocks for developing static websites, namely HTML, PHP and CSS. Then after a thorough discussion on skinning brochure websites, we introduce MySQL and techniques for building data-driven websites. With the help of JavaScript and the magical XHR, we can transform old fashioned web applications into Rich Internet Applications (RIA). The last few chapters are dedicated to building these RIAs.

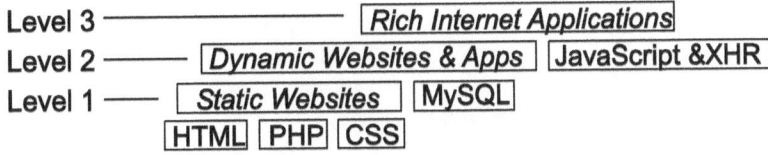

1.0 Understanding the Web

It is safe to assume that you have used a web browser such as Internet Explorer, Firefox, Opera, Chrome or Safari. We will later discuss the anatomy of web browsers, as it's important to understand their roles and the root causes of compatibility issues.

I'd also like to assume that at some point, you have tinkered with some aspect of web development. Maybe you edited the HTML source of certain page, moved around files via FTP, or hacked through the myriad of CSS declarations trying to make a Word Press website look different.

Web sites and web applications function as a symphony of communication protocols, server software, networking hardware, programming languages and so on. To become a master web developer, you must understand the fundamental mechanics of the web. I suggest you put aside any development tools you might have been using, and look beyond programming conventions and techniques. Let's focus on the principals of the web first.

1.1 The "Trace"

My usual approach to figuring out the mechanics of a system is to perform a trace from the entry point, in this case, the point where the user enters a request URL in his web browser. We'll see how his request travels through all the other elements and how he gets his response, namely a rendered web page.

Abstractly speaking, we know somewhere on the inter-web, there's some "server" that handles the request, and generates a response. And the browser then displays the response. But how exactly does this happen?

Machines on the Internet locate and communicate with one another by IP addresses, not by names. Take www.google.com for example: one of Google's servers has an IP address of 193.194.32.104 (at the time of this writing). The address can change at any time, and your computer may not know the latest address. This is one of the reasons why we don't type IP addresses directly in our browser. Other key reasons are human readability and virtual host (will be covered in later chapters).

The process of translating URL strings to IP addresses is called "name resolution". A server that is responsible for resolving domain names such as www.google.com is called a Domain Name Server, or DNS.

Without complicating matters any further at this stage in the book, I ask you to accept the following "facts" for now:

1. Your computer, as long as it has internet access, knows a DNS server
2. An IP address uniquely identifies a machine in the public network
3. Knowing the destination IP address, requests from your browser can somehow find their way to the web server

When I say server, I mean either the software that responds to requests, or the physical machine on which the server software is running. For clarity, we call the latter "host".

With the help of DNS, your browser finds out the IP address of the host, and with the help of routing services, the request arrives at the host.

Usually there's one IP address associated with each physical or virtual network adapter. There can be a number of applications running on the host, all communicating with other parts of the Internet. These network applications share the bandwidth, but on a programming level they have exclusive use to their allocated resource. This is achieved by ports. Web servers typically listen on port 80. If a different port number is used, the request from the browser has to declare it: www.google.com:8080.

Picture the host machine as a parking lot. Each slot in the parking lot has a number – a port number. When the delivery truck, also known as the Apache Web Server, is parked on Port 80, no other truck can park there anymore. A host can have a number of IP addresses, just like a parking lot may have multiple entrances. Regardless how you enter the lot, the truck is still parked on Port 80. In other words, ports on the host machine are valuable real estate[1].

It's also important to understand that an IP address is often not specific enough to identify a website because multiple websites can reside on the same host AND on the same port. In addition to the parking lot analogy, we can see a host as a house. The IP address helps locate the house, and each

---

[1] Virtual machines allow multiple ports; virtual hosts use the same port for multiple domains.

entrance to the house is a port. Each tenant in the house can use the shared main entrance and pretend that he is the sole owner of the place when the pizza delivery guy shows up. The pizza is the web request.

This is exactly how virtual hosts work. In the HTTP request header there's a "host" field that identifies which specific website the server should retrieve. Virtual host is a way to share ports and physical hosts. It is also why typing the IP address in the browser address bar is not the same as entering the domain name. You can observe this more easily on websites that are using shared hosting.

The core functionality of a web server is very basic. It returns the content of a file that is requested in the URL.

For example, http://www.google.com/intl/en/about.html asks for a file named about.html that's located in the /intl/en/ directory. If the server fails to locate such file, it returns a "404 – Page Not Found" error page, which you have undoubtedly seen before.

In the file name component is not specified in the request URL, the server uses the default home page which is specified in server settings. The default page, such as index.html, index.php, default.aspx, etc., can be omitted from the request URL.

It's important to understand that domain name by itself is not a complete request. Even when you omit the file name[1], there should still be a forward slash (/) separating the domain and file name.

Type www.google.com in your web browser and look at the address bar when the page is loaded. You'll see the slash is automatically added. This correction is done by most modern web servers.

Often times, the server does not directly return the content of the request file. Based on the file extension, the server handles the files differently. Image files (.jpg, .png, etc.) and plain HTML files are directly returned. Along with the response content the server sends the Content Type in the response header, telling the browser how to deal with the response.

For example, the Content Type for landscape.jpg is image/jpeg. The Content Type for index.html is text/html.

---

[1] Technically it's the resource name, as the server does not always just return a file.

I need to stress the importance of seeing this as a two step process. At first, the server needs to know how it deals with the file. This is indicated by the file name extension. The extension to server handling mapping is called a MIME Type. The concept of file is lost in the server response. It is just "content". The browser doesn't look at file extension in a server response. It follows the Content Type response header.

Plain HTML files and images are usually returned directly, and therefore they are referred to as "static resources". In other words, the server doesn't have to "think". It simply regurgitates the content.

If you have an image file, or a HTML file on your local hard drive, and you open them in a browser using the local file path, e.g. C:\sites\index.html, you'll see the response the same as hosting and requesting the file from, say, http://www.mydomain.com/index.html. The content type determining process in this case is very different! The browser looks at the file extension and asks the operating system (Windows, Linux, Mac OS, etc.) for file association. The browser installers usually create such associations, so that HTML files are assumed to contain text/html content. It just so happens that web servers have the same setup for static files. I cannot stress enough times, that when an image loads under the URL www.mydomain.com/banner.jpg, it is NOT because your computer maps .jpg files to the image/jpeg content type.

Some file contents are not returned as is by the server. They are not static. They are dynamic. PHP scripts fall in this category. The server is configured to treat .php extensions as application/x-httpd-php, a MIME type the web server doesn't natively understand unless the server is otherwise extended in functionality. The PHP handler is a module that is embedded in Apache[1]. It is up to the PHP handler's to return the content type, as it has taken over the control of the web server. As a matter of fact, a PHP script has significant control over the response header, so a .php "page" could be a text/html page, or an image/jpeg photo, or anything it needs to be.

Again, the file extension only matters to the server and the browser only cares about the content type, which is provided by the response header, which is further determined by server, or manipulated by server-side scripting languages like PHP on behalf of the web server.

---

[1] For now we ignore the technical details of such extension. If you're curious, search for CGI and SAPI.

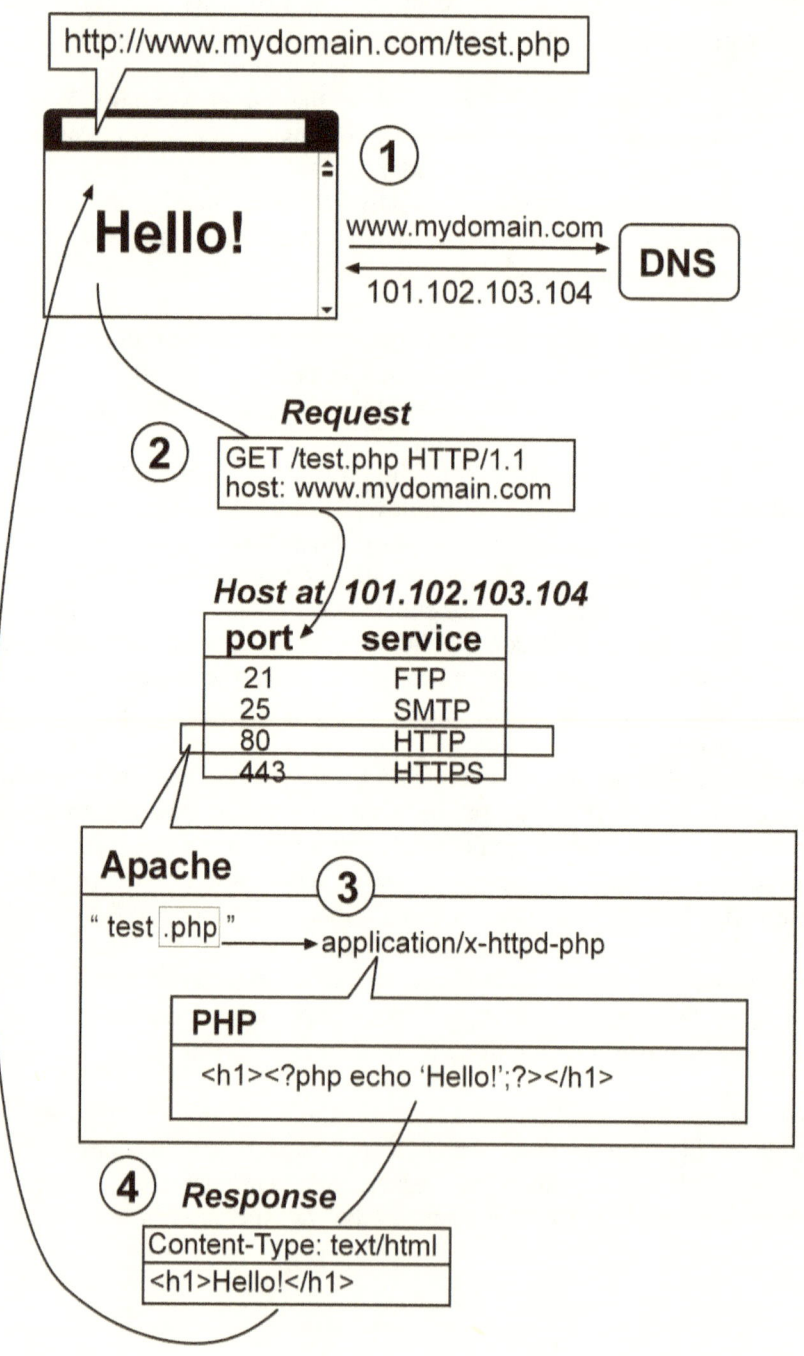

http://www.mydomain.com/test.php

Hello!

(1)

www.mydomain.com
101.102.103.104

DNS

Request

(2)
GET /test.php HTTP/1.1
host: www.mydomain.com

Host at 101.102.103.104

port	service
21	FTP
25	SMTP
80	HTTP
443	HTTPS

Apache
(3)

" test .php " ────► application/x-httpd-php

PHP

<h1><?php echo 'Hello!';?></h1>

(4) **Response**

Content-Type: text/html
<h1>Hello!</h1>

Now go to a web site you often visit, and use the above diagram to trace your request. Ask yourself the following questions:

1. What is the IP address of the Host?

You can go to the command prompt[1] and type in:
```
ping www.domain.com
```

In the above line, replace "www.domain.com" with an existing domain. For example, "www.google.com". Not all servers respond to pings, though the output gives away the IP address of the target server.

2. What are the typical URL structures of the web site?

Click around the web site and look at your browser address bar. Do links have extensions such as .php, .aspx, .jsp? Or the pages are static content and the extensions are .htm or .html? Is there a question mark somewhere in the URL?

3. What are the content types of the web pages?

Use an online tool such as http://web-sniffer.net/ to look at both the Request and Response headers. Isolate the "GET" and "Host" fields in the request headers. Look at the Content-Type in the response header. While you are at it, see whether the server response header also reveals the type of server the web site is running on.

1.2 Setting up Apache and PHP

In this section, we will set up a web server on your computer, so that you don't need Internet connectivity to develop web applications. Localizing the development environment has many benefits, which you will naturally appreciate once you start to deploy your product on a remote server.

If you look at the "Trace Diagram" in the previous section again, there's nothing that says the web browser and the server cannot be on the same machine. Every computer has a special loop back IP address to call itself: 127.0.0.1. On most operating systems, the hostname "localhost" is also bound to 127.0.0.1. Once you have your web server (Apache) running, you

---

[1] "Terminal" in Linux and Mac OS

will be able to reach your local web content by entering http://localhost/ in your browser.

If you just want to set up Apache and PHP[1], you can follow one of the hundreds, if not thousands of online configuration guides. There are even all-in-one packages that take care of all the installation tasks. As much as I want to give you a development environment / laboratory / playground, I want the process of server installation harness the concepts that are explained in Section 1.1.

Assuming you don't already have a local web server running, go to http://localhost/. After a bit of wait, the browser gives up and complains about the server not being available. Some browsers might try to correct the URL by submitting the term "localhost" to their default search pages. In any case, this is well expected, as we don't have a server running locally. To be more exact, the browser tried to establish a network connection from 127.0.0.1 to 127.0.0.1 on Port 80, but no program is listening or responding to that port.

Now download and install the Apache server. The official name is Apache HTTPd. Web servers communicate in the HTTP protocol, and the letter D stands for "daemon", which is a running process. In the context of server applications, this daemon actively listens on the port that's associated with its protocol. For example, an FTP server process is commonly called FTPd.

The official web site for the Apache HTTP Server Project is located at http://httpd.apache.org.

Installing Apache on Windows is a straightforward process. I don't want to impose my specific way of setting up Apache on you, but as a word of warning, using the default settings will set your Apache folder to an inconvenient location – something like C:\Program Files\Apache Group\Apache Server. I do a lot of work on the command line, and cannot be bothered with long directory names. So I set the target directory to C:\apache2.

The Apache installer, regardless of the operating system, does essentially three things. It copies the files to the target directory. It registers Apache HTTPd as a service (or daemon), and it starts the service.

---

[1] Usually MySQL is also part of the set up. For the sake of simplicity, we'll set up MySQL later.

If you have any other program running on Port 80, the service registration will fail. The top three reasons Port 80 is blocked are:

1. An Apache server is already running on Port 80
2. Another web server, such as IIS, is using Port 80
3. Check if your Skype is running

Keep in mind, it is just a *convention* that HTTPd runs on Port 80. You can make Apache run on most other non-used ports. A common alternative is Port 8080. For the same reason, the chat program Skype scans ports that are not in use during initialization, and it often lands on Port 80.

Make sure **none** of the web servers or Skype is running during Apache installation. If you're running Windows Vista or Windows 7 and have user access control (UAC) enabled, run the installer as administrator, or the UAC will interfere with the service registration.

On Windows, the Apache folder contains typically the following subfolders:

bin – executable files
conf – configuration files
logs – default log file directory
htdocs – default server content root, maps to / of the server

On Linux, these folders are mapped to different locations:

bin/httpd.exe – /etc/init.d/apache2
conf/httpd.conf – /etc/apache2/sites-available/default
logs – /var/log/apache2/
htdocs – /var/www/

Upon successful installation of Apache, the HTTPd service should be running and listening on Port 80. Go to your browser again, and type in http://localhost/.

If Port 80 is blocked during an Apache installation on Windows, the NT service that runs the web server will fail to register. If this happens, you have to manually register the service by going to the command prompt:

```
> cd \apache2\bin
> apache -k install -n ApacheServer
> apache -k start
```

The first link switches the working path to the Apache executable directory. Change the path accordingly if your Apache is installed elsewhere.

The file that runs the Apache server may be *apache.exe* or *httpd.exe*, depending on the version. Run the one you have with the -k switch to indicate the service mode and the -n switch to specify a service display name. You can use a friendlier service name such as MyWebServer or "My Apache Server" (with quotation marks to enclose the spaces).

After registering the service you can start it by entering the 3rd line in the above script.

Once the service is running, go to the localhost on your browser. If for any reason your web server is not responding, check the content of the error log. The error log is usually located at the *log* folder under the name *error.log*.

Your task now is to modify the content of this web page. First locate the file that is responsible for the content. Since the URL http://localhost/ doesn't specify a file name, the directory is in the web root, i.e. htdocs/, and the file is the default index page. In the case of a freshly installed Apache server, we are looking at index.html.

Change the file content in index.html. Save the file and reload the page in your browser. Make sure you see that changes.

In some versions of Apache the default starting page is a collection of index pages. If this is the case, delete all the files in the htdocs folder (not the folder itself) and create index.html. If you use Notepad to create the file on Windows, use quotation marks around the file name, e.g. "*index.php*" instead of just *index.php*, so that the file is saved with the proper php extension. Failing to quote the full filename will save the file as *index.php.txt*.

Now change the file name from index.html to index.php. The file manager in your operating system such as Explorer or Finder tends to hide the file extensions. Make sure index.html is not changed to something like index.php.html. In Windows explorer, there's a setting for "hiding file extensions for known filenames". Disable this setting first before you can view and change file extensions properly.

Reload your browser again. The original page is gone. In place is a list of files. One of the listed files should be index.php.

By default, Apache returns the directory listing if the default page (index.html) is not found in the requested directory. One of the three parts of setting up PHP is to set index.php to be one of the default pages.

Edit the httpd.conf file and locate the following line:

```
DirectoryIndex index.html
```

Change it to:

```
DirectoryIndex index.php index.html
```

Notice the order of files matters. In the above configuration, the server looks for index.php first. If no such file exists, it then retrieves index.html.

Every time you change the server settings (e.g. httpd.conf) you need to reload Apache for the changes to take effect. After reload, refresh the browser. You should see two possible outcomes. Depending on the version of Apache you have installed, you either see the content of index.php, as if it's the same as index.html, or you are prompted to download index.php as some unknown file type. In the former case, Apache sets the default content type to be text/html. At this point, Apache doesn't know how to handle .php files.

I will explain what exactly PHP is in later chapters. It is similar to an HTML document, except that the page content can be dynamically calculated. For example, you could write an HTML page with the following content:

```
<div>Today is December 25, 2011.</div>
```

Every day, your web page goes out of date, and you need to modify the page with the new date stamp.

The PHP script tells the server to generate the content. Your browser still gets the HTML code like the above, except you only need to write the script once:

```
<div>Today is <? echo date('F j, Y');?>.</div>
```

Look at Step 3 in the Trace diagram. Apache passes the control to PHP, and PHP spits out the text in the script unchanged, until it enters the <? ?> tags. PHP uses the instructions inside these tags to calculate the HTML content. It then gives back the generated content to Apache. Apache then sends the response back to the browser, as illustrated in Step 4 in the Trace diagram.

We need to load the PHP module in Apache. First read the following documentation and pick the right version of PHP to download:

http://php.net/manual/en/install.windows.manual.php

In short, you should pick the **thread-safe** version that's compiled in **VC6** if you run PHP on Apache.

Add the following line to httpd.conf:

```
LoadModule php5_module c:\windows\php5apache2.dll
```

Technically you may add the above line anywhere in the file (except in virtual host containers). However, the default conf file already loads a number of modules. Locate the section where the modules are loaded and add the above line. This organizes your modules better.

If your PHP files are not located in C:\Windows, copy the following files to the Windows folder:

```
php5apache2.dll *
php.ini
php5ts.dll
...
```

Different servers use different extension methods and therefore require different modules. Even within the Apache product line, a specific handler file needs to be picked. It could be *php4apache2.dll*, *php5apache2.dll*, *php5apache2_2.dll*, *php5apache2_filter.dll*, etc. When in doubt, copy over all the dll files that look like a handler.

The default config file, *php.ini*, is optional for PHP to run. The PHP package contain 2 sample files, one for development, one for production. You may rename the development file and copy it to the Windows folder.

1.0 Understanding the Web

If you cannot locate any Apache handlers in the PHP package, you may have downloaded the wrong file. Use the thread safe version and you shall have all the files.

Now the PHP module enables Apache to handle a MIME type named application/x-httpd-php.

Next we need to tell Apache to treat .php files as PHP files. This seemingly redundant step is necessary. PHP files are not always called .php. Sometimes extensions like .php3 and .php5 are used. At times, .php files are disguised as other extensions, too. Add the following line in httpd.conf that binds .php to the PHP handler:

```
AddType application/x-httpd-php .php
```

PHP is now enabled in your Apache server. To test whether it works properly, change the content of index.php to the following:

```
<?php
phpinfo();
?>
```

Reload the server (as you have made changes to httpd.conf), and refresh the browser. You should see the following page:

PHP Version 5.2.11

System	Windows NT CAVE 6.1 build 7600
Build Date	Sep 16 2009 19:39:11
Configure Command	cscript /nologo configure.js "--enable-snapshot-build" "--enable-debug-pack" "--with-snapshot-template=d:\php-sdk\snap_5_2\vc6\x86\template" "--with-php-build=d:\php-sdk\snap_5_2\vc6\x86\php_build" "--with-pdo-oci=D:\php-sdk\oracle\instantclient10\sdk,shared" "--with-oci8=D:\php-sdk\oracle\instantclient10\sdk,shared"
Server API	Apache 2.0 Handler
Virtual Directory Support	enabled
Configuration File (php.ini) Path	C:\Windows

In sum, there are three key steps in setting up PHP in any web server:

1. enable the PHP handler
2. map the MIME type of .php files to application/x-httpd-php

3. set index.php as the direct index page (aka. default page)

You may have heard of the acronym LAMP, which stands for Linux, Apache, MySQL and PHP, and its Windows counterpart WAMP. MySQL will enter the picture at later chapters. The database is not tied to the server-side scripting engine such as PHP, and PHP doesn't only run on Apache. Apache has been ported to many operating systems and is definitely not coupled to just Linux or Windows.

2.0 HTML Basics

The Hyper-Text Markup Language (HTML) is the lingua franca of the web. A web page is an HTML document. It doesn't matter what server-side language is used, or what objects are embedded. When you load a page in a web browser and view the page source, you see HTML code.

2.1 HTML Syntax

First of all, let's explore some basic characteristics of HTML.

Line breaks and spaces are treated as spaces. Multiple spaces are condensed to one.

In the Apache web root folder (htdocs), open the default index page (index.htm or index.php) in a text editor. Type in the following lines:

```
This is Line 1.
This is Line 2.
```

Now load http://localhost/ in your browser. You'll see the above page is rendered as following:

```
This is Line 1. This is Line 2.
```

HTML uses tags to mark different parts of a document, so that the browser renders them differently according to the attributes of a tag. In the above example, the line break tag is needed to separate the lines:

```
This is Line 1.<br>
This is Line 2.
```

Tags are written in angled brackets. Here's another example use of tags:

```
<div id="menu" class="navigation"> Menu <span>Items</span>
</div>
```

HTML tags usually come in pairs. Each pair of tags contains a piece of the document. The marked up section is called an "element" or "node"[1] in the document. You can wrap one or more nodes in another pair of tags, creating a new "parent node" for all the "child nodes". Note that the node is a logical concept. Tag pairs are used to express a node. In the above example, the entire line represents a node with the content:

```
Menu <span>Items</span>
```

And the content of the node represents the plain text "Menu" and another node, whose content is "Items", denoted by the pair of *span* tags.

The first tag in the pair is called the opening tag. Each opening tag has a corresponding closing tag. The closing tag begins with a slash followed by the tag name. For example, the closing tag for <div> is </div>, and the closing tag for <p> is </p>.

Important: Some tags do not have closing counterparts. Each of these tags denotes a node by itself. These tags (and their represented nodes) are called "empty elements".

```
<br>     <img src="logo.png">     <input name="email">
```

I know many developers who have worked with XML have the misconception that all tags need to be closed, and that a tag pair can be condensed to one if there is no content. This is wrong, because HTML is not XHTML. XHTML applies the XML syntax to HTML, meaning in terms of functionality, XHTML documents are like HTML documents, except that they follow the XML syntax. HTML is not XML.

```
Wrong: <img src="logo.png"></img>
Wrong: <img src="logo.png" />
Wrong: <div id="banner" />

Correct: <img src="logo.png">
Correct: <div id="banner"></div>
```

Also remember, the first tag that's opened is the last tag that is closed:

```
<div> <span> <a>Link</a> </span> </div>
```

---

[1] "Node" and "Element" will be used interchangeably throughout this book.

And one last note about syntax: keep all tag names and attribute names in lowercase. If you have the following bad habits, it's time to drop them now:

```
Wrong: <DIV>Test</DIV>
Correct: <div>Test</div>
```

```
Wrong: <a onClick="alert('a');">Test</a>
Correct: <a onclick="alert('a');">Test</a>
```

The opening tag can carry additional information that describes the behavior and appearance of the enclosed element. For example:

```
<div style="margin:0;" onclick="alert('a');" id="a" class="t">
```

In the above example, "style", "onclick", "id" and "class" are attribute names. Attribute values are declared in double quotation marks, separated by the equal signs. The order of attributes doesn't matter. You can declare *style* before *onclick* and vice versa. Attributes should not have the same name. For example, the following declaration is incorrect:

```
<div id="x" id="y">...
```

An element can have only one ID, so the above node has to take either "x" or "y". The event handler, on the other hand, can be combined:

```
<div onclick="alert('a'); alert('b');">...
```

Before discussing the attributes in more details in later chapters, I'd like to give you a quick taste of how they enhance HTML files with expressive graphics (CSS) and rich user interaction (JavaScript).

In the past, the look of an element is controlled by its encapsulating tags or special (now deprecated) attributes. For example:

```
<span><font color="red"><b>Red Text</b></font></span>
```

The Cascading Style Sheet (CSS) provides a powerful mean to describe the appearance of an HTML node. The above line can be converted to the following:

```
<span style="color:red;font-weight:bold;">Text</span>
```

This is called "inline styling".

In practice, many elements share similar appearance traits. Some element also inherits the look from its parent node. The "id" and "class" attributes allow CSS to generalize, match and externalize the definition of styles. Consider the following lines of code:

```
<style>
      #menu{border:solid 1px; padding:10px;font-size:20px;}
      .item{text-decoration:underline;color:#ffab00;}
</style>
<div id="menu">
      <span class="item">Home</span>
      <span class="item">About Us</span>
      <span class="item">Help</span>
</div>
```

The pound sign (#) tells the browser to style the element with an ID "menu" with a border and 10 pixels of content padding. The font size of this element and all its child nodes is 20 pixels.

The dot (.) matches the style by class name. The three elements inside the *menu* node are styled to have the orange text color and underlines.

#menu and *.item* in the above example are called CSS selectors. We'll learn more about CSS in later chapters.

With the help of JavaScript, an HTML element also responds to various events. For example, the *onclick* attribute specifies the action that needs to be taken when the element is clicked on:

```
<div onclick="alert('Hi!');"> Click me </div>
```

You may have noticed the "Click me" text doesn't look like it can be clicked, but it can be. The look is controlled by CSS. For now we focus on the event handling.

The actions you perform on the web page are called "client-side events". Event handlers that are declared as tag attributes take the prefix on–. Their names are usually self-explanatory. For instance, *onclick*, *onmouseover*, *onmouseout*, *onkeyup*, *onkeydown*, *onfocus*, *onblur*, *onscroll*, *onresize*, etc.

Again, these are attribute names, and should be written in all lower case. Do not write them as onMouseOut, onKeyUp and so forth[1].

Now that we've had a glimpse of the interaction between HTML, CSS and JavaScript, let's put them together in our first properly structured HTML document. You can either save it as index.php in the htdocs folder, or save it under a different name.

```
<html>
<head>
        <title>Test</title>
        <style>

        </style>
</head>
<body>

        <div>some text here...</div>
        <button>Button</button>

        <script>

        </script>
</body>
</html>
```

An HTML document has a "head" and a "body" section. Both sections are enclosed by the <html> tags.

The *style* and *script* blocks may be declared in many locations. For reasons I'll explain later, it's optimal to place the script blocks at the bottom of the page, right before the *body* tag closes.

The *style* blocks can also occur in the HTML head, or even almost anywhere in the body, but it's best to declare styles before the content, i.e. at the beginning of the page.

---

[1] Java programmers have a strong tendency to do so because of the Java camel case naming convention. Attribute names are not function names!

We have already seen, from a previous example, how HTML tags label a document into elements. The opening tags for each element carry attributes that tell JavaScript and CSS handle events and appearance respectively. As much as you should pay attention to the interplay of these components, it's equally important that you focus on their separation of duties.

Load the file you just edited in a browser. You'll see the page title is set to "Test", and the page content has one line of text: "some text here", followed by a button. Change the code to the following:

```
<html>
<head>
        <title>Test</title>
        <style>
        #header{font-size:20px;color:#ff0000;}
        </style>
</head>
<body>

        <div id="header">some text here...</div>
        <button onclick="sayhi();">Button</button>

        <script>
        function sayhi(){
            alert('Hi');
            alert('Bye');
        }
        </script>
</body>
</html>
```

As you see, both the inline styling and inline JavaScript can be relocated outside the attribute value quotes. This allows great programming flexibility. You can also store these declarations in external files so that different HTML pages can share common look and behavior.

```
<html>
<head>
        <title>Test</title>
        <link rel="stylesheet" href="mystyles.css"
type="text/css" />
```

```
</head>
<body>
    ...
    <script src="myscripts.js"></script>
</body>
</html>
```

The last two examples may seem redundant – they focus on different matters. The first example explains "who does what". HTML marks the sections; CSS pretty up the elements; JavaScript deals with the events and actions. The second example stresses on "what goes where". It puts the style and script blocks in the context of a HTML document in its entirety.

2.2 Tags with Special Abilities

HTML tags share many common traits. For example, each element can declare its own unique ID; specify a class name for styling. They also share most of the events such as *onclick*. The most "plain" tags are <div> and <span>. All they do is to form a conceptual container by enclosing content in their tag pairs. <div> breaks the content into a new line whereas <span> keeps the content flow uninterrupted. The difference between <div> and <span> will be explained further when we study CSS.

There are also other vocabularies in the HTML language – tags other than <div> and <span>. These tags are like specially shaped pieces in a Lego set that serve special functions.

For a complete list of standard HTML tags and their complete attributes, please refer to an online HTML reference such as www.w3schools.com.

The Anchor Tag – <a>

The <a> tag defines an "anchor". Maybe it is better explained as a combination of two names: "link" and "bookmark".

The most common use of <a> is to place a link to another page:

```
<a href="about.php">About Us</a>
```

or another web site address:

```
<a href="http://www.google.com/">Search</a>
```

There are two common mistakes associated with the URL format. One is the use of relative location. If the page that contains the <a> tag is called *index.php*, and the target *about.php* is located in the same directory, a relative path is recommended, as illustrated in the above example.

When referring to an external page, however, "http://" must be added to the full address. If your domain is called mydomain.com, the link

```
<a href="www.google.com">Search</a>
```

will point to a non-existent page: mydomain.com/www.google.com/

Sometimes you'll want to open the target document in a different window. This is done through the *target* attribute:

```
<a href="http://www.google.com/" target="_blank">Google</a>
```

The <a> tag is a common container for menu items as well as other elements the user can click, known as "affordances":

```
<a onclick="alert('Hi');">Say Hi</a>
```

Sometimes both a target link and event handler is given, but the event handler suppresses the link:

```
<a href="sayhi.php" onclick="alert('Hi');return false;">
Say Hi
</a>
```

In the above example, if JavaScript is enabled in the browser, click on the Say Hi link will prompt a message box. If JavaScript is disabled, the page is then redirected to sayhi.php, presumably a page that displays the same greeting that's otherwise displayed in the JavaScript call. We'll discuss more of this later. I'm throwing this here because you might have seen it in other places before.

The second use of the <a> tag is to place a bookmark, or a "landing target". Imagine you have a very lengthy page of Terms and Conditions (terms.php), and you want to jump into a specific section from an external page:

```
...
<div>2. Copyright Information</div>
...
<a name="warranties"></a>
<div>7. Warranties</div>
...
```

Now you can link to Section 7 directly from within the page:
```
<a href="#warranties">See "Warranties"</a>
```

or from an external page:

```
<a href="terms.php#warranties">See "Warranties"</a>
```

The pound sign (#) is also used to denote the current page, forming a "null target link", meaning clicking on the link doesn't really move away from the current page.

```
<a href="#">Back to Top</a>
```

Note clicking on the # link will move your view point to the top of the page, as if a new page is loaded and that you start reading from the beginning.

The <a> tag is also used to implement hover over effects that require no JavaScript. This is done by taking advantage of the *a:hover* CSS selector. We'll revisit this magic ability in later chapters.

Images – <img>

The <img> tag places an image in the document. In its simplest form, the <img> tag finds its image source in the *src* attribute:

```
<img src="banner.jpg">
```

Although the HTML standards require the width and height of the image to be explicitly specified, the browser can figure out the native image dimension automatically. For example, a 320x100 banner may be inserted as following:

```
<img src="banner.jpg" width="320" height="100">
```

If the width attribute has a different value than the actual image width, the browser will automatically scale the displayed image. The omission of the other dimension (e.g. width, height) tells the browser to keep the aspect ratio. For example, the following code implies the height is "50":

```
<img src="banner.jpg" width="160">
```

If you want to comply with the standards, you'll have to calculate and specify the height:

```
<img src="banner.jpg" width="160" height="50">
```

Imagine you are displaying a series of images of slightly different aspect ratios. Perhaps thumbnails of user profile pictures in a forum? You need the images to have the same width, say 100 pixels, and you're okay with slight variations in their heights, as longs as they're not distorted. Still want to comply with the standards? Tough luck. My point is there are times when "being right" and "being correct" have conflict meanings. You'll be making "moral choices" like this from time to time.

The <img> tag carries some attributes that controls its basic appearance. For example, <img> and <a> are often used in conjunction, but the <a> tag automatically places an ugly border around the image. The <img> tag then needs to override the border settings:

```
<a href="index.php"><img src="logo.jpg" border="0"></a>
```

You can also make the text flow around the image:

```
<img src="redcap.jpg" align="left"> Once upon a time...
```

The align="left" attribute makes the image float on the left side of the text. Ideally you'd also want some spacing between the image and the text:

```
<img src="redcap.jpg" style="float:left;margin-right:10px;">
...
```

If you are wondering how to create elements with background images, the <img> tag is not the right tool. We'll explore better ways in the CSS related chapters.

2.0 HTML Basics

Headings – <h1>, <h2> …

The headings tags mark the outline of a document. Section numbers and subsection numbers are typical examples of headings. Browsers have different visual interpretations on what each level of headings should look like. In general, the heading tags are displayed in large, bold fonts with extra margin around them.

The appearance of heading tags can be easily implemented by plain <div> tags. Consider the following code:

```
<h1>Chapter 1</h1>
   <h2>Section 1</h2>
```

And its replacement using <div> and CSS:

```
<style>
.chapter, .section{font-weight:bold;margin-bottom:10px;}
.chapter{font-size:20px;}
.section{font-size:16px;}
</style>

<div class="chapter">Chapter 1</div>
   <div class="section">Section 1</div>
```

The latter produces far more consistent and manageable results.

The reason we still use heading tags is because they give web crawlers like Google bots a cue of the structure of the document. The <h1> tag, in particular, plays an important role in search engine optimization (SEO). Later we'll look at scenarios where the <h1> tag is in the HTML source but displayed differently, if at all, on the rendered page.

Ordered and Unordered Lists – <ol>, <ul>, <li>

The <ol> tag creates an ordered (or "numbered") list; the <ul> tag creates an unordered list, i.e. bullet points. The <li> tag defines a list item inside the list.

Place the following the code in a web page and view it in a browser:

```
<ol>
   <li>Item 1</li>
   <li>Item 2</li>
   <li>Item 3</li>
</ol>

<ul>
   <li>Item 1</li>
   <li>Item 2</li>
   <li>Item 3</li>
</ul>
```

Again, with careful design, the <ul> tag can be implemented with just the <div> tag and proper CSS declaration. One of the benefits of using the <ul> tag is that it provides tag name variety which simplifies the CSS selectors. More discussion on this topic in the CSS related chapters.

Click me! – <button>

Want a button? Use the <button> tag. Like the <a> tag, <button> serves as affordance containers:

```
<button onclick="alert('Hi!');">Say Hi</button>
```

The <button> tag looks differently from the <a> tag, and doesn't take the *href* attribute.

If you see a "native button"[1] on a web page, it could be made of a <button> tag, if not one of the form control elements[2].

Picture in Picture – <iframe>

The <iframe> tag embeds another page inside the current page. For example:

```
<iframe src="http://www.google.com/"
```

---

[1] Buttons that are directly drawn by the browser, not the ones that are emulated by JavaScript and image sprites.
[2] See "Form Controls".

```
width="800"
height="500">
</iframe>
```

Remember to always close the <iframe> tag even though there's nothing in between the tags. Also don't spell <iframe> as <iFrame>. It is not an Apple product!

When you follow the links on the page inside the iframe container the new page loads within. This "stay-in-the-same-page" nature is the key ingredient of many stunts such as cross domain data transfer. It was even used as a predecessor of the XMLHttpRequest Object – a vital component of what we consider today to be "AJAX"[1]. For the same reason, <iframe> is used to implement AJAX file uploaders.

Of the many talents of <iframe>, page layout composition is not one of them. I have seen sites that brutally duck tape iframe views as different sections of a web page. I hope this book stops you from becoming "one of them".

"Neutral" Tags – <div>, <span>

The power of <div> and <span> tags is that they have no special power. Special power comes with side effects. Sometimes we just need generic tags to mark up a section of the content, so that we can apply styling and click handling. Combined with CSS and well crafted image sprites, the <div> and <span> tags can achieve a wide range of visual effects.

"Unnatural" Tags – <object>, <embed>

Before HTML 5 was supported by most modern browsers, web pages had no standard way to display video or dynamically generate graphics and advanced visual effects. Flash objects were commonly embedded in <object> and <embed> tags, depending on the browser[2]. HTML 5 tags such as <video>, <audio> and <canvas> offer a more organic approach. After learning the skills from this book, you'll find picking up HTML 5-specific tags a piece of cake!

---

[1] See "XMLHttpRequest Object" in "There's no AJAX".
[2] <object> and <embed> tags are usually nested to support both IE and Firefox.

2.3 Using Tables

Because of its history, wide misuse and abuse and controversial "ban" in the CSS realm, the HTML table system deserves a section of its own.

First, let's look at how the table tags work. An HTML table defines a grid of rows and cells inside each row. The table starts and ends with the <table> tag. Each row is defined by the <tr> tags. Cells are defined by the <td> tags.

To display the following grid,

```
1  2  3
A  B  C
x  y  z
```

we first write the raw content just like the above, and wrap it in a pair of <table> tags. Then wrap each row with <tr>:

```
<table>
    <tr>1  2  3</tr>
    <tr>A  B  C</tr>
    <tr>x  y  z</tr>
</table>
```

Now per each row, wrap each column, or "cell" with the <td> tags:

```
<table border="1">
    <tr><td>1</td><td>2</td><td>3</td></tr>
    <tr><td>A</td><td>B</td><td>C</td></tr>
    <tr><td>x</td><td>y</td><td>z</td></tr>
</table>
```

The above code generates a table like the following. To make the grid line visible, the border attribute is set to 1:

1	2	3
A	B	C
x	Y	z

For better readability, the code is written in expanded form:

```
<table border="1">
    <tr>
<td>1</td>
<td>2</td>
<td>3</td>
    </tr>
    <tr>
<td>A</td>
<td>B</td>
<td>C</td>
    </tr>
    <tr>
<td>x</td>
<td>y</td>
<td>z</td>
    </tr>
</table>
```

Sometimes a cell can take multiple rows or columns. This is expressed by the *rowspan* and *colspan* attributes:

1	2	3
	B	C
	y	z

```
<table border="1">
<tr><td
rowspan="3">1</td><td>2</td><td>3</td></tr>
<tr><td>A</td><td>B</td><td>C</td></tr>
<tr><td>x</td><td>y</td><td>z</td></tr>
</table>
```

To expand a cell, first remove the cells that are "in the way". Then count the total cells in the original grid. If the expansion is vertical, use *rowspan*; use *colspan* for horizontal expansion:

1	2	3
	B	
	y	z

```
<table border="1">
<tr><td
rowspan="3">1</td><td>2</td><td>3</td></tr>
<tr><td colspan="2">B</td><td>C</td></tr>
<tr><td>y</td><td>z</td></tr>
</table>
```

2.0 HTML Basics   31

The <table> tag itself carries three other important attributes that usually need to be normalized. Normalization means setting explicit values to override the otherwise inconsistent values in different browsers. These attributes are "border", "cellpadding" and "cellspacing". Edit an HTML page and play with these attributes.

Now that you get a hang of the tables, it's time to discuss when it's appropriate to use them. By definition, tables are great for displaying tabulated data. It also comes in handy when you need the content in one cell to "stretch" the conceptual grid, especially when the length of the content is unknown. For this very reason, tables are commonly used to build registration forms, where the form labels and input fields fit in a grid:

First name:	_____
Address:	_____
Phone:	_____

Here's when not to use tables. Tables are not supposed to be used to implement page layouts when imposing a grid makes no sense. Many types of element composition can be better done in CSS.

I know people who take great pride in the fact that their entire web site has no use of tables. Some even use the existence of tables to judge the quality of a website's implementation. I find this too extreme. I call these people the "table Nazi".

The reason we shouldn't implement page layout using tables is not because it is frowned upon, or that it is "impure". It's because from the stand points of content representation, code maintenance and graphical modeling, it doesn't fit.

To make a concrete example, let's look at a typical page header. The following header has a few visual elements: a banner image, a logo and a navigation menu.

If we were to implement the above banner using tables, we'd probably come up with the following nested grid system:

The thick borders represent tables, and the thin lines show cell divisions.

Admittedly, there's no need to place the logo and menu in two rows in a single-column table. We could have declared them one after another. If you have the unfortunate experience of reading some "old fashioned" websites, you'll see the entire site is in one giant table. Inside the table are more embedded tables that further enclose even more tables.

One of the reasons "grid fitting" was so prominent at one point was because people didn't know better. They looked into the source code of one table-based web site, and accepted it as the standard practice. The use of grid has been baked into the graphic design – implementation workflow. Both Photoshop and Dream Weaver offer utilities to slice a page!

The use of tables or more specifically, the imposing of grid has transformed the simple content into a forest of table tags. The logical content contains a logo, the gradient background color (maybe hard to see in this print), a list of menu items and two links for selecting editions. That is three items in total. Inside the menu there are 9 tabs. The code for this content is diluted with <tr>s and <td>s. Such dilution makes it very painful to maintain the code. Every cell you edit is inside a <td>. How many <td>s are there in the row? You don't know. You have to count the number of cells in other rows. Is it inside another table? You don't know. You have to scroll the code up and down, trying to reconstruct the grid lines in your head.

What's worse is when the design of the banner changes. Maybe the logo is moved to one side, the background changed, etc. You'll have to re-slice the banner image again! The process of slicing merges a layered design to a flat image. The use of tables enforces such incorrect flattening.

So when you consider using tables, think carefully. In later CSS related chapters, I'll show you the proper ways to build typical page layouts.

2.4 Form Controls

Form controls include text field, radio buttons, checkbox, and submit buttons. These controls are all variations of the <input> tag:

```
Phone: <input type="text" name="phone">

<div>
Gender:
<input type="radio" name="gender" value="male"> Male
<input type="radio" name="gender" value="female"> Female
</div>

<div>
Age:
<input type="radio" name="age" value="0"> 0-20
<input type="radio" name="age" value="1" checked> 21-50
<input type="radio" name="age" value="2"> 50+
</div>

<input type="submit" value="Submit">
```

Phone: [   ]

Gender: ○ Male ○ Female

Age: ○ 0-20 ● 21-50 ○ 50+

[Submit]

You can change the input type from *radio* to *checkbox* and see how the output changes.

Radio buttons allow one choice in a group. In the above example, there are two groups of radio buttons. Choices within the same group share the same *name* attribute. When you change the radio buttons to checkboxes, make sure you give each <input> a different name.

You can pre-select or check the radio button or checkbox by adding the "checked" attribute.

A non-<input> form control is the drop down list, using the <select> and <option> tags:

```
<select name="country">
   <option value="ca">Canada</option>
   <option value="us" selected>USA</option>
</select>
```

Note the pre-select attribute in a drop down list (also known as a combo box) is "selected", not "checked".

Each variation of these control tags has its own special attributes. You can research online to find out how to mask the password fields, how to tell the browser not to remember entered values and how to make a dropdown into a multi-select menu.

Form controls are usually enclosed in the <form> tag:

```
<form action="formtest.php" method="POST">
   <input type="text" name="phone"><br>
   <input type="radio" name="gender" value="m"> Male
   <input type="radio" name="gender" value="f">Female
   <input type="submit" value="Try it!">
</form>
```

When the "Try It!" button is clicked, the data entered in the form is sent to the page that's indicated by the *action* attribute. If *action* is missing, the data is set to the current page.

Assuming you have entered the phone number "1234" and picked "Male" in the above form. The browser will encode the data as following:

```
phone=1234&gender=m
```

Remember in Step 2 of the Trace diagram, the browser sends a request to the server? When a form is submitted, a new request is generated. The *method* attribute in the <form> tag sets the request method. Common request methods are "GET" and "POST". Request methods are always in all caps.

The request generated by following hyperlinks is GET. For example, the request to load www.google.com looks like the following:

```
GET / HTTP/1.1
```

2.0 HTML Basics   35

```
Host: www.google.com
User-Agent: Mozilla/5.0
...
```

Create a file called formtest.php. Make sure the above code is in a different page, say, form.php. Change the form method to GET:

```
<form action="formtest.php" method="GET">
```

Hit the "Try It!" button. And the following page is loaded:

```
http://localhost/formtest.php?phone=1234&gender=m
```

This is because the server responded to the following request:

```
GET /formtest.php?phone=1234&gender=m HTTP/1.1
Host: localhost
...
```

Now set the form method to "POST" and submit the form again. You'll see form.php is redirected to formtest.php, but the data you entered is invisible.

Here's the request that's set to the server:
```
POST /formtest.php HTTP/1.1
Host: localhost
...

phone=1234&gender=m
```

So far formtest.php is empty. Write the following lines in formtest.php:

```
<pre>
<?php print_r($_POST); ?>
</pre>
```

The <pre> tag is an HTML tag that tells the browser to render the source code as is. Line breaks will be line breaks; multiple spaces stay multiple spaces. It is a convenient way to debug.

Post the form again, and you'll see the following output:

```
Array(
    'phone'=>'1234',
    'gender'=>'m'
)
```

This shows that formtest.php has received the form data, even though it is not showing in the URL string.

Before I conclude the chapter of HTML Basics and move on to PHP, I want you to install two plugins for your Firefox: Firebug and HttpFox.

Firebug extends Firefox to a versatile web development tool. It lets you inspect page elements, debug JavaScript calls and much more. You can get Firebug at http://getfirebug.com/.

HttpFox doesn't have its dedicated web page at the time of this writing. You can easily find it in Firefox's Add-Ons directory. HttpFox monitors and analyzes all incoming and outgoing HTTP traffic between the browser and the web servers. After installing HttpFox, post to the form test page again. And see the request header yourself. Set the form to both POST and GET to experiment.

3.0 Introducing PHP

By now you have come across PHP a number of times. The PHP interpreter runs inside the Apache web server. It "calculates" the response for Apache to return to the browser. To put things in perspective, the following diagram re-illustrates Step 3 in the Trace.

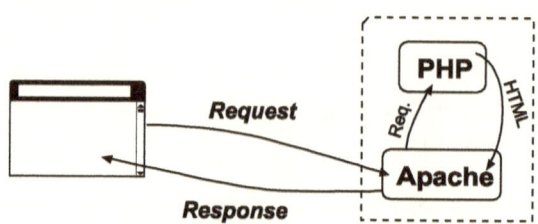

It's important to note that once a web page is displayed, the network connection is no longer needed until the next request. If the HTML content that's generated by PHP (and subsequently returned by Apache) contains affordances to make more requests, such as links to click on, or web forms that collect user input, then more requests are potentially sent to the server. PHP will then calculate more content for Apache to return. This cycle goes on and on until the user stops interacting with the browser. This cycle is regarded as a "user session".

The reason I'm pointing this out even before you're formally introduced to PHP is because I want you to see PHP in **context**. You already know a fair amount of HTML, and you have a local server set up, running Apache and PHP. I expect you keep the above feedback loop in mind when you learn PHP.

If you are completely new to PHP and procedural programming in general, I suggest you read the Language Reference at the official PHP website:

http://www.php.net/manual/en/langref.php

The following sections put you on a fast track. They are by no means replacements of the Language Reference.

3.1 Mixing with HTML

As you have seen in the examples in previous chapters, PHP code can be embedded, or more precisely, interweaved, with HTML page. Run the following script:

```
<html>
<?php
    $now=date('H:i:sa');
?>
<head>
    <title><?php echo $now;?></title>
</head>
<body>
    <h1>The time now is <?php echo $now;?></h1>
</body>
</html>
```

The above code displays the current time in both the page header and content. View the source of the page in the browser. You'll see by the time the browser gets the response, the content is already plain HTML.

In an HTML page, you can enter the PHP mode through the "<?php" tag. Once you're done with your business in PHP, you can escape back to HTML by closing the tag, using "?>". On most servers, the "<?php" tag can be shortened to just "<?".

The context switching between HTML and PHP can be viewed as an unprepared weatherman giving a live forecast. He uses PHP, his magic power to freeze time, so that he can look up the sheets in front of him. His audience is completely unaware of any interruptions in his HTML weather report.

This weatherman also has the ability of speaking to our reality of HTML from his dimension of PHP, using the "echo" command. In the above example, he paused to look at his watch and remembered the exact time. He then recited the time twice in his weather report. Once in the header; another time in the report content.

3.2 Variables

PHP mixes well with HTML. But these two languages are from very different families. HTML is a declarative, markup language. PHP is procedural language.

Imagine an HTML document as a sculpture that conveys certain message. Once it's built, it's built. You can't really have a conversation with the sculpture. PHP, on the other hand, is more like a sculptor you can talk to.

First there are variables. Variables are like pronouns: "you", "he", "it", etc. In PHP, variable names begin with dollar signs ($). The following are some sample variable names:

```
$db, $result, $directory_handler, $file3
```

Variable names cannot contain spaces or arithmetic operators. They can contain numeric symbols as long as they don't start with numerals.

Both variable and function names in PHP are case sensitive. I recommend using all lowercase names to avoid inconsistency and misspelling.

PHP is a loose typed language, meaning the data type of a variable doesn't have to be explicitly declared. The value of a variable can also be changed to a different type at any time. Think variables as Tupperware containers. You can use them to contain water, or grapes, or pushpins, etc. When you dump out the water from the liquid container and put in pushpins, the container becomes a stationary container.

```
  <pre><?php
1 $value="Hello World!";
2 var_dump($value);

3 $value=12;
4 var_dump($value);

5 $value="12";
6 var_dump($value);
  ?></pre>
```

In the above example, we use the <pre> tags to preserve all the line breaks in the output. Inside the PHP tags, each statement ends with a semi-colon. In the above example, each line that's given a line number is a statement. You may have multiple statements in one line. PHP can tell them apart by the semi-colons between them:

```
$value=12; var_dump($value); $value="12"; var_dump($value);
```

The *var_dump* function is very similar to *echo*. It outputs the content of the variable. It also displays the data type of the variable.

Here's the output of the above code:

```
string(12) "Hello World!"
int(12)
string(2) "12"
```

You can see that although PHP variables are flexible to contain different data types, the variables are not ignorant of what they are assigned to. There is still a distinction between integers and strings. If you used *echo* to display the output of Line 3 and Line 5, you'll see they both print out the text "12". Yet it's important to know the internal representations of those variables are different. You can perform arithmetic operations only on numeric types; string functions only work with strings; array functions expect their input to be arrays, etc.

3.3 Strings

In PHP you'll be doing a lot with strings. Sooner or later it'll become apparent to you that the sole point of PHP's existence is reformatting strings. Yes there are some internal calculations, and complex data structure may be summoned and dismissed, but in the end, HTML code is returned to the browser (HTML text are strings), or files are created or modified (file content are expressed as strings in PHP), or some database gets updated (database queries are strings).

Strings are expressed in quotes. Either single or double quotation marks can be used, as long as they pair up:

```
$str1="This is a string";
```

```
$str2='This is also a string';
$str3="I'm a string";
$str4="He says \"$str3\". ";
$str5='You said "Hello"';
$str6="\$str1 says $str1";
```

The above lines show some typical forms of quotations. When a quotation mark literally needs to be in a string, it needs to be escaped, as in *$str4*.

You can get away from quotation mark escaping by using a different set of quotation marks, as shown in *$str3* and *$str5*.

Note the double and single quotations are not completely interchangeable. Look and *$str4* and *$str6*. The values of the quoted variables are in place of the variable names. If you want to print out the variable name literally, you can use a slash to escape the dollar sign as in *$str6*. You can also escape just the dollar sign by using an extra dollar sign:

```
$price=12.95;
$str="The price is $$price"; //The price is $12.95
```

Of course you can use the old fashioned way by concatenating strings and variables. In PHP the concatenation operator is the dot.

```
$str='$str1 says '.$str1."!";
```

If you worked with some other languages such as C++ or Java, the above line is equivalent to the following:

```
str = "$str1 says "  + str1 + "!";
```

Note the single quote always outputs its content exactly as is. And yes, you can mix single and double quotation pairs in a series of string terms concatenated by dots.

You'll see later that the direct value replacement in double quotation marks makes writing SQL queries much easier. Compare the following statements that produce the same result:

```
$query="select * from users where userid=$uid and age=$age";
$query="select * from users where userid=".$uid." and
age=".$age;
```

Another important use of double quote is line breaks. A logical break between two lines can have different underlying implementations. You have already seen that in HTML, the line breaks are represented by <br> tags. In text document, the line breaks are denoted by a special character called "new line", or "\n". Consider the following lines:

```
$str1='Line1\nLine2';
$str2="Line1\nLine2";
```

In the above example, *$str1* has the literal value of "Line1\nLine2" while *$str2* represents two lines: "Line1", line break and "Line 2".

In Windows, line breaks use two special characters: "**ne**w line" \n and "carriage **re**turn" \r.

```
$win_str="Line1\r\nLine2";
```

In the old days, the "enter" key on your keyboard had a different label. It was called "return", which stands for "carriage return". This traces back further to the typewriter days, when starting a new line involved two steps: pushing back the carriage to the left most side, and rotating the carriage so that more paper is fed through. The technical term for "new line" is "line feed", as in feed in the paper. The term "new line" is easier to remember, because it has the letter N. Later models of typewriters automatically combine the steps. When the handle on the carriage is pushed to the left, the carriage also spins to get more paper. This is why carriage return proceeds the line feed.

The carriage return – line feed combo is commonly written as CR LF. Many network protocols are plain text based. Some use LF as line breaks, and some use CR LF.

Single quotation marks have their own merits. For one, there are times you want to quote content literally. When you type \n, you really mean to output a slash followed by the letter N, not to mention you don't have to hold down the "shift" key so often just to enter the double quotation mark.

Benchmarks on most PHP versions show that single quotes are marginally faster than double quotes. In the grand scheme of things, this little gain doesn't really matter, although I do have the habit of using single quote whenever I don't need the double ones.

3.0 Introducing PHP   43

I also want you to think why it is natural to believe that single quote *should* be faster than double quote. Imagine you are getting letters from two mail boxes in your house. Yes, real mails, not emails. One box is the single quote mail box where all the letters are addressed to you. The other box is the double quote box. It contains most of your letters, but from time to time, the neighbor's letters are mixed in. To grab letters from the single quote box, you simply take everything. For the double quote box, you do have to sift through every mail. The double quotation marks also make you a nosy neighbor, meaning whenever you see the neighbor's letter, namely a variable name, you also open the letter and look into its content.

My point is sometimes when you put yourself in the machine's shoes, you can naturally feel what can potentially slow you down.

Now that you can print strings using *echo*, and you know how to declare strings in various ways, what can you do with them? There are some typical string operations in PHP.

You can find the length of a string using the *strlen* function:

```
$str="This is a test string";
echo '$str has '.strlen($str).' characters.';
```

Sometimes you need to replace one type of character in the string with another. The following code adds a slash in front of all single quotes. You'll see later that this is important step when preparing SQL queries:

```
$message="The Conan O'Brian show is at 11 o'clock.";
$sql_message=str_replace("'","\'",$message);
```

You'll see more uses of strings in later chapters, in the context of building web applications.

Heredoc Syntax

The code below outputs text directly:

```
<?
$name='John';
$role='tour guide';
?>
```

"Hi, my name is <?echo $name;?>.
I am your <?echo $role;?> for the day."
<?

What if we want to assign the text to a string variable instead of direct output? We could use a single quote:

```
$name='John';
$role='tour guide';
$paragraph='"Hi, my name is '.$name.".\r\n";
$paragraph.='I am your '.$role.' for the day."';
```

Or double quote syntax:

```
$paragraph="\"Hi, my name is $name.
I am your $role for the day.\"";
```

Escaping special characters can be annoying for large amount of text. The *heredoc syntax* allows us to define our own quotation identifier:

```
$paragraph = <<<YourOwnIdentifier
Hi, my name is $name.
I am your $role for the day.
YourOwnIdentifier;
```

Although you can spell the identifier however you want, it's common to see "EOT", which stands for "end of text":

```
$paragraph = <<<EOT
Hi, my name is $name.
I am your $role for the day.
EOT;
```

When using heredoc syntax we have to be very careful with whitespace. The quoted text won't end until the identifier is reached **at its own line** with **no spaces or tabs in front**. A line break should also immediately follow the identifier that starts the quote.

3.4 Numeric Operations

Addition, subtraction, multiplication and division are expressed in plus (+), minus (-), asterisk (*) and slash (/) signs respectively.

```
$unit_price=20;
$quantity=5;
$shipping=15.75;
$discount_rate=0.1; // 10% off
$tax_rate=0.13;

$subtotal=($unit_price*$quantity+$shipping)*(1-
$discount_rate);
$total=$subtotal*(1+$tax_rate);
```

The code above makes common sense. Values of variables are defined first before being used to calculate the subtotal and total. In practice, the variable values are usually retrieved from a database or user input that's gathered from HTTP GET or POST.

Statements in the above code are called "assignments". They assign values to variables. Note that the equal signs are not the same as the ones in a mathematical equation.

```
$x=5*$y+2;
```

means store the value of the sum of 5 times y and 2 to variable x.

It doesn't mean solving an equation where x is unknown. So the following statement is incorrect:

```
$x-2=5*$y;
```

If you mean to compare the value of x-2 and 5*y, use the double equal signs:

```
($x-2==5*$y)
```

We'll talk more about value comparison in the Boolean Operations section.

PHP offers a wide range of math functions that are documented on this page:
http://ca3.php.net/manual/en/ref.math.php

Realistically, in the context of web sites and applications, you won't see many mathematically expressions in PHP code. The following are the most common "math operations":

```
$x=$x+1; // incrementing values in loops, etc.
$x++; //shorthand for the above
$content=$pages[$index-1]; // array offsetting
```

When a variable is used in the expression on the right hand side and assigned to the same variable, its original value is first retrieved. After the entire expression is calculated, the value is stored in the variable. The original value is then lost. The following code swaps the values of two variables, using the help of a temporary variable.

```
$a=12; $b=47;
$t=$a; // now $t is 12
$a=$b; // now $a is 47

//$b cannot read from $a because $a's original value is lost
$b=$t; // use $a's original value that's stored in $t
```

Another very important operation is modulo calculation, using the percentage sign (%):

```
$a1=0%3; $a2=1%3; $a3=2%3; $a4=3%3; $a5=4%3; $a6=5%3;
```

Values of $a1 to $a6 are 0, 1, 2, 0, 1, 2 respectively. Modulo calculation is useful for confining numbers to a "ring" of values. You can view the base of the mod (the value after the %) as the size of a wheel. This wheel rotates on a belt of a sequence of numbers.

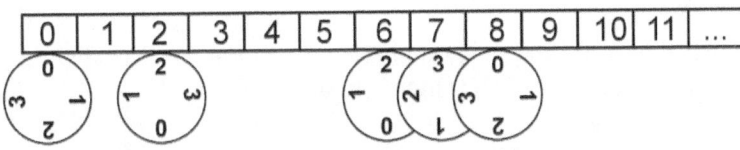

As illustrated by the above diagram, 0 mod 4 = 0, 7 mod 4=3.

3.5 String-Numeral Conversions

You can easily convert a numeric variable to a string representation by concatenating it with a string:

```
$price=20;
$price=$price.'';
```

The second line in the above code "morphs" the numeric variable *$price* to a string. Now you can perform string operations on *$price* such as measuring the string length or taking a substring.

Keep in mind the above conversion loses the original numeric copy. If you want to use the numeric variable again, you should keep the original, and store the string version in a separate variable:

```
$price=20;
$dprice='$'.$price;
```

The D in $dprice stands for "display". It's my own convention. You can name it anything you find convenient.

Conversely, a string that logically represents a number can be easily converted to a numeric variable.

```
$a="12";
$a=$a+0;
$b=5;
$c=$a+$b;
```

The second line in the above example converts *$a* from a string to a numeral. Note the conversion is triggered by the numeric operator (+). If you omit the second line, *$a* will be converted automatically when calculating the value of *$c*.

The technical term for the string-numeric conversion is "Type Juggling". The official PHP documentation has more on this topic:

http://www.php.net/manual/en/language.types.type-juggling.php

Juggling from strings to numbers conveniently sanitizes user input. The following example ensures the input is an integer between 0 and 3:

```
$mode=$_GET['mode'];
$mode=$mode+0;
$mode=$mode%4;
```

You can condense the above codes into one line:

```
$mode=($_GET['mode']+0)%4;
```

3.6 Comments

There are times when you want to write additional lines in the script for your own information. You want the processor of the script to ignore such lines. These lines, or comments, are expressed in certain formats in various languages.

In PHP, comments begin with /* and end with */. For example:

```
$base_price=20;

/*
Starting April 2010, the General Sales Tax (GST) and
Product Sales Tax (PST) are combined to
Harmonized Sales Tax (HST) in Ontario, Canada
*/
//$gst=0.5;
//$pst=0.8;
//$tax=$gst+$pst;

$hst=0.13; // as of 2010; subject to change
$tax=$hst;

$total=$base_price*(1+$tax);
```

The above example also demonstrates another form of commenting – inline comments that begin with two slashes (//). It's common practice to use inline commenting to quickly enable and disable lines of code during debugging. To efficiently comment out a block of code, use the /* */ commenting style.

While we're at the topic, let's also talk about commenting in HTML. HTML comments begin with <!-- and end with -->. For example:

```
<div id="canvas">
...
...
</div><!-- canvas -->
```

The above comment helps identify the pairing of div tags. The browser treats <!-- canvas --> as comment and ignores it.

Note it is a common mistake to use HTML commenting to hide or disable lines of code, as we did with PHP. The following example demonstrates the misuse:

```
<div id="userinfo">
      Name: John Smith<br>
      Gender: Male<br>
  <!-- SSN: 384-12-8493<br> -->
</div>
```

Although the browser doesn't display the now supposedly hidden social security number, the information is still generated, consuming network bandwidth and browser rendering time. Worse, it compromises privacy by failing to hide sensitive information.

You can use PHP commenting to properly comment out HTML code:

```
<div id="userinfo">
      Name: John Smith<br>
      Gender: Male<br>
  <?
  /*
      SSN: 384-12-8493<br>
  */
  ?>
</div>
```

In the above example, PHP considers the HTML code in bold to be PHP code. Normally this causes syntax error because HTML code is not PHP code. However, PHP's multi-line commenting ignores the HTML code.

If you just want to quickly disable some HTML code for the sake of testing or debugging, you can use inline CSS to hide the line:

```
<div id="userinfo">
      Name: John Smith<br>
      Gender: Male<br>
  <span style="display:none;">SSN: 384-12-8493<br></span>
</div>
```

3.7 Boolean Operations

Boolean variables store logical "True" or "False" values. Boolean expressions are like arithmetic expressions, except that they calculate True/False results instead of numeric values.

In PHP, you assign Boolean values using the *true* and *false* keywords, all in lower case, no quotes. For example:

```
$hungry=true;
$thirsty=false;
```

Boolean operators are And (&&), Or (||) and Not (!).

```
$full=!$hungry; // false
$uncomfortable=$hungry||$thirsty; // true
$just_need_a_drink=$thirsty&&!$hungry; // false
$spare_time=true;
$grocery=$spare_time&&($thirsty||$hungry); // true
```

The double ampersand and double pipe signs are called "logic and" and "logic or" respectively. The negation sign is expressed by a single exclamation mark.

Negation has the highest precedence, followed by logic ands and then followed by logic ors. Similar to arithmetic expressions, you can use brackets to override the precedence in a logical expression.

Comparisons of math expressions are also Boolean expressions. The following example evaluates whether a point, expressed in separate variables x and y, is within a bounding box:

```
$left=10; $right=200; $top=40; $bottom=80;
$x=32; $y=43;
$inside=$x>=$left&&$x<=$right&&$y>=$top&&$y<=$bottom;
```

Comparison operators are greater than (>), less than (<), greater than or equal to (>=), less than or equal to (<=), equal to (==) and not equal to (!=).

The following two lines are functionally equivalent:

```
$a=$x!=$y;
$a=!($x==$y);
```

Some very important points to note: The single equal sign is for assigning value to variables from the expressions on their right hand side. The double equal sign is for value comparison. The first line is the recommend form for testing inequalities because it is easier to read. Do not mix the second line with the following use:

```
if (!$f=fopen('test.txt','rt')) ...
if (!$myrow=mysql_fetch_array($rs)) ...
```

Both lines in the above example assign the return value of a function call (*fopen*, *mysql_fetch_array*) to a variable. The true or false of these assignments are evaluated. This is not comparing variables and function calls. The first line opens a file in text mode. If this operation is successful, f will be holding the file handle. Otherwise, the variable holds a *null* value. Similarly, the second line attempts to populate the *$myrow* variable with the next record in a database result set. If the operation is unsuccessful, *$myrow* won't be populated. The assignment gives *$myrow* a *null* value. When a null value is used as a Boolean expression, it is logically false.

You can view the above two lines as shorthand of the following lines:

```
$f=fopen('test.txt','rt');
if (!$f) ...
```

```
$myrow=mysql_fetch_array($rs);
```

```
if (!$myrow) ...
```

In case you are wondering what a *null* value is, it explicitly means nothing. Picture your variables as empty containers. After you have assigned them with values, the containers are full. Subsequent assignments will only replace the containers with updated values, but the containers are still filled. You can empty the containers by assigning them *null*:

```
$a=null;
if (!$a) // not-null is true
```

You may be confused at why both *null* and *false* are, logically speaking, false. How about I tell you the numeric value 0 can be also considered logical false?

True, False and Null are all 0s in disguise. In the eyes of computers, variable values are just data. On most machines, a *byte* is the smallest storage unit. A byte has 8 bits; it is capable of representing numbers from 0 to 255.

If you don't know how binary numbers work, look it up and learn about the conversions between binary and decimal numbers. I'll take a stab at explaining it in an extremely concise fashion.

The number system we use to count, namely the decimal system, is base-10. We use 3 digits to express the number 214 because

$$214 = 2*10^2 + 1*10^1 + 4*10^0$$

If the base of the number system is bigger, we have more expressing power per "digit". 214 in Base 10 is D6 in Base 16, also known as the hexadecimal system.

$$214 = 13*16^1 + 6*16^0$$

When writing hexadecimal numbers, we want each digit to be represented by single digits, because otherwise the sequence 13, 6 would be confusing. Letters from A to F denote numbers from 10 to 15, respectively.

Computers process binary data, so each digit is base-2, expressing numbers from 0 to 1. To express 214 in Base 10, the binary system needs 8 digits:

$$214=1*2^7 + 1*2^6 + 0*2^5 + 1*2^4 + 0*2^3 + 1*2^2 + 1*2^1 + 0*2^0$$

3.0 Introducing PHP

The relation between a byte and its 8 bits can be viewed as a pack of hot dog buns. Each bun can contain 0 or 1 sausage, but you cannot buy individual hot dog buns. They come in bags of 8.

A Boolean value cares only about 0 or 1. If the number is 1, it is true; otherwise it is 0. When PHP checks the logical value of a variable, it checks whether any of the 8 buns contains at least one hot dog. In other words, **the Boolean value of a number is true if the number is non-zero**.
The story with null value is similar but not exactly the same. The difference between null and zero is beyond the scope of this book. One thing for sure, there's no hotdog in the "null" bag of buns that sets the Boolean test positive.

3.8 If-Statements

PHP executes code one line after another. Sometimes we want to conditional run, or not run certain lines of code. Sometimes we need to repeat or reuse certain logic. This is called Control Flow.

The if-statement allows for conditional execution of code fragments. An if-statement has the following format:

```
if (condition) statement_1; else statement_2;
```

The condition is a Boolean expression. If the expression is evaluated as true, *statement_1* is executed; otherwise *statement_2* is executed. Subsequent lines are run regardless. The "else" sub-statement is optional.

```php
<?php
$a=10;
echo "Line 1<br>";
if ($a>5) echo "Line 2A<br>"; else echo "Line 2B<br>";
echo "Line 3<br>";
?>
```

Output of the above script:

```
Line 1
Line 2A
Line 3
```

3.0 Introducing PHP

It's a common mistake to forget the semicolon after the statement before "else". The Boolean expression *always* needs to be in a pair of brackets in an if-statement, regardless how many Boolean terms it contains.

To include multiple lines under either if- or else- branch, use the curly brackets to group the code:

```php
if ($raining){
      bring_umbrella();
      cancel_trip();
} else {
      bring_sunscreen();
      visit_beach();
}

buy_grocery();
```

According to the above pseudo code, different items and actions are taken based on whether it is raining. Groceries, however, has to be bought regardless because the statement is outside of the if-else blocks.

The if-statement is suitable for switching between two choices – left or right, black or white, etc. When it comes to more than two choices, you *could* use nested if-statements. The following code prints out the soup of the day based on the day of week. Cream of mushroom is offered on weekends; Tomato soup is on Monday, Wednesday and Friday. Beef stew is served on Tuesday and Thursday.

```php
if ($day==0||$day==6)   $soup='Cream of mushroom';
else {
      if ($day==2||$day==4) $soup='Beef stew';
      else $soup='Tomato soup';
}
```

The braces in the above example are optional. They're there to make the code easier to read. The above example can be better written using the "switch" statement.

3.9 Switches

The last example in the if-statement section can be re-written as the following:

```
switch ($day){
        case 0: case 6: $soup='Cream of mushroom'; break;
        case 2: case 4: $soup='Beef stew'; break;
        default: $soup='Tomato soup';
}
```

The key components in a switch structure are written in bold in the above example. Note the "break" statements are needed at the end of each "case"; otherwise the statement from the previous case will fall through.

There is no code written to handle *case 0*, but since there's no break after *case 0*, the execution falls through the next case – *case 6*.

The *default* clause is optional. It catches any scenario that hasn't been predetermined. For example, if, for some unexplainable reason, there's an eighth day in a week, tomato soup will also be served on that day because it is in the catch-all clause.

3.10 Loops

PHP offers 4 types of looping structures.

1. The **for**-loop works like a racing track that counts the number of laps.

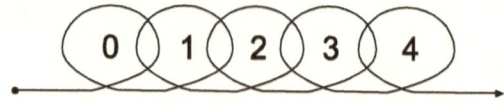

Example:

```
for ($i=0; $i<5; $i++) echo "Line $i<br>";
```

2. The **while**-loop enters the loop conditionally and checks the condition every time for subsequent re-entries.

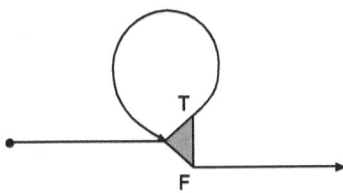

Example:

```
$i=0;
while ($i<5){
        echo "Line $i<br>";
        $i++;
}
```

3. The **do-while** loop enters the loop unconditionally. Exit condition is checked at the end of each loop.

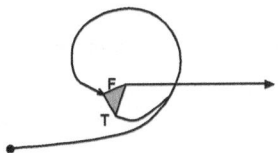

Example:

```
$i=0;
do{
        echo "Line $i<br>";
        $i++;
} while ($i<5);
```

4. The **foreach**-loop works great for iterating through a collection of items. We'll talk more about for-each-loops after learning "PHP Arrays". For the sake of completeness, here's an example that's functionally equivalent to the previous loops:

```
$lines=array(0,1,2,3,4);
```

```
foreach ($lines as $line) echo "Line $line<br>";
```

All 4 examples from above output the following text in a browser:

```
Line 0
Line 1
Line 3
Line 4
```

Regardless of which loop structure you use, a looping mechanism requires the following components:

- an iterator
- a target to loop through
- entrance and/or exit conditions

In the first three loop examples, the loop target is the number range from zero to four. The iterator is the variable i.

The for-loop can be viewed as a short hand of the while-loop. The three sub-statements in its loop condition expression define the initial value of the iterator, exit condition and increments on the iterator.

It's important to ensure that the loop exits, unless of course you intend to have an infinite loop. The following for-loop doesn't ever end:

```
for ($i=0;$i<10;$i--) echo 'a';
```

When using while- or do-while loops, make sure the iterating variable is initiated before entering the loop, and that it is incremented within the loop.

The following example calculates the sum of 1, 2, 3, ..., 100:

```
$sum=0;
for ($i=1;$i<=100;$i++) $sum=$sum+$i;
echo "Total: $sum";
```

And another snippet that you'll see very frequently in later chapters:

```
while ($myrow=mysql_fetch_array($rs)) {...}
```

When you are inside a loop, you can either skip to the next iteration or escape from the loop as a whole. This is done by *continue* and *break* respectively.

```php
$i=0;
while ($i<10) {
      $i++;
if ($i%2==0) continue;
      echo "Line $i<br>";

      if ($i>5) break;
}
```

The above code outputs the following lines:

```
Line 1
Line 3
Line 5
```

Let's examine the code. The iterating variable starts with 0. The first line inside the loop outputs the value of the iterator. Module 2 of this iterator is then calculated and compared against zero. This checks whether the iterator holds an even number. If so, the remaining statements in this loop are skipped over.

The last statement in the loop checks whether the iterator is greater than 5. If so, the loop is terminated even before $i is incremented to 10. The above example is just to illustrate the use of *continue* and *break*. It can be better written using the do-while loop structure:

```php
$i=0;
do {
      $i++;
if ($i%2==0) continue;
      echo "Line $i<br>";
} while ($i>5);
```

It's very important not to call *continue* before incrementing the iterating variable. Otherwise, the iterator will never get updated, making the loop infinitely running.

3.11 Arrays

Until this point, variables have been able to hold only single values. Arrays make it possible to store series of data.

Consider calculating the sum of your grocery bill using simple variables:

```
$orange_juice=5.95;
$milk=6.75;
$chicken_wings=9.99;

$total=$orange_juice+$milk+$chicken_wings;
```

What if you are adding more items? For now let's not care about the names of the item. Even using generic variable names is difficult:

```
$item0=5.95;
$item1=6.75;
$item2=9.99;
$item3=5.99;
$item4=10.00;

$total=$item0+$item1+$item2+$item3+$item4;
```

Using arrays, the above code can be written as the following:

```
1  $items=array(5.95,6.75,9.99,5.99,10.00);
2  $total=0;
3  $count=count($items);
4  for ($i=0;$i<$count;$i++) $total+=$items[$i];
5  echo "Total: $total";
```

Line 1 declares a "simple array" – a sequence of numbers. Each item in the array is assigned an index number, starting from 0. You can view the above array as a spreadsheet of one column of item prices. The index of each item is the row number:

0	5.95
1	6.75
2	9.99

3	5.99
4	10.00

The size of an array is retrieved by the *count* function, as shown in Line 3.

The value of an array item can be read and set using the square bracket syntax. For example, to change the third item in the above list to $1.00:

```
$items[2]=1;
```

To get the price of the 5th item:

```
$chicken_wings=$items[4];
```

Note the index numbers in a simple array are 0-based, so the 3rd item has an index of 2.

Elements in an array can also be arrays. The following code extends the one column spreadsheet to two columns:

```
$items=array(
        array('orange juice',5.95),
        array('milk',6.75),
        array('chicken wings',9.99)
);
```

We can print out the above array using a simple for-loop:

```
for ($i=0; $i<3; $i++){
        $name=$item[$i][0];
        $price=$item[$i][1];
        echo "$item: $price <br>";
}
```

For better readability, the above code is rewritten as the following:

```
for ($i=0; $i<3; $i++){
        $item=$items[$i];
        $name=$item[0];
        $price=$item[1];
        echo "$name: $price <br>";
```

```
}
```

Alternatively, you could define the spreadsheet by an array of two sub-arrays, where each sub-array is a list of item names and prices respectively.

```
$items=array(
        array('orange juice', 'milk', 'chicken wings'),
        array(5.95, 6.75, 9.99)
);
```

Then the code to print the array would be written differently:

```
for ($i=0; $i<3; $i++){
        $name=$items[0][$i];
        $price=$items[1][$i];
        echo "$name: $price <br>";
}
```

Although the above two examples are functionally equivalent. The former declares an array of sub-arrays where each sub-array represents an item; the latter represents a column in the spreadsheet in each sub-array. In practice, the former method should be used because it encapsulates the attributes of an item (e.g. name, price) to an item record (a sub-array).

It is also customary to use plural forms to denote array variables, so that it is clear that the variable is a collection of values.

The *echo* command that we have been using to print out variable values does not display the content of an array. Instead, it only prints the text "Array". To display the content of an array, use the *print_r* function:

```
echo '<pre>';
print_r($items);?>
echo '</pre>';
```

The above code shows the internal representation of the *items* array:

```
Array
(
    [0] => Array
```

```
        (
                [0] => orange juice
                [1] => 5.95
        )

    [1] => Array
        (
                [0] => milk
                [1] => 6.75
        )

    [2] => Array
        (
                [0] => chicken wings
                [1] => 9.99
        )

)
```

print_r is a powerful command that allows you to inspect PHP objects that have unknown structures.

So far we have been dealing with "classic arrays", where elements are associated with numeric indices. A PHP array is actually an *ordered map*. In programming, a *map* can be viewed as a dictionary. Words in such dictionary are called *keys*, and the definition of a word is called the *value* of the word, or key. If you have studied algorithms and data structures before, you'll be glad to know that PHP arrays can be used as many storage structures such as *list, hash table, stack, queue, trees* and more.

If you are learning about arrays for the first time, don't be intimidated by the above list of unfamiliar terms. The essence of PHP arrays can be understood by learning the key-value syntax:

```
$person=array (
'name'=>'John',
        'phone'=>'416-123-4567',
        'age'=>42
);
```

In the above example, the *person* array has three elements: *name*, *phone* and *age*. Compare this to a previous example:

```
$items=array(5.95,6.75,9.99);
```

The above line implies the following:

```
$items=array(
      0=>5.95,
      1=>6.75,
      2=>9.99
);
```

The => operator defines a key-value pair. If the key is missing in an array element definition, a numeric key is automatically assigned.

The same index-based array accessing syntax works for the non-numeric keys[1]:

```
$item=$items[0]; //first item
$name=$person['age'];
$phone=$person['phone'];
```

In order to iterate through an array that has no sequential numeric keys, you need the for-each loop:

```
$items=array(
      'orange juice'=>5.95,
      'milk'=>6.75,
      'chicken wings'=>9.99
);
```

**foreach ($items as $name=>$price) echo "$name $price
";**

If you don't care to retrieve the keys, you can use the simplified form:

```
foreach ($items as $price) echo "$price <br>";
```

---

[1] The technical term for numeric key-based arrays are "indexed arrays"; key-value-based arrays are called "associative arrays". In PHP, indexed and associative arrays are the same type.

Just to further illustrate the use of PHP arrays as a key-value store, here's another example:

```php
$cars=array(
    array('make'=>'Toyota', 'model'=>'Corolla', 'year'=2002),
    array('make'=>'Nissan', 'model'=>'Maxima', 'year'=2001),
    array('make'=>'Ford', 'model'=>'Focus', 'year'=2006)
);

foreach ($cars as $car){
    $make=$car['make'];
    $model=$car['model'];
    $year=$car['year'];
    echo "$make, $model, $year";
}
```

Feel free to run *print_r* on the above array so that you can see the internal storage structure.

Sometimes an array is declared as an empty storage; its content is populated during the code execution. For example:

```php
$car=array();

$car['make']='Honda';
$car['year']=2006;
$car['model']='Civic';

array_push($cars,$car); // assuming $cars already exists
```

The above code shows two ways of adding to an array – adding with, or without a key. In either case, the variable has to be declared as an array, even if it's empty.

The above code can be shortened as the following:

```php
array_push($cars,
array(
'make'=>'Honda',
'year'=>2006,
```

```
'model'=>'Civic'
)
);
```

Note keys in an array are unique. If you assign values to an already existing key-value pair, the old value will be overwritten.

If you retrieve values of a non-existing key, PHP will return an empty (null) value with a warning. To test whether a key-value pair exists, use the *isset* function:

```
if (isset($person['age'])) echo "Age: ".$person['age'];
else echo "Age: N/A";
```

You can also test whether a variable holds a proper array object:

```
if (!is_array($cars)) echo "Error setting cars info";
```

We will revisit PHP arrays in the context of real-life application development in later chapters.

3.12 User-defined Functions

So far we have already been using some pre-defined PHP functions. For example:

```
$length=strlen('this is a test');
$size=count($items);
print_r($items);
php_info();
$str=str_replace('x','y',$str);
```

The above are examples are *function calls*. Function calls are invoked by the function name followed by a pair of parentheses that enclose a list of *parameters*, also known as *arguments*. Some functions require no parameter so they are called by an empty pair of parentheses. Some functions take several parameters that are separated by commas.

The *return value* of a function can be assigned to a variable for further processing. If the function doesn't return a value, it should be called directly, as shown in the 4th line in the above example.

You can organize your code into reusable modules by defining your own functions. A function is declared by the *function* keyword, followed by the name of the function, then a list of argument names in a pair of parentheses, and then the function body that's enclosed in a pair of curly braces:

```
function sayhi($name){
        echo "Hello $name!<br>";
}
```

The above function can be declared anywhere in the PHP script, preferably at the beginning of the script. Try calling the above function with the following lines:

```
sayhi('Jerry');
sayhi('George');
```

You can see the *sayhi* function separates the logical functionality from implementation. If later on we decide to change the behavior of greeting, we only need to change the function itself, not how it is called. The process of identifying repeatable code and restructuring them in custom functions is called *code factoring*.

The use of parameters / arguments allows the same function behave differently based on the value of the input parameters. The function name and the list of parameters the function takes are collectively called a *function signature*, or *prototype*. The process of introducing new parameters to extend the flexibility of a function is called *parameterization*. For example, we can parameterize the *sayhi* function so that the greeting phrase "hello" can be customized:

```
function sayhi($name, $phrase){
        echo "$phrase $name!<br>";
}
```

To call the above function, we now need to pass in the secondary parameter to specify the greeting phrase. The order of parameters in the function signature needs to be consistent with the argument values in the function call. We can call the above function like the following:

```
sayhi('Jerry', 'Hi');
sayhi('George', 'Howdy');
```

In the first line, the value Jerry takes the position of the first parameter, so inside the function, the variable *$name* takes the value of "Jerry". Similarly, the variable *$phrase* takes the value of "Hi". Looking from the function caller's perspective, the values are *passed in* to the function. Looking from the inside the function, the variables are said to be *bound* to the passed-in values.

PHP supports default parameter values, so that when a parameter is omitted, or null, the default value is used instead. For example, the greeting phrase can default to "Hello" unless otherwise specified:

```
function sayhi($name,$phrase='Hello'){...}

sayhi('John'); //outputs Hello John!
sayhi('Dave', 'Hi'); //outputs Hi Dave!
```

It is customary to put mandatory arguments before optional ones, so that your code is more concise and readable.

Missing parameters and null values are different. If the parameter you need to skip is not the last argument, you can use the *null* value as a place holder and handle it like the following:

```
function sayhi($phrase, $name){
    if ($phrase==null) $phrase='Hello';
    echo "$phrase $name!<br>";
}
```

When a variable is passed to a function, PHP automatically makes a copy of this variable. Changing its value from inside the function does not change the original variable. This is called "passing by value".

```
function double_size($n){
    $n=$n*2;
}
$num=100;
```

```
double_size($num);
echo $num; // still outputs 100, not 200!
```

Earlier in the Arrays section, we came across the following function:

```
array_push($car_brands, 'BMW');
```

Calling the above line adds the string "BMW" to the array of car brands. So it should be possible for a function to modify the original variable.

We can achieve this by adding an ampersand sign in front of the parameter name:

```
function double_size(&$n){
   $n=$n*2;
}
```

Now when you run double_size($n) where $n=100, it changes $n to 200.

The ampersand (&) denotes an alias, or "passing by reference" instead of "passing by value".

The following call to the above function now becomes illegal:

```
double_size(100);
```

PHP will throw an error because 100 is not a variable that the *double_size* function can modify.

Alternatively, we could use the return value of a function instead of changing the variable directly:

```
function double_size($n){
   return $n*2;
}
$n=100;
$n=double_size($n); // $n is now 200
```

In general, a function shouldn't change the value of input variables, especially when it returns a value. The following code does exactly the opposite just to illustrate the undesirable side effect:

```php
function double_size(&$n){
    $value=$n;
    $n=0; // empties input variable
    return $value*2;
}

$num=100;
$result=double_size($num); // $result is 200, but $num is 0
```

For beginners, stick to the rule of "function not changing input values". Given the choices of

```php
double_size($n); // function changes $n to 2x$n
```

and

```php
$n=double_size($n); //assigns the return value to $n
```

, always pick the latter style.

If you are curious why PHP changes the variable value in the *array_push* function instead of returning a new array, compare the following function signatures their calls:

```php
function my_array_push_a(&$array, $item){...} // Option A
function my_array_push_b($item){...} // Option B

my_array_push_a($brands,'Brand A');
$brands=my_array_push_b($item);
```

Option A is essentially identical to the native *array_push* function in PHP. It changes the array variable directly.

Option B makes a copy of the array first and then returns the modified array object. Option B is not as memory efficient as Option A.

In fact, in many languages such as C/C++ or Java, function parameters are passed by value for simple variables, or by reference for complex variables. Simple variables include numeric and string variables. Arrays and objects are complex variables.

Now another rule of thumb: whenever writing a function that manipulates the content of a collection, such as an array or object, pass the parameter by reference (i.e. denote the argument with an ampersand), and modify the input value directly.

3.13 Variable Scopes

The scope of a variable is the context in which the variable was created, and in which it can be accessed. PHP has two variable scopes: Global and Local.

Local variables are created inside functions, and can be accessed from within the function.

```
function show_value(){
      $value=100;
      echo "Value is $value<br>";
}

show_value();
echo "Value is $value";
```

The above script displays the following:

```
Value is 100
Value is
```

Because *$value* is only accessible inside the *show_value* function, the second line fails to print properly. This is called accessing variable out of scope – a programming error we should avoid.

Global variables are created outside function blocks. Consider function blocks as houses, global variables live in streets where as local variables stay inside the houses. Global variables are accessible from anywhere in the script.

To access the global variable from outside a function, just use the variable directly. To access the global variable from within the function, however, you need to declare that the variable has a global scope. Back to the housing analogy, things in the street (global variables) can be picked up by anybody, but you have to open the door first (declare global scope).

Consider the following example:

```
$value=100;

function show_value(){
    global $value;

    echo "Value is $value<br>";
    $value=10;
}

show_value();
echo "Value is now $value";
```

The above code gives the following output:

```
Value is 100
Value is now 10
```

As you can see, the value of *$value* can be read and modified from inside a function. Now remove the line in bold, which declares $value as a global variable, and run the script again. You'll get the following output instead:

```
Value is
Value is now 100
```

PHP assumes variables inside a function to be local unless otherwise declared. If you have worked with other languages such as C, Java or even JavaScript, you should note that the need to declare global variables inside a function is unique to PHP. In most other languages, global variables are directly visible inside functions.

This behavior of PHP effectively avoids accidental name collisions. Imagine a function unintentionally modifies the value of a variable, which is used by other functions? In later chapters you'll see the same issue is handled rather differently in JavaScript.

Now that you understand how global variable works, it's important not to misuse them. In general, global variables are used as "contextual variables". For example, a database connection or general settings that are frequently accessed throughout the script. It would be otherwise clumsy to pass these variables as parameters in individual functions. Communication among functions, however, is better implemented as parameters.

3.14 Query Parameters

PHP offers a special kind of global variables that are accessible everywhere even without being declared the global scope inside functions. These variables are called the "superglobals". Their variable names begin with an underscore and are in all uppercase letters. For example, *$_GET*, *$_POST*, *$_COOKIE*, *$_FILES*, *$_SERVER*, are all superglobals.

We will discuss the use of each super global variable in later chapters. For now, let's look at the *$_GET* parameters.

The full URL of a web page contains the protocol (http, or https), optional port number, domain name and full path to the web page:

http://www.google.com/search?q=query+parameters&hl=de

Additional information can be added to the URL after a question mark. In the above example, "q=query+parameters&hl=de" is the encoded string of query parameters. It describes the following key-value mapping:

q	query parameters
hl	de

If Google's search page were written in PHP, you'd extract the above info with $_GET:

```
$keyword=$_GET['q'];
$language=$_GET['hl'];
```

As an exercise, try to build a page that displays the sum of two input numbers. The page is called by a request like the following:

```
http://localhost/add.php?a=20&b=75
```

Here's a simple implementation:

```php
<?php
$a=$_GET['a'];
$b=$_GET['b'];
echo $a+$b;
?>
```

The above script can be improved in a couple of ways. First of all, we know parameter "a" and "b" should both be numeric values. We need to make the script robust enough so that it doesn't "crap out" when non-numerals are used. Remember in PHP when two terms are connected with the plus sign, they are converted to numerals first. Non numeric variables are set to zero. The output line in the above example is already immune of bad input value, but just to be safe, it's good practice to convert the $_GET parameters right away:

```php
$a=$_GET['a']+0;
$b=$_GET['b']+0;
```

Also there are times, especially when writing AJAX request handlers as we'll see later on, when we need to return the output without extra white spaces. In the above example, if you include a few line breaks after ?>, the output will contain both the calculation result and the unwanted white spaces.

The easiest way to ensure there's no white space artifact is not to get out of the PHP context. In other words, do not end the <?php tag.

Now *add.php* has become the following:

```php
<?php
$a=$_GET['a']+0;
$b=$_GET['b']+0;
echo $a+$b;
```

3.15 Include Files

A PHP script can be split and stored in separate files, so that common code and functionality are shared among other scripts.

Include files are used to divide a static HTML page into reusable components. For example, instead of writing the following lines of code in every web page:

```
<html>
  <head>
    <title>Page Title</title>
  </head>
  <body>
  <h1>Welcome!</h1>
  </body>
</html>
```

We can use an include file to define just the header section in *header.php*:

```
<html>
  <head>
    <title>Page Title</title>
  </head>
  <body>
```

And the footer section is defined in *footer.php*:

```
</body>
</html>
```

Now all the pages in the website can reuse the header and footer.
For instance, index.php:

```
<?include 'header.php';?>
<h1>Welcome!</h1>
<?include 'footer.php';?>
```

And the code for contact.php:

```
<?include 'header.php';?>
```

3.0 Introducing PHP   75

```
<h1>Contact Us</h1>
<?include 'footer.php';?>
```

The process of organizing a set of static HTML files into PHP files that share common visual elements is called "templatizing". We will discuss later in much greater details about the process and art of creating templates.

Note the filename of the include file can take any name, as long as they exist. Once a file is included, it is treated as if it's a PHP script. In the above example, the component files do not have the PHP tags, so the role of PHP is simply putting the pieces together.

Another important use of include files is packaging user functions into libraries. Syntactically speaking there is no difference in how you include the files. But when a file contains user functions, it is used differently.

First of all, this file cannot be included twice, because you cannot declare the same function twice. Picture the following block.php where a red block is directly displayed:

```
<div style="width:50px;height:50px;background-color:red;">
</div>
```

To display 3 blocks, we can simply include block.php three times:

```
Block 1: <?include 'block.php';?>
Block 2:<?include 'block.php';?>
Block 3:<?include 'block.php';?>
```

If we define a function that displays a block as following:

```
function show_block(){
?>
<div style="width:50px;height:50px;background-color:red;">
</div>
<?
}
```

Then we need to include the function declaration only once, and then call the function 3 times:

```
<?include 'block.php';?>
Block1: <?show_block();?>
Block2: <?show_block();?>
Block3: <?show_block();?>
```

There are many reasons why we would want to define and reuse components one way or the other. There are many architectural advantages of wrapping the output in a function call, such as allowing parameterization, name space protection and separation of the representation from content. We will explore these concepts in later chapters. Directly including static output still has its place, especially in creating HTML templates.

In the above example, we can make the show_block function show blocks of different colors in different sizes. In *block.php*:

```
function show_block($size=50,$color='red'){
?>
<div style="width:<?echo $size;?>px;
height:<?echo $size;?>px;
background-color:<?echo $color;?>;">
</div>
<?
}
```

Now the function can be called in the main script that includes *block.php*.

```
<?include 'block.php';?>
Block1: <?show_block();?>
Block2: <?show_block(100,'green');?>
Block3: <?show_block(150,'#ffab00');?>
```

Note the use of default parameter values comes in handy.

Remember: do not mix function declarations and function calls in the same include file. An include file either defines a function (or functions) to enable the calling script additional abilities, or generates output in forms of either HTML output or returns values for other functions to use.

So far we've only covered the basics of PHP. You should be able to follow code snippets that appear both in later chapters of this book and examples in php.net, the official PHP documentation.

Do not be discouraged if you tried and failed to understand PHP code from open source projects, for the following reasons:

1. You are only taught the syntax of the language. A programming language allows you to express your thoughts, or "algorithms". Software architecture and algorithm design are topics we have not explored yet. You'll also need to put in many hours practicing coding.

2. Reading the code of one script does not reveal the overall design of a big project, unless you are experienced to reverse engineer the author's intent, or familiar with the project's architecture. You're not there yet.

3. Many open source projects have bad structure and bad style. Read them just to identify the topics we have covered in this chapter. I hope you do not pick up the bad coding habits from these open source projects.

4.0 CSS Basics

Cascading Style Sheet (CSS) is a style sheet language that describes the appearance of HTML pages. CSS is designed to separate the document content (HTML) from document presentation.

Before the standardization and wide acceptance of CSS, HTML tags are used to change the look of parts of a document. For example, setting the text color of a word in a paragraph:

```
This is an important message.
```

Without using CSS:

```
This is an <font color="red">important</font> message.
```

If the color of important phrases needs to be changed later, you'll have to modify the HTML document directly. You might even have to modify multiple places in different pages in a web site.

In CSS, you can mark sections of a document and define "appearance rules" for the marked sections. For example:

```
This is an <span class="important">message</span>.
So is <span class="important">this one</span>.
```

Now you can use CSS to highlight both words that are marked *important*:

```
.important {background-color: #ffff00;}
```

Before I explain in detail where to put CSS rules in an HTML document, here's a simple example:

```
<html>
    <head>
        <style>
        .important {background-color: #ffff00;}
        </style>
    </head>
```

```
<body>
    This is an <span class="important">message</span>.
    So is <span class="important">this one</span>.
</body>
</html>
```

4.1 Where to Declare CSS Rules

There are three ways to insert CSS rules into an HTML document: inline CSS, block declaration and external style sheet.

Inline CSS defines styles as the "style" tag directly in an HTML tag:

```
<div style="border: solid 1px;">sample text</div>
```

Comparing inline CSS with the previous example, inline CSS doesn't isolate appearance from the document. Although inline CSS is often considered "bad style", it is highly effective for prototyping and debugging. It is also used for sections that do not share common visual features. We'll discuss more about this in later sections.

Block CSS declares CSS rules inside the <style> block. These rules match certain patterns in the HTML document, changing the look of matching elements. The example in the previous section demonstrates the use of block CSS. The <style> block can occur anywhere in the HTML document. To avoid confusion, it's best to have only one instance of style block, and declare it at the beginning of the document.

External CSS is functionally identical to block CSS, except that it is declared in an independent CSS file, with the *.css* extension. Once the style rules are stored in one file, multiple HTML pages can link to the same style sheet, sharing common visual features. This is how CSS enables a consistent look throughout a web site.

External style sheets can be referenced by adding the following tags in the header section of an HTML document:

```
<html>
  <head>
    <link rel="stylesheet" href="style.css" type="text/css" />
```

```
</head>
```

Multiple style sheets can be used by declaring multiple *link* tags.

4.2 CSS Syntax

Each CSS rule is described by a selector followed by a semi-colon delimited list of attribute-value pairs. For instance,

```
#banner span, .intro {
    color: red;
    font-weight: bold;
}
```

#banner span and *.intro* are both selectors that match specific patterns in the document.

Inside the curly braces is the list of styles. Each style is a pair of style name (attribute), and style content (value). For example, *color, width, background* and *font-weight* are all common style attributes. All attributes are in lowercase. Attribute names cannot have spaces, so a hyphen is used to connect two-word attributes so that they are still legible to human readers. Examples are *font-weight, text-decoration* etc.

Attribute names and values are paired up and separated by a colon. This is conceptually similar to the key-value array declaration we discussed in the PHP section. Consider the syntax of the following array:

```
$car = array {
        'make' => 'Ford',
        'model' => 'Focus',
        'year' => 2006
};
```

And later in the book you'll see the format of a JavaScript object:

```
var car = {make: 'Ford', model: 'Focus', year: 2006};
```

The key-value list syntax effectively describes an object or a set of rules in an easy-to-process fashion. The precise syntax, especially in terms of delimiters (e.g. comma, semi-colon, double-arrows, etc.), may vary, but the principle is the same across multiple programming disciplines.

It is also important to note the syntactical difference between a CSS rule definition from a PHP/JavaScript object declaration.

In the above examples, the PHP and JavaScript objects are declared in an assignment statement. Each ended with a semi colon.

In CSS, a rule ends with a closing curly bracket. The additional semi-colon is not only unnecessary, but will invalidate the rest of the style sheet!

So don't ever end a CSS rule with a semi colon like the following:

```
#banner {color: red; font-weight: bold;};
```

Now a note about white spaces; the line breaks between attribute-value pairs, and the spaces before the opening bracket or after the commas/colons/semi-colons are optional. They are ignored by the browser, which is responsible for parsing the style sheet and rendering your document. Therefore, white spaces only exist to make the code more "readable".

Personally I prefer to write CSS rules with few, if any, spaces or line breaks. Each CSS rule takes up one line instead of a block of several lines - beginners might find this hard to follow or consider the code to have poor readability. Once you are familiar with the common styling patterns, however, you can easily parse the single-line rules. When managing more complex style sheets or source code in general, it's better to fit more lines in one screen. We can compare this to a painting: verbose code gives more emphasis to each stroke, whereas compact code moves the painting farther away from the audience so that they can see more strokes, and hence the overall picture.

4.3 Inline vs. Block Elements

You have probably already noticed that when a portion of HTML code is wrapped around by certain tags, the enclosed content takes a line on its own; some other tags, however, keep the content flowing in the same line.

For example, the *div* tag breaks the following content in 3 lines:

```
This is Line 1. <div>This is Line 2.</div> This is Line 3.
```

The *span* tag, on the other hand, doesn't break the line:

```
This is Line 1. <span>This is Line 2.</span> This is Line 3.
```

Tags such as *div, p, form, ul*, and *table* are **block elements**.
Tags such as *span, a, b* and *input* are **inline elements**.

Note the distinction between block and inline elements has nothing to do with inline or block CSS declaration.

The default display mode of an element can be overridden. For example, we can force a *div* tag to behave like a *span* and vice versa:

```
This is Line 1.
<div style="display:inline;">This is Line 2.</div>
This is Line 3.
<span style="display:block;">This is Line 4.</div>
```

Later in Chapter 4.15.1 we'll see the benefit of overriding display types. For now, we just need to know the defaults can be changed.

Apart from taking up a line on its own, a block element differs from an inline element in several other ways. For one, the *margin* property makes sense for only block elements. The differences between block and inline elements are rooted from their different box models, which we'll explore further in the Box Model section (Chapter 4.5).

4.4 The Document Tree and Inherited Rules

An HTML document can be styled with various visual elements. We look at web pages as collections of conceptual components: header, footer, navigation menus, etc.

A web browser looks at the document differently. In order to effectively command the browser to render the page the way we want, we need to understand how a document is perceived in the "mind" of a browser.

To a browser, an HTML document is a hierarchy of tag-defined elements, which can be best described as a tree. The root of the tree, as far as CSS is concerned, is the document body.

Consider the following code snippet:

```
<body>
    <div id="banner">
        <div id="logo">...</div>
        <div id="menu">...</div>
    <div id="content">
        ...
    </div>
</body>
```

The above code is visualized as a tree:

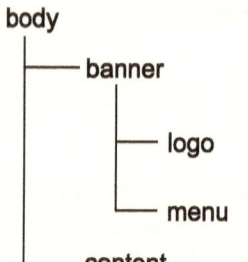

Certain CSS attributes in a document node are automatically inherited by the node's child nodes. For example, if the *color* of the *banner* element is set to red, the text inside *banner*, *logo* and *menu* are all displayed in red, unless the color is otherwise overridden. Text color in the *content* block is not affected, because *content* is not a child node of *banner*.

If the *color* attribute of the *logo* element is set to blue, the text color of the *menu* block stays red, because *menu* is a child node of *banner*, not *logo*.

Note the *background-color* attribute is not inherited. The default background color of an element is transparent. If a block has the same background color as its parent node's background color, it is only a visual effect. Do not confuse this with inheritance.

The process of implementing graphics with CSS takes a layered approach. Start with common attributes on the top-most elements. As these attributes trickle down to child nodes, use more specific definitions. This is very similar to painting where you set the tone of the background first and then

4.0 CSS Basics

use fine paint brushes to touch on the details. It is also similar to the concept of clip art – elements encapsulate or stack on top of one another. We can represent the above tree structure in a series of containers. This could better emphasize the effect of inherited rules:

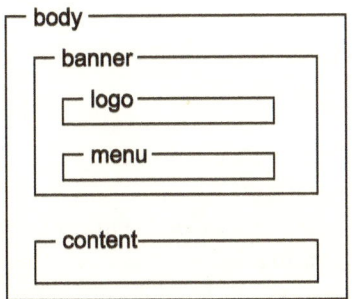

4.5 The Box Model

The dimensions of a block element, e.g. div, are measured by the following properties:

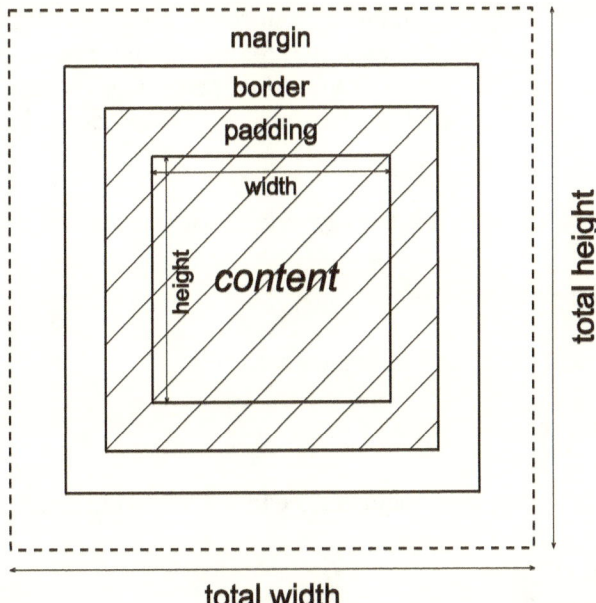

According to the W3C standard, the total width of an HTML element is the sum of content width, padding, border and margin. The background image or color applies to the content and padding, as illustrated in the shaded area in the above diagram.

Note that not all browsers follow this standard. We'll discuss more about this right after a brief introduction on some basic syntax.

The four sides of padding, border widths and margins around the element can be assigned separately. For example:

```
padding: 10px; padding-left: 100px;
```

When the *padding* attribute is described with only one value, all sides take the same measure. The *padding-left* attribute sets the padding only on the left side. When both attributes are declared in the same line, the most recently declared one trumps the previously defined rules. In the above code, the left padding is overridden to 100 pixels while the other sides remain 10 pixels.

In addition to *px*, which stands for "pixels", other units such as *em* and *pt*, can be used. You can also use percentage instead of fixed values.

We'll see in later chapters, and also from real-life practice, that using pixel measure tends to give you fewer browser-compatibility issues. It also helps, in many occasions, to refrain from using percentage values, or explicit measures entirely. The benefits of using implicit values will be discussed later.

If the length measure is 0, it is usually written without the unit. For example:

```
    margin: 0;
```

There's a shortcut to define padding on each side:

```
padding: 10px 0 50px 20px;
```

The above code is a compact equivalence to the following code:

```
padding-top: 10px;
padding-right: 0;
padding-bottom: 50px;
padding-left: 20px;
```

An easy way to remember the order of the 4 parameters is to start from the top and rotate clockwise – top, right, bottom, left.

The same format applies to margin settings.

If there are only two values in the padding or margin styles, the first value is used by the top and bottom, and the second value denotes the left and right side.

For example:

```
margin: 0 auto;
```

The above line set the top and bottom margin to zero pixels, and let the browser to determine the left and right margin. This code is commonly used to center an element.

If you are curious about how 3-value shorthand works with padding and margins, feel free to look it up online. If you find the explanations too complicated to follow, stick with the simpler formats, such as uniform value with explicit overrides, the 4-value shorthand or the 2-value shorthand.

For the sake of completeness, here's the format of the border attribute:

```
border: style width color;
```

If the third parameter is omitted, the default color is used. The default color of an element is its parent node's color. If the parent node's color is unset, the color is black.

The border descriptor is analogous to a paint brush. The common styles are *solid*, *dashed* or *dotted*; the width is usually expressed in pixels; and the color takes the format of either a simple color word such as "red", or a hexadecimal value, e.g. #ffab00.

The following two lines of border examples:

```
border: solid 1px;
border-right: dashed 1px #ffab00;
border: none;
```

The third line in the above code is used to clear an existing border.

Calculating the Width and Height

As mentioned earlier, the total width of an element is the sum of the content width, border width, padding on the left and right sides, and margins on the left and right sides – at least per standards.

Unfortunately most versions of Internet Explorer do not follow the standards closely. Unless a *doctype* is set, the *width* attribute denotes the total width instead of content width.

For instance, on IE 6 without *doctype*, the following element takes up a total of 100 pixels, and the content width is cut down to 80 pixels:

```
width: 100px; padding: 10px;
```

The common solution is to use a *doctype* to tell the browser to conform to standards, and implement various patches so that the code works, hopefully, on more browsers. This solution only works with "modern browsers". Support for older versions of Internet Explorer is usually dropped.
A much more elegant solution indeed exists. It works on all browsers without hacks or patches. Before I explain how this solution works and what on earth this *doctype* thing is about, let's go back in time and look at the root cause of browser compatibility issues, which continues to plague today's developers.

Before the standardization of HTML and CSS, browser vendors had their own interpretations. The expected behaviors of most tags are obvious, and therefore consistent in all browser versions. During the Internet Explorer versus Netscape Navigator battle, proprietary document model and tags were introduced to allow competitive features. Many of these proprietary features were later deprecated from HTML. With the introduction of CSS, and the subsequent isolation of content and presentation, most of the "specialty tags" can be implemented in CSS.

Before the CSS specifications were finalized, browser vendors were again steps ahead. Certain ambiguous terms such as *width* are given inconsistent interpretations. Developers tend to build a website in one browser, just to find out the layout is completely broken in another.

The Firefox browser gained significant popularity when many of the web standards were finalized. Apart from being a more standard compliant browser, there're other reasons why Firefox became developers primary browser. Most of the reasons are linked to a better JavaScript debugging environment. For example, IE evaluates the entire JavaScript code and instantly complains about any mistakes upon page load, whereas Firefox reports error as a specific piece of code is triggered by an event, such as a mouse click. Firefox extensions such as Firebug further secured Firefox's dominant position as a developer's browser.

If the developer cares at all about cross browser support, he'll eventually check his site in Internet Explorer, just to find out that "everything is broken in IE".

You'll be surprised to find out that 90% of the layout issues are related to the definitions of *width* and *height*, and another 9% caused by relative dimension and positioning settings, which we'll discuss later.

As a rule of thumb, do not ever style the same element with both explicit width/height and padding at the same time. Use a nested *div* block instead.

For example:

```
<div style="width:100px">
    <div style="padding:10px;"> Content </div>
</div>
```

The outer *div* in the above code confines the total occupied width to 100 pixels. The 10-pixel padding is carved out of the 100. There's no way to misinterpret the intent of the above code, and therefore, the code behaves the same in all browsers, including the now hard to find IE 5!

What most other books will teach you is what I call a "political approach". Instead of writing code that's naturally compatible to all browsers, a *doctype* line is added to the beginning of the HTML document, telling the browser to comply with standards. There are so many revisions of standards and hence document types that it's overwhelming and at the same time, practically irrelevant.

Without the *doctype* line, browsers will render the document in standard mode, also known as the "quirks mode". In most cases, if your code withstands the test of quirks mode, it'll almost certainly still work when a *doctype* is added to the document.

4.0 CSS Basics

We'll see later, that the declaration of *doctype* will also change the Document Object Model (DOM) to some degree.

Also document type is no guarantee that the browser will comply. For example IE 7 still considers padding to be part of the *width* attribute.

If you ever wonder why IE treats padding differently, it's because Microsoft actually got it right and implemented its logically correct understanding in its browsers. And *then* the standards came out, defining it otherwise. Just look at the CSS box model as a wooden crate. The dimension of the box is described in width and height, and the clearance around the box is the margin. If we need to protect the fragile content in the box, we buffer it with pillows on all sides, but this padding takes up space. So a 100x100 box has a content capacity of 80x80, assuming the pillows are 10 pixels thick.

4.6 Basic Matching Rules

So far you've seen CSS examples in the form of inline styling. Inline CSS could significantly speed up the prototyping and debug process. In live sites, however, it's usually better to store the CSS rules outside of HTML tags. This allows more flexibility and eliminates redundant declarations.

For example, a list of items that are rendered with red underlines:

```
<div style="border-bottom: solid 1px red;">Line 1</div>
<div style="border-bottom: solid 1px red;">Line 2</div>
<div style="border-bottom: solid 1px red;">Line 3</div>
```

The above code can be factored as the following:

```
<style>
.lineitem{border-bottom: solid 1px red;}
</style>

<div class="lineitem">Line 1</div>
<div class="lineitem">Line 2</div>
<div class="lineitem">Line 3</div>
```

If the look of *lineitem* is changed in future, you only need to modify that in one place. This also reduces the size of the HTML document, reducing bandwidth consumption.

Elements are matched with CSS rules through CSS selectors – the phrases in front of the opening curly braces. In this section, we'll look at three basic forms of matching: by tag name, by class and by ID.

Tag matching is usually used to override the default behavior or normalize browser differences while retaining the semantics of the tag. For example, *h1* tags identify Level 1 headings. An *h1* element is bold and comes with some margins. If you want to reset the heading to normal font weight and absolutely no extra spacing, you can assign the CSS rules to the *h1* tag:

```
h1 {padding:0; margin:0; font-weight:normal;}
```

A specific element can also be labeled with a *class* attribute. Selectors for classes begin with a dot. For example:

```
.menuitem {display:block; color:red;}
```

And to apply the *menuitem* class:

```
<div class="menuitem">Home</div>
```

Similarly, an element with an id attribute can be matched with an ID selector, which is expressed by a pond sign:

```
#menu {background-color:black; color:white;}
```

In an HTML document, each element's ID, if it exists at all, should be unique. This is not only a matter of convention, but also required for the JavaScript function *document.getElementById* to work properly, as you'll see in later chapters. The *class* attribute, on the other hand, can be assigned to multiple instances. For example:

```
<div id="menu">
        <span class="menuitem">Home</span>
        <span class="menuitem">Products & Services</span>
        <span class="menuitem">Contact Us</span>
</div>
```

When multiple rules are matched, and therefore applied, to the same element, the non-conflicting rules are combined. More specific rules trump the more general rules. The following code shows that IDs are more specific than classes; and classes are more specific than tag rules:

```
<style>
#c{color:green;}
.b{color:blue;}
div{color:red;}
</style>

<div class="b" id="c">
Test
</div>
```

When conflicting selectors are equally specific, the more recently declared rule wins. And inline declaration overrides any externally declared rules.

If multiple CSS rules share the same definition, you can combine them.

Consider the following example:

```
.c1{text-decoration: none; color: red; font-size:12px;}
.c2{text-decoration:none; color:green; font-size:12px;}
```

Since *c1* and *c2* have quite a few common attributes, we can address both of them at the same time:

```
.c1, .c2 {text-decoration:none; font-size:12px;}
.c1 {color:red;}
.c2 {color:green;}
```

We can further reduce the above code to the following two lines:

```
.c1, .c2 {text-decoration:none;font-size:12px;color:red;}
.c2 {color:green;}
```

The first line sets both classes to the same style, but the second line then overrides the text color, achieving the same effect as the previous code block.

The goal of refactoring is not to reduce the sheer number of lines. It reduces the needs to make changes in multiple places.

Note the selectors are separated by commas. Missing this separator will bring a completely different meaning to the CSS selectors.

When selectors are separated by spaces, the "path" of the elements matches against the entire pattern. For example:

```
#menu span .current {...}
```

Matches the following element in bold:

```
<div id="menu">
  <span><a class="current">Home</a></span>
  <span><a>About</a></span>
</div>
```

The above selector applies to only the *current* class that's inside a span that immediately follows the *menu* element. The matching rules are powerful and can be quite confusing for beginners. The key is to keep the path short, and always experiment with a browser instead of just logically verifying the code with a reference book.

If an element is incorrectly targeted, it could be missed or over-matched. Over matching can be easily prevented by using class names or IDs. Mismatching on the other hand can be frustrating because the targeted element doesn't seem to pick up any changes. A handy trick is to temporarily hide the element. For example, is the following line targeting all the *p* tags inside *div* tags?

```
div p {display:none;}
```

Before adding the above line, load the page in a browser first, then add the line and refresh. If the targeted elements disappear, then the selector pattern matches the target element.

A dedicated CSS book or reference will teach you more complex rules, such as matching the first class in an ID but not the subsequent classes. Some of these rules are not correctly implemented in all browsers, so special "hacks" are often used, making the code even more confusing.

The good news is that you don't have to make your life complicated than it has to be. As a web developer who has complete control over the HTML content, you can label your elements with attributes that allow simple matching patterns. The reason CSS supports complex rules is because of the assumption that HTML content cannot, or should not be modified. And the reason the CSS code in many open source projects are convoluted is because the developers run into the exact said situation, namely no control over HTML content and therefore no means to mark the elements for more convenient styling.

If you see the value of a class attribute is a list of space-separated terms instead of just one term, do not confuse this with a matching pattern:

```
<div class="type1 type2">...</div>
```

The above line means to apply both type1 and type2 classes:

```
.type1 {font-size:20px;}
.type2 {color:red;}
```

Again if you have total control over HTML, especially when the content is dynamically generated in PHP, you can stitch an inline style instead of using multiple classes.

4.7 Styling Links

If you ever tried to style a page with hyper links, you'll notice that these links seem to have a mind of their own. For example, the following code attempts to set the link color to red, but doesn't quite work:

```
<style>
a{color:red;}
</style>
<a href=#>Test Link</a>
```

In IE, once you click on the link, which has a default blue color, the link turns purple, which is the default color for visited links.

The reason links don't obey styling rules in the above code is because the CSS selector is not addressing all the states the link can be in.

The following code will set the link of all states to red:

```
a, a:link, a:visited, a:hover {color:red;}
```

In many designs, the hyper links are styled not to have the underline, unless it's hovered over by a mouse cursor. We can remove the underline for all states, and then override the setting just for the hover state:

```
a, a:link, a:visited, a:hover
{text-decoration:none; color:black;}

a:hover {text-decoration:underline; color:red;}
```

The above code set the link color of the entire document to black, and their hover color to red, with an underline. If you want links in different sections of the page look differently, nest the links in a *div* wrapper:

```
<style>
footer a, footer a:link,
footer a:visited, footer a:hover
{text-decoration:none; color:black;}

footer a:hover{text-decoration:underline; color:black;}
</style>
```

The selector after the semi-colon is called a "pseudo class". In quirks mode, IE only renders pseudo classes for hyper links correctly, and only if the link has a *href* attribute set. Because of this compatibility issue, the following code doesn't work:

```
<style>
.test:hover {color:red;}
</style>

<a href=# class="test">Test</a>
```

The above code needs to be fixed to the following:

```
<style>
.test a:hover{color:red;}
</style>

<span class="test"><a href=#>Test</a></span>
```

In addition, you may want to further disable the hyper link. Even though the hash (#) refers to the same page, if you are at the bottom of the page, it gives an unwanted scroll-up effect as the link redirects to the top of the page. You can disable the redirect like this:

```
<a href=# onclick="return false;">Test</a>
```

Another thing you might have noticed when clicking on a link is the dotted border around the link. There are many reasons you may want to get rid of this artifact, especially when the link is styled with background images, as we'll see in later chapters. You can remove the border with the following code:

```
a:active{outline:0;}
```

However, the border is there for accessibility reasons. If you hit the tab key, you'll see the same type of border cycles around all the links on the page. This allows the user to navigation the site without using a mouse. The link that has a border around it is said to be in focus. In the Chrome browser, the *input* element has a yellow highlighting border when it's in focus. We can eliminate the borders and highlights in both states:

```
a:active, a:focus{outline:0;}
```

A link is in the *active* state when the link is clicked on. If the link redirects to a different page, you'll see the effect of the *active* state for a short period of time, before the new page is loaded.

Now that we have removed the visual cue for keyboard navigation, we need to provide a visual alternative in order to preserve accessibility.

```
a:active, a:focus{outline:0;}
a:active, a:focus, a:hover {color:red;}
```

The above code set the focus indicator to the same style as mouse hover, so that the visual cues are consistent.

4.8 Using Float and Clear

So far we've seen two types of simple layouts: flowing text and links that are implemented by inline elements, and stacked up blocks by block elements.

A typical web page usually has a non-linear layout. In many cases, the page has a columned layout or some form of side-by-side content:

CSS is very limited in expressing layouts. It uses *float* and *clear* to emulate column layouts.

The *float* attribute is assigned to a block element to prevent it from forming a new line. It is also used in junction with the *width* attribute.

```
<div style="width:250px">
    <div style="width:100px;float:left;">A</div>
    <div style="width:100px;float:left;">B</div>
    <div style="width:100px;float:left;">C</div>
</div>
```

In the above code, three left floating blocks try to fit in a 250-pixel wide container. You can see that Block C fails to fit in and snaps into the next line.

If you change the container width to 300 pixels, the three blocks will be laid out side by side.

Another common use of float is wrapping text around images. By default, text and image are aligned on the bottom, or baseline. Try the following code:

```
<img src="logo.png"> Test message
```

You can make the text flow around the image by setting the image afloat:

```
<img style="float:left; margin:10px;" src="logo.png">
Test message
```

You can anchor the image to the right by setting *float* to *right*. The image element should still come before the text.

Note when wrapping text, the text itself doesn't require a float. Columned layout, on the other hand, requires each column container to be left floating.

It's important to remember to complete, or "seal" the floating chain with a *clear* attribute:

```
<div style="background-color:red; width:100px;">
        <div style="float:left; width:20px;">
             A1 <br> A2
        </div>
        <div style="float:left; width:20px;">
             B1 <br> B2
        </div>
        <div style="clear:both;"></div>
</div>
Footer Text
```

You can see the importance of the bolded line in the above code by removing it. Test the above code in Firefox. Without a clearing div, the container's background fails to "stretch down" to the bottom, and the text after the containing block continues to float.

The literal meaning of the clear attribute can be understood as clearance. For example, *clear:left* means no elements should be arranged to the left side; and *clear:both* is a combination of *clear:left* and *clear:right*.

4.9 Position Types

Another way to implement non-linear layout is to use the *position* attribute. This technique is extremely useful for building web applications as it gives you total control over the placement of elements.

The position attribute takes the following values: "relative", "absolute", "static" and "fixed". Let's talk about relative and absolute positioning first. By default, a DOM element is positioned "static".

The best way to understand absolute positioning and relative positioning is to treat them as completely different words.

From now on, read position:relative as "reference point".
And treat position:absolute as "coordinates and reference point".

Consider the following snippet:

```
A<br>B<br>C<br><br>
<div style="position:relative;">
    <div style="position:absolute; top:100px; left:100px;">
        X
    </div>
    <div style="position:absolute; top:0; left:0;">
        Y
    </div>
</div>
```

Label X is placed at (100, 100) using the top left corner of its containing block as a reference point. The three lines before the container make the role of the reference point more obvious.

Similarly, Label Y is placed at the top left corner of the containing block because its offset coordinates are both set to zero.

Note that *left*, *right*, *top*, *bottom* attributes only make sense when the position type is *absolute*.

Also be very careful with the *right* and *bottom* attributes. Use them only if the width and height are either explicitly set or agreed upon by all browsers in quirks mode.

In Firefox, absolutely positioned elements do not take up space in their containing block. Try adding a border to the containing div and you'll see this block is not stretched by its content at all. Unlike *float*, you cannot use a *clear* to "stretch it down". A specific height has to be assigned to the outer div if you want to render the background color or image properly.

In general, the relative-absolute positioning pattern is used for implementing web applications while floating columns are for textual web pages.

Internet Explorer sometimes has glitches rendering relatively positioned elements. You'll see the entire content disappear. Make sure you test often on all major browsers. If the glitch happens, try also setting the parent element to relatively positioned, or set positioning to a different element, until the problem's resolved.

Fixed positioning works very similar to absolute positioning. A fix positioned container serves as a coordinate reference for its child nodes. Note that *position:fixed* only works in standard rendering mode, i.e. not quirks mode. A fix positioned element keeps its position relative to the browser viewport. This makes this position type useful for hovering menus and other overlay effects.

4.10 Stacking Orders

When elements are displayed in a linear fashion, be it top and bottom or side by side, they don't overlap each other. Absolutely positioned elements, on the other hand, are layered on top of other elements.

The order in which elements are piled up is called the stacking order, as the elements form a stack.

In general, absolutely positioned elements are on top of relatively positioned elements, and the most recently declared elements are displayed on top.

```
<style>
.block{
  position:absolute;
  top:10px;left:10px;
  width:100px;height:100px;
}
</style>
<div style="position:relative;">
  <div class="block" style="background-color:red;"></div>
  <div class="block" style="background-color:green;"></div>
  <div class="block" style="background-color:blue;"></div>
  This line is covered by a colored block.
</div>
```

In the above code, the inline style overrides the background color for individual elements, and the common visual effects are set by a CSS class.

Since all three blocks are in the exact same position, only the blue block is visible as it is the last element.

Although the text "this line is covered by a colored block" is declared after the blue block, it is relatively positioned, so it is still covered by a previously declared element.

Overlay popup boxes and custom context menus can be implemented with absolutely positioned elements. Since they are visually on top of anything else, they should be placed at the end of the document.

Now I'm very hesitant to tell you about Z-Index, a mechanism to override the stacking order, so that the latest declared element is not necessarily placed on the top.

I'll explain how Z-Index works first, then why we should avoid using it when possible.

In the previous example, the blue block is declared after the green block, which is declared after the red block. As a result, the red block is covered by the green block, which is further covered by the blue block.

We can alter the arrangement with Z-Index:

```
<div class="block" style="background-color:red;z-index:3;">
</div>

<div class="block" style="background-color:green;z-index:2;">
</div>

<div class="block" style="background-color:blue;z-index:1;">
</div>
```

Now the red block is on the top most, followed by the green block, and then the blue block. Higher Z-Index values bring the element closer to the front.

Consider the following code:

```
<style>
.block{
  position:absolute;
  top:10px;left:10px;
```

```
    width:100px;height:100px;
}
</style>

<div style="position:relative; z-index:2">

<div class="block" style="background-color:red;z-index:3;">
</div>

</div>

<div style="position:relative; z-index:1">

<div class="block" style="background-color:blue;z-index:100;">
</div>

</div>
```

The blue block is given a higher Z-Index value, but is still covered by the red block. This is because the parents of these blocks have formed their individual **Stacking Contexts**.

A stacking context is formed when an element is either absolute or relative positioned, and is assigned a Z-Index value.

Child elements inherit from the parent's Z-Index, behaving as if it's one unit. So in the above example, the high Z-Index of the blue block means nothing outside of the stacking context. Its parent loses the battle for visibility against the red block's parent.

If you add a green block at the same level as the red block but with a slightly higher Z-Index value, the green block will trump all the other blocks.

It's also worth nothing that in Mozilla browsers such as Firefox, elements with an opacity value less than 1 also form stacking contexts.

When the Z-Index value is negative, the element is placed behind any elements that have undefined or positive Z-Index values. However, negative values are known to cause rendering glitches in various browsers, so try to avoid using negative Z-Index values.

Now that we've explained how Z-Index works, there are two ways to implement an "overlay popup" – an element that hovers on top of all other elements, which looks like a dialog box. We could declare this absolute positioned element at the end of the document, right before closing the *body* tag; or we could place the element anywhere that has an undefined stacking context, and assign a Z-Index value to this element.

If you have total control of the generated code, you should definitely use the first approach. By the way, the "natural" stacking order where the later declared elements are brought to the front is called the **Source Order**.

There are times when the top most elements have to be declared before other elements. In this case you'll have to resort to Z-Index. But remember, if you can somehow engineer the code to use source order, managing stacking orders could be so much simpler.

In general, if an element is unexpectedly covered by other elements, or unexpected revealed, it indicates an incorrect stacking order. We can fix the issue by either rearranging the elements, or assigning Z-Index to the proper stacking context. There is, however, one exception.

In some older version of IE, the dropdown list (the select tag) always stays in front of any other elements. This bug is rooted in the internal implementation of the dropdown element. While all other elements are rendered as graphics by the browser, the dropdown is a window by itself. Imagine you have two browser windows: it doesn't matter which element is the top most; once you drag another window on top of it, it covers everything! This is exactly the case with the select tag.

If you care at all about legacy browser support, you can either try to avoid using an overlay popup and dropdown list on the same page or you can dynamically hide the dropdown list elements, or you can use an iframe object as a background. An iframe is also implemented as a window so it'll cover the dropdown list.

4.11 Changing Visibility

The visibility of an element can be altered through either the *visibility* or *display* CSS attributes.

The necessity of showing or hiding an element becomes more obvious when the visibility style is changed dynamically via JavaScript, as we'll see in later chapters.

To hide an element, we can set the *display* to *none*, or *visibility* to *hidden*:

```
<div>Line 1</div>
<div style="display:none;">Line 2</div>
<div>Line 3</div>
<div style="visibility:hidden;">Line 4</div>
<div>Line 5</div>
```

Try the above code in a browser. You'll see that both Line 2 and Line 4 are invisible. However, the space that Line 4 takes up is preserved. The space for Line 2 is completely gone.

In other words, hiding with *display* is visually equivalent not having the element at all. Hiding with *visibility* hides the content without collapsing the space.

If an element is hidden through *visibility*, you can turn it back on by setting the *visibility* to *visible*:

```
<style>
#logo{visibility:hidden;}
</style>

<div id="logo" style="visibility:visible;">Test</div>
```

The above code is unlikely to exist in real life applications because the default visibility of an element is normal, and there's no point to hide and show the same element in the same page at the same time. We'll see in later chapters that the *visibility* attribute is dynamically set to *normal*, as a way to implement some toggling visual effects.

If the element is hidden through *display*, you'll have to set the *display* attribute to the elements original display mode, which is either *block* or *inline*. As discussed earlier, a block element takes up a line by itself while an inline element flows. By default, the *div* elements are block and *span* elements are inline.

4.12 Working with Fonts

When we talk about fonts in the context of web design, we usually mean text treatment, which is part of a much broader scope – typesetting. Font handling has a level of complexity that potentially deserves a book on its own. Since type setting is beyond the scope of this book, we only cover the basic CSS vocabulary and concepts that allow you to manipulate certain aspects of text.

Font Size Units

In CSS, the font size is defined as a numeric value and a unit:

```
<span style="font-size:12pt;">Test</span>
```

There are two main types of units: Relative (or Scalable) and Absolute.

Relative units are em, ex and px;
Absolute units are in, cm, mm, pt and pc.

Personally I find the notion of relative or absolute confusing because these concepts are defined in reference to print. For instance, in, which stands for inches, is considered to be an absolute unit because regardless what your screen resolution is, the browser will attempt to render a 1in text to a character frame of about 1 inch tall. To me, this is Relative, because I've been working with digital graphics, and I care about the number of pixels. The same 1 inch text requires different number of pixels on different screen resolutions. How is that Absolute, if you use screen as the point of reference?

To avoid confusion, I'd like to call "relative units" "**screen units**"; and "absolute units" "**print units**".

Print units are easy to explain. Inches (*in*), centimeters (*cm*) and millimeters (*mm*) are the physical measurement we use. Points (*pt*) and picas (*pc*) are defined in the print industry. As of CSS 2.0, one point is $1/72^{th}$ of an inch. One pica is equal to 12 points. It's worth noting that the typical screen resolution is 72 dpi, or dots per inch. The "dot" in dpi is the point.

Now let's talk about screen units. Consider the following code:

```
<div style="font-size:20px;font-family:arial;">
  20px: MmEeXx
  <div style="font-size:2em;">
```

```
    2em: MmEeXx
    <div style="font-size:2em;">
      2em: MmEeXx
    </div>
  </div>
  <div style="font-size:5ex;">
    5ex: MmEeXx
  </div>
</div>
```

The output is measured in the following diagram:

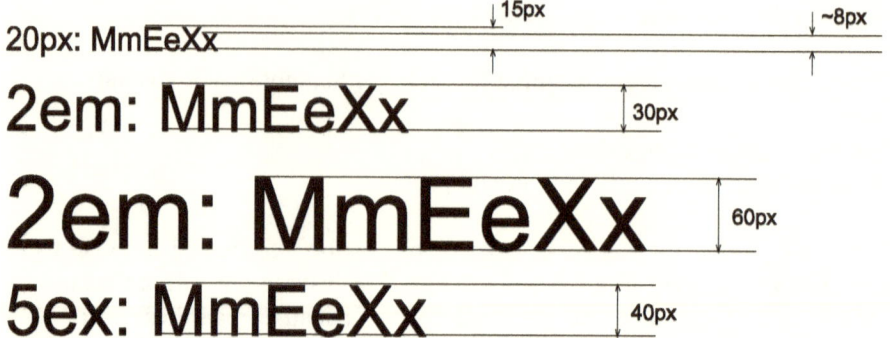

Note the lower case in the 20px line is actually measured in 10px. For the sake of explanation, let's treat it as 8px for now.

Also note the second line of "em" text is nested in another 20em block. Comparing this to pixel unit, the result is intriguing.

A 20-pixel "M" would have the same size everywhere on the same page, assuming the same font face. The EM measure is defined on the *current* font size, in particular the height of the current capitalized E, or the width of the current capitalized M.

When we first set the text to 2em, the font height becomes twice as tall as the previous E, which is 30px instead 15px. When we set the font size to 2em instead an already 2em block, the 30px font is doubled in size again. If you want to explicitly set the font size of the inner block to the same size, use *1em* instead.

Similarly, the unit EX is defined by measuring the lowercase e, or lowercase x. The measurement is applied, still, to the uppercase E in the targeted text.

The reason capitalized letters E and M, and lowercase x are used is because they better represent the average case of letter dimensions. Letters I and H tend to be too narrow (undershoot) whereas letters A and O tend to be too wide (overshoot).

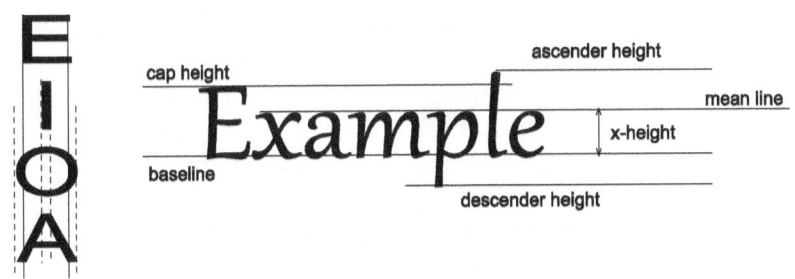

Are you still wondering why, in the previous code example, the font size is measured as 15 pixels although we specified 20 pixels, and why the *x* is 10 pixels instead 8?

Different typefaces are designed differently. They vary in the measures that are illustrated in the above diagram. The Arial font has the same cap height and ascender height, but an x-height that's slightly taller than how tall the browser thinks an *x* should be. What this means is that to determine the pixel measure of a font size, we'll have to try and err a bit to get the exact size in the mockup that's provided by the graphic designer.

You may have heard from other sources that *em* and *ex* provide better accessibility and that they should be preferred units for screen viewing. I personally find these units too clumsy to use. As demonstrated in an earlier example, the actual size of the text, when described in *em*, depends on the context. This means if I move the text around, I may have to recalculate its font size in order to retain the same look. This goes against code portability.

The drawback of using pixel unit is that when you increase the font size setting in the browser, the text stays the same, and this is not as accessible as *em*-based text. However, most modern browsers now scale the text even if it's expressed in pixels. For building web applications, I absolutely prefer *px* as the unit.

The *font-family* Attribute

The typeface of an element can be set using the *font-family* style property. This attribute takes a list of font family name or generic font family name.

There are five generic font families: *serif, sans-serif, cursive, fantasy* and *monospace*. Typical typefaces for each generic font are Times New Roman, Arial, Script and Comic Sans respectively.

The exact font you wish to use may not be available on the target computer. The font family list provides a mechanism to fall back on to more generic fonts. For example, fewer computers have Helvetica installed, but most of them do have Arial. Just in case Arial is also not available, we let the browser to choose the most suitable font from the sans-serif font family:

```
body{font-family: Helvetica, Arial, sans-serif;}
```

Always leave the generic font to the end of the font list.

If the font name has a space in it, put the font in quotation marks:

```
body{font-family: Georgia, 'Times New Roman', serif;}
```

However, never put generic font names in quote. Otherwise, the browser will look for a font called, for instance, "serif" and fail to find the font. This defeats the purpose of having generic fonts.

Using Embedded Fonts... Or Not

Proposed by CSS2 and now fully adopted by CSS3, the font-face attribute provides a mechanism to define a typeface through an external font file.

Imagine we have designed an awesome font called Alien. If we include the font directly like we did in the previous examples, the font wouldn't work because the users' computers don't have Alien installed.

Now we save the font file (*alien.otf*) in the web root directly, which is in the same folder as the main CSS file. Then declare the custom font face:

```
@font-face {
    font-family: Alien;
    src: url(alien.otf);
```

```
}
body: {font-family: Alien, 'Comic Sans', fantasy;}
```

Note there're no quotation marks around the file name in the URL resource.

Embedded fonts seem like an elegant solution, but they're by no means a silver bullet. If I can get away with web safe fonts or image replacement, as we'll soon discuss, I would always avoid embedding fonts.

First of all, the *@font-face* attribute is **not universally supported** by all browsers. If your font looks drastically different from the backup fonts, a lot of your users are in for a surprise. Different browsers support **different font formats**, so you'll need to provide **multiple sources** for each browser. Also some font files are large. Downloading them tend to **make the browser unresponsive**. There's also a **controversy around font licensing**. Free fonts are not as well designed as professional fonts. But professional fonts cost money, and the download mechanism of embedded font allows everyone to easily steal the font.

Considering all the drawbacks, embedding font isn't really worth the trouble in my opinion.

Image Replacement

Before CSS3 perfects the embedded fonts, we have to resort to alternatives. There are many techniques for replacing text with images. Some even use JavaScript to dynamically detect and replace the text. Here I'll show you how to use background image to replace text. This technique was first used by Todd Fahrner, so it's called Fahrner Image Replacement (FIR).

The way it works is quite simple. Pick your favorite typeface in your image editor and save the text as an image. Take note of the dimension of the text image. Let's say the text is "About Us" and the dimension of the image is 320 by 140.

```
<style>
#aboutus{
   background-image:url(aboutus.png);
   width:320px; height: 140px;
}
#aboutus span{
```

```
    display:none;
}
</style>
<div id="aboutus"><span>About Us</span></div>
```

The above code performs two tasks. It hides the text inside the *span* tag; it also displays the text image as the background image. The effect is that the user will see the graphic version of the text banner, and search engine robots can still see the text version. You can find more about using background images in Chapter 4.13. The technique of using the *span* tag is also discussed in Chapter 4.15.1.

Note that this replacement method is known to fail certain screen readers. If accessibility is important to your website or application, you'll have to research more on other techniques.

Bold, Italic and Underline

The attributes for setting a piece of text to bold, italic and underlined are *font-weight*, *font-style* and *text-decoration* respectively.

The *font-weight* attribute takes the value of either *normal* or *bold*. Of course some other values, such as "*bolder*", are also supported, but because of browser differences, and the lack of variation in the typeface you choose, you may get inconsistent results.

As for *font-style*, use either *normal* or *italic*. You may have seen another option "*oblique*". The difference between italic and oblique is that italic is a font variation, and oblique is a text treatment. An italic *K* looks slanted, but it is a font by itself. Setting the letter K to oblique means get the upward K from the font, and then transform the image so that the K looks slanted. Note this is a theoretical difference. Most browsers treat *italic* and *oblique* the same, if they support *oblique* at all. Again, reduce the vocabulary and save yourself some trouble.

The underline is added to text by the *text-decoration* property. Earlier in Chapter 4.7 we have already seen *text-decoration* in action:

```
a, a:visited, a:line {text-decoration:none;}
a:hover {text-decoration:underline;}
```

Text Transform

You can change the letter casing of an element without modifying its text. For example, we can display the following item in uppercase:

```
<span style="text-transform:uppercase;">Test message</span>
```

Other values the text-transform property can take are *capitalize, lowercase* and *none*. When we say "capitalizing a text" we often mean putting the text to all caps, i.e. *uppercase*. The *capitalize* option only promote the first letter in each word to uppercase. In other words, *capitalize* means "title case".

Next time when you decide to make all the links in your web page footer all caps, use *text-transform* instead, as it preserves the original information.

White Spacing

Another handy CSS property for handling text is the *white-space* attribute. It takes the value of *normal, nowrap, pre, pre-line* and *pre-wrap*. You can look up each value in a CSS reference. What we're really interested here is the *nowrap* option.

When the text is longer than the width of its container, it breaks into the next line. Sometimes we do not want this behavior. We want to limit the text to one line, and cut off the excessive characters. Chapter 4.15.3 talks about the *overflow* property. In order to properly "trim" or "clip" text, both *white-space* and *overflow* need to be used in conjunction.

```
<style>
.clip{
    width:100px;
    overflow:hidden;
    white-space:nowrap;
}
</style>
<div class="clip">
This is a very long test message that goes on and on and on
</div>
```

Try disabling the *white-space* property and you'll see the default text wrap behavior renders the overflow (clipping) useless.

4.13 Background Images

In CSS, you can specify the background image of an element. It is common practice to use a block element such as a *div* block as a medium.

```
<style>
#banner{
    background-image: url(images/banner.png);
    width:300px; height:100px;
}
</style>
<div id="banner">Test Message</div>
```

Prepare a 300x100 image file and save it as *images/banner.png*. The banner container in the above example is configured to have the exact dimensions as the image.

Try setting the banner container's size to 50x50; then set its size to 600x200.

You can see that unlike the *img* tag, a background image does not stretch the container. Picture the *div* container as a wall, and the background image is one piece of a tiled wall paper. If the wall is smaller than the wall paper image, you see only part of the wall paper; if the wall is larger than the wall paper image, the wall paper tiles up, or "repeats" itself in both horizontal and vertical directions. Later we'll see that this tiling behavior can be customized.

The syntax of the *background-image* attribute is simple but shouldn't be overlooked. Beginners tend to make two types of mistakes. They either forget to specify the type of data source, namely wrapping the filename with the term "url" and brackets, or they put the filename in quotation marks.

```
background-image: url(banner.png)      /* correct */
background-image: banner.png           /* wrong */
background-image: url("banner.png")    /* wrong */
background-image: url('banner.png')    /* wrong */
```

The path of the image file is relative to the location of the CSS file.

Another important difference between CSS background image and the *img* tag is that CSS background image changes the appearance of an existing element while the *img* tag introduces a new element. In the above example, the text "Test Message" is a child element of the banner container, so the text is displayed on top of the background image. You could emulate the stacking effect by absolutely positioning an *img* element and the text overlay inside a relatively positioned container. But this approach introduces unnecessary complexity.

CSS background image also provides powerful tiling and cropping control.

You could look up the following attributes in a reference book:

```
background-color
background-image
background-repeat
background-attachment
background-position
```

Or you could learn about the *background* property, which is a shorthand property that combines all of the above settings.

Here's an example of *background*:

```
background: transparent url(logo.png) no-repeat top left
```

The first parameter is the background color, followed by the background image, then the tiling settings, and then the anchoring position.

Now let's discuss each parameter.

It's a common misconception that the term "transparent" makes the background image transparent. When an element has both background color and background image, the background color becomes a "filler color".

Use the above example on an oversized *div* container. Make the container much bigger than the background image, and disable tiling by using "no-repeat". Instead of using "transparent", use "black". You can see the margins of the background image are painted in black. If the background-color is set to transparent, it simply means do not fill the gaps with a solid color.

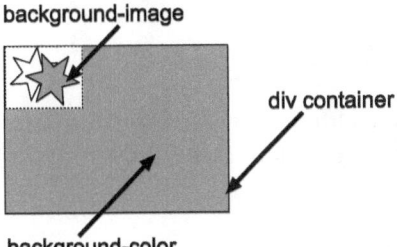

background-image

div container

background-color

The background-image and background-color combination has one non-trivial application, which we'll see after we've covered the *image-repeat* attribute.

The background of an element takes the following *repeat* values: *no-repeat*, *repeat*, *repeat-x*, and *repeat-y*.

There are times when you want to tile an image only in one direction. The attribute values *repeat-x* and *repeat-y* are for horizontal- and vertical-tiling respectively.

Horizontal tiling, or repeating, is commonly used to implement gradients.

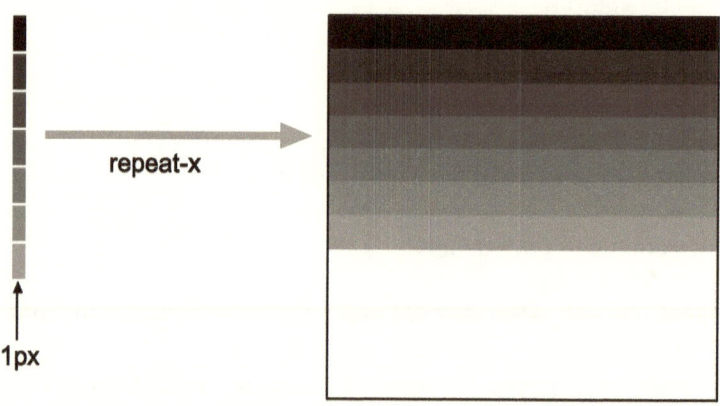

Prepare a gradient image that is 1 pixel wide. Stretch the image as the background of the document body:

```
<style>
body{
  padding: 0; margin:0;    /* reset default white spaces */
  background: transparent url(bg.png) repeat-x top left;
}
</style>
```

The above approach not only saves the bandwidth and time to download the background image file, but is also adaptive to the width of the container (in this case, the body of the document).

As illustrated in the above diagram, the gradient doesn't end gracefully. This is where the *background-color* attribute comes in handy:

```
<style>
body{
  padding: 0; margin:0;    /* reset default white spaces */
  background: #808080 url(bg.png) repeat-x top left;
}
</style>
```

Use a color picker in your image editing program to find the hex code of the exiting color of the gradient, i.e. the color of the bottom pixel. The above code assumes the color to be #808080.

The background color and image work together to create a seamless gradient background:

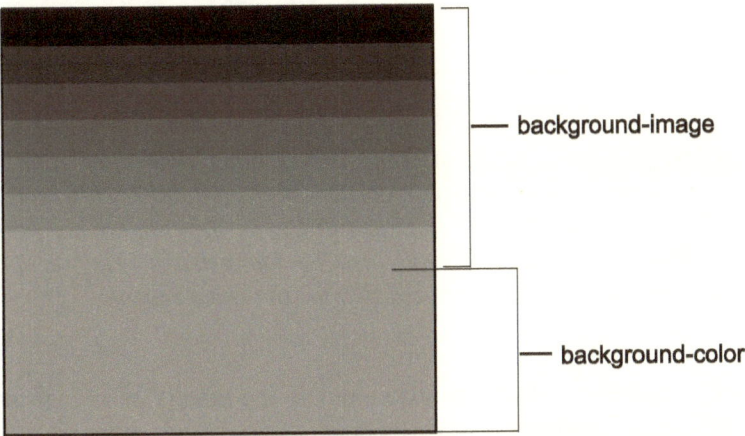

The document body grows with the content, so does the background color coverage.

The last set of parameters in the *background* shorthand is *background-position*.

The position settings in the previous examples are "top left", meaning if the container is larger than the image, then the image is placed on the top left corner of the container.

The following code puts the image on the vertical center, but right edge of the container:

```
<style>
#logo {
width:100%;
height:200px;
background:transparent url(logo.png) no-repeat center right;
}
</style>
<div id="logo"></div>
```

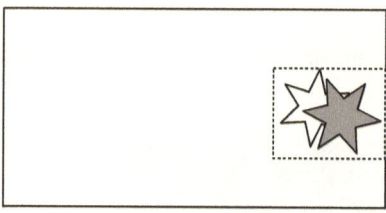

Be very careful when using positioning values other than "top" and "left".
All browsers agree on the top left corner of a container. However, if the
width or height is implicit and calculated different, then the anchor points for
right and bottom, respectively, will also be inconsistent. The vertical and
horizontal-centers could be miscalculated for the same reason.

The *image-position* attribute can also emulate the effects of an icon pack or
even CSS-based animation. We'll cover CSS-based animation in the
JavaScript section. For now let's take a look at the icon pack.

In a web application, there're usually many graphic icons and they tend to be
small. For example, the Google Docs application uses the following icons:

If we were to use the conventional method, we'd have a separate image file
for each icon, and display them using either the *img* tag or background
image.

When a browser displays a web page full of small images, it simultaneously opens several connections. For simplicity, we can assume that each image corresponds to a separate connection. A web application with 20 different visible icons would initiate 20 connections all at once, not counting the page itself and other external files such as CSS style sheets and JavaScript files.

Connections are a very expensive resource. Regardless of network speed, the number of connections per page request directly affects the concurrency level of a server. Concurrency level is the number of users the server can support at the same time.

In order to reduce the number of connections, we could put all the icons in one image file. Then we use a container that is smaller than the icon image. By manipulating the position of the background image, we can align the logical icon in the icon set with the target container.

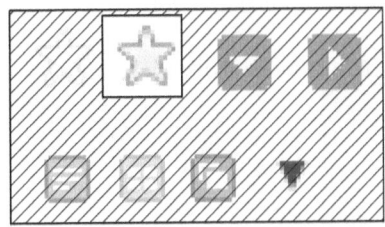

To display a star, we have a div element that's 32x32 – the same size as the icon. The star icon is positioned at (36,5) according to the above diagram.

```
<style>
.star{
width:32px; height:32px;
background:transparent url(icons.png) no-repeat -36px -5px;
}
</style>
<div class="star"></div>
```

Note the coordinates in *image-position* are measured relative to the top left corner of the container. Therefore, negative values are used.

Another way to look at this is to treat the page as a layered birthday card. The top layer is the container – the card cover with a hole. The background image lies behind the cover. In order to reveal the icon at (36,5), you'll need to pull the back card up by 5 pixels (-5px) and to the left by 36 pixels (-36px).

Realistically speaking, connection saving through this technique is "nice to have" but not absolutely necessary. Modern browsers are smart at caching image resources. CSS background images are more likely to be cached, and in a more persistent manner. Clipping from an icon set requires the container to have a fixed width and height; this might pose constraints in other aspects of coding. So combine the images only when it's convenient to do so.

4.14 Overflow

An element container that has no explicit width or height expands itself to accommodate the content. When explicit dimensions are set, and that the content takes up more space than the container's size, overflow occurs.

Compare the rendering result of the following code in various browsers:

```
<style>
#container{
    width:100px;
    height:100px;
    border:solid 1px;
}
</style>
<div id="container">
    Hello<br>
    <img src="300x300.jpg" width="300" height="300">
</div>
```

On most standard compliant browsers such as Firefox, you'll see that the container remains its original size, and the content "spills" out of the container:

On some versions of IE, the container grows to its content size, acting as if the width or height was not specified in the first place:

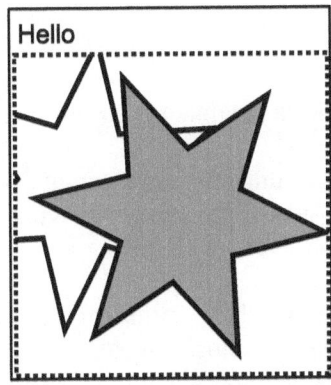

In either case, it's wrong to allow the content to take up more space its fix-sized container – unless a proper overflow behavior is specified.

There are two overflow modes: one clips the content, and the other generates scrollbars. There's also an automatic mode that generates scroll bars only if the content is larger than the container. In practice, clipping and auto scrolling are commonly used.

Use *overflow:hidden* to clip the content; use *overflow:auto* to enable auto scrollbars.

```
<style>
#container{
    width:100px;
    height:100px;
```

```
        border:solid 1px;
        overflow:hidden;
        position:relative;
}
#content{
        position:absolute;
        top:0px;
        left:0px;
}
</style>
<div id="container">
        <div id="content">
                Hello<br>
                <img src="300x300.jpg" width="300" height="300">
        </div>
</div>
```

The above code emulates a "clipping view port".

Go to Google Maps and drag the map around. You'll see the map view is contained on the right side of the screen. Moving the map to the left doesn't cover the left side of the screen with the map.

Similarly, you can change the position of the view port by changing the coordinates of the *content* block. Note the relative-absolute positioning combo is used, as explained in Chapter 4.9.

The clipping view looks something like the following:

Since the content is larger than the container, a set of scrollbars shows up when we set the overflow property to *auto*:

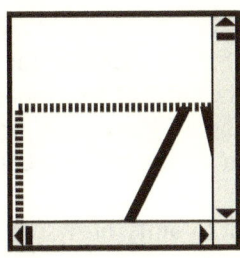

Note on a mobile Safari that's running on an iPhone or iPad, the scrollbars are not visible even when the overflow is set to auto. However, the user can still scroll the inner content by swiping with two fingers. Although the overflow attribute is a great way to implement view ports, content panels or whatever you wish to call it, it makes a clumsy user interface on a touch device. So if you want to optimize for iOS devices, avoid inner scrollbars.

You can also specify overflow modes independently by using the overflow-x and overflow-y attributes. For example, you can scroll vertically but clip horizontally.

4.15 Notable Quirks

A quirk is an unexpected behavior in a specific browser. In other words, the look of a web page may be inconsistent in different browsers; these inconsistencies are traced back to various quirks.

As mentioned in Chapter 4.5, the declaration of document type at the beginning of the HTML document is an attempt to ensure that all browsers behave the same way, so that developers don't have to bother all the quirks.

Unfortunately, *doctype* is ineffective for two main reasons.

First older versions of browsers, especially ones in the IE family, do not fully comply the standards that are specified in the *doctype* header. Many of these browsers are being used by a significant number of users. For many public facing websites, dropping support for old browsers means dropping a sizable share of the potential market.

Second, there are still many holes in various HTML standards. Even with a document type, browsers still disagree on many undefined behavior.

Realistically, to ensure maximum compatibility, a web developer needs to be immensely knowledgeable of the version of the standards he's targeting in addition to all the browsers he intends to support. At the end of the day, it comes down to the website being knowingly broken in some old browsers versus unknowingly broken in some old browsers.

I find it ironic that the attempt to unify browsers has, to some extent, brought far more complexity to web development. If a page can be made to look consistently in quirks mode, that is, without specifying a document type, then it's almost safe to say that this page is "naturally compatible" to all browsers.

Before we go through the list of notable quirks, let's look at the "genetics" of browsers. It may seem like there are many brands and versions of browsers, there are only a few "blood lines", or layout engines. A layout engine is the component that parses HTML and CSS code, generates the internal tree of DOM notes, composing them on a web page and rendering them with the proper visual styles.

Many embedded web browsers behave exactly like Internet Explorer because they all use the Trident layout engine. The Gecko layout engine is used by Firefox, Camino and all Mozilla based browsers. Both Safari and Google Chrome use the WebKit engine while Opera has always been powered by the Presto engine.

Thanks to the trend of open source, standardization and code reuse, new browsers tend to inherit the features and quirks of one of the above said layout engines.

4.15.1 Padding and Widths

Do not mix explicit width (or height) and padding in the same element. It may seem logical to do, but as explained in Chapter 4.5, the calculation of the total width (or height) is ambiguous.

Consider the following code:

```
<div style="width:200px;background-color:#dedede;">
    This is a test message
</div>
```

The text doesn't have any breathing room to the left. We need to give it, say, 10 pixels of left padding so that it looks more pleasing.

Resist the urge of adding that 10px left padding on the same element! Instead, create a nested layer of *div*, which I call the "padding shell".

```
<div style="width:200px;background-color:#dedede;">
    <div style="padding-left:10px;">
        This is a test message
    </div>
</div>
```

If you want to avoid in-line CSS, you can use the "span shell" technique as illustrated below:

```
<style>
#test{
    width:200px; background-color:#dedede;
}

#test span{
    display:block;
    padding-left:10px;
}
</style>
<div id="test">
    <span>
        This is a test message.
    </span>
</div>
```

The *span* tag is used instead of *div* so that the id-span pattern can be easily described in the CSS selector. Remember, by default, a *span* is an inline element; we override it to behave like a *div* by setting it to a block element. Next time when you see a *span* tag immediately follow an opening *div* tag, there's a high chance it's a padding shell.

4.15.2 Centering

There are times when we need to place an element in the center of the page, or the center of its containing element. Traditionally people have been using the *center* tag, which is now deprecated.

Unless explicitly specified otherwise, centering an element means placing it in the horizontal center. The spacing on the left of the element should be the same as the spacing on its right.

Translating the above definition literally, here's what most people do to center an element:

```
<style>
#main{
    /* empty for now */
}
#content{
    margin:0 auto;
}
</style>
<div id="main">
    <div id="content">
        Put me in the center of the page!<br>
        But do not center-justify the text.
    </div>
</div>
```

The above code doesn't work. Not even in any browser.

The first thing that's missing is an explicit width. Without the width, the content div is as wide as its container, so the definition of "having the same spaces on both sides" wouldn't make sense.

```
#content{
    margin:0 auto;
    width:300px;
}
```

The content may seem to be still off centered. This is because the said width is larger than the actual visible content. The more accurate the estimate is, the more centered the element looks. In practice, the content is usually more than just a blob of text. It's often the case that the element to be centered has a known width.

Once you have a width set, centering is fixed… at least in Firefox.

The code still doesn't work in IE, because the Trident family has a different approach to centering. The term "center" is a relative concept. It takes a host, or container, and an object, or content.

The element in Firefox says: Put me in the center of my container.
And the container in IE says: Put all my stuff in my center.

```
#main{
    text-align:center;
}
```

Text align is an inherited attribute. It affects not only text but all the elements inside the container. This means the above code change will correctly put the content *div* in the center; however, it will also make the text inside the content *div* center-justified. To correct this side effect, we need to override the inherited rule:

```
#content{
    margin:0 auto;
    width:300px;
    text-align:left;
}
```

Now the entire code looks like this:

```
<style>
#main{
    text-align:center;
}
#content{
    margin:0 auto;
    width:300px;
    text-align:left;
}
</style>
<div id="main">
```

```
    <div id="content">
        Put me in the center of the page!<br>
        But do not center-justify the text.
    </div>
</div>
```

Just to recapture the ingredients that are needed to center an element properly in all browsers, here's a checklist:

- Set a fixed width
- Use *margin:0 auto* to center in Firefox
- Use *text-align:center* on container to center in IE
- Override with *text-align:left* in current element

Next time when your centering is not working, use the above list and see what's missing.

Centering Absolute-Positioned Items

An absolute-positioned item does not respond to *margin:auto* well. In a composite layout where *position:absolute* is used, set the element's width to 100%, and place it on the left edge of its container. The content of the absolute-positioned element is then centered using previously discussed techniques:

```
<style>
#abs_{position:relative;}
#abs{
      position:absolute;
      top:10px;left:0;width:100%;
      text-align:center;
}
</style>
<div id="abs_">
      <div id="abs">
            Text to Center
      </div>
</div>
```

4.15.3 Overflow and Explicit Height

In Chapter 4.14 we discussed browser's different reactions to overflowing content. If the container has an explicit height without overflow setting, and that the content takes up more space, the content either "spill" out of the container, or "stretches" the container, depending on the layout engine.

| stretch | spill | implicit |

The above diagram illustrates a very common scenario of a messed up layout. The graphic designer might have not provisioned the long menu titles. The web developer then measures the height of the menu item. When the menu title becomes too long, such as in the case of "Products & Services", it first wraps to two lines because of the explicit width, then either stretches or spills.

This is one of the few cases when an improper implementation looks more broken in Firefox than in IE. But if you pay attention to the spacing in IE, it's also not so correct.

The root problem is design itself. Either the layout or content needs to be changed. If we have to make the best of the worst, we'll have to use implicit height.

Before the fix, the code looks something like the following:

```
<style>
.menuitem{
    background:transparent url(dots.png) repeat-y top left;
    width:250px;
}
.menuitem span{
    display:block;
    padding-left:10px;
```

```
        height:16px;
}
</style>
<div class="menu">
    <div class="menuitem">
        <span>About Us</span>
    </div>
    <div class="menuitem">
        <span>Products & Services</span>
    </div>
    <div class="menuitem">
        <span>Careers</span>
    </div>
    <div class="menuitem">
        <span>Contact Us</span>
    </div>
</div>
```

Except for the fixed height bug, the above code is an excellent example of implementing menu items. It exemplifies the use of a padding shell, as we have discussed in Chapter 4.15.1. It also uses repeat-y to tile the background images.

To apply the fix, we'll just need to drop the explicit height, and add spacing to the natural height of the content.

```
.menuitem span{
    display:block;
    padding-left:10px;
    height:16px;
    font-size:12px;
    padding-top:3px;
    padding-bottom:3px;
}
```

One line of text of font size 12px takes up about 12 pixels in height. Adding the padding from top and bottom gives a total of 16 pixels in height. This is nearly visually identical to the previous implementation.

When the text wraps into multiple lines, however, the content height expands, and the clearance on top and bottom of the text is still the same. The text seems vertical aligned. Considering the design itself could have been better, this implementation is good enough.

4.15.4 Floating

There are two common mistakes when using float. The first one is not having the float attribute on all floating elements; the other is not clearing the float. When either of the mistakes is made, browsers, IE and Firefox in particular, could render the page differently.

Compare the output of the following code in IE and Firefox:

```
<div style="float:left;">abcd</div>
<div style="float:left;">xyz</div>
<div style="clear:both;"></div>
<div>123</div>
```

Remove the left float in the second element "xyz". In IE, you'll see a gap between "abcd" and "xyz"; this gap doesn't exist in Firefox.

To further magnify the issue with the missing float, let's emulate a two column layout in a fixed width container. Add the following bolded lines to the above code:

```
<div style="width:300px;">
    <div style="float:left;width:100px;">abcd</div>
    <div style="width:100px;float:left;">xyz</div>
    <div style="clear:both;"></div>
</div>
<div>123</div>
```

Now the two columns are spaced apart. Without the help of a snapping tool and image editor to measure the exact pixels, the inconsistency between two browsers may go undetected. As a matter of fact, many websites suffer from this subtle bug.

Let's make the issue even more visible by tighten the container width to exactly 200 pixels – the sum of the two columns.

Quite expectedly, the 2-column layout "snapped" in IE. A common remedy is to reduce the width of one of the columns until they fit again. This approach is wrong because it dials us back to the previous "extra gap" scenario.

What's really missing is the left float we struck out in the code. Once we give it back, the problem's solved.

Similarly, when the chain of floating elements is not ended with a clearing element, the output could be different in browsers.

Remove the clearing element from the above example:

```
<div style="width:300px;">
    <div style="float:left;width:100px;">abcd</div>
    <div style="width:100px;float:left;">xyz</div>
    <div style="clear:both;"></div>
</div>
<div>123</div>
```

Compare the output in maximized windows, so that the content space is enough to accommodate the two columns and the text "123".

In Firefox, "123" is displayed as a third column whereas in IE, "123" is displayed in the next line as if the clearing element weren't removed at all. This is another one of the few scenarios where a page may look fine in IE but noticeably broken in Firefox.

Moral of the story: **assign floats to all elements, and always, always clear the float in the end.**

4.15.5 Small Containers

Try creating a red *div* block that's 5 pixels tall and 5 pixels wide.

```
<style>
.block{
    width:5px;height:5px;
    background-color:red;
}
```

```
</style>
<div class="block"></div>
```

Now view the above code in IE... Surprise!

The red block is much taller than 5 pixels. It's not a square at all.

My *hypothesis* is that IE somehow uses invisible filler content (text in particular) inside empty *div* elements. We have discussed in Chapter 4.15.3 about explicit height and overflow. In this case, we limit the height of the container to 5 pixels, but the content is taller than that, so the container is stretched to the content height.

Now it all makes sense, and we can fix the issue by making the content size smaller than its container. We set the font size to 1 pixel only:

```
.block{
    width:5px;height:5px;
    background-color:red;
    font-size:1px;
}
```

Note this is only necessary for containers with explicit, small heights. An empty *div* without explicit height takes up no space, not even in IE.

4.15.6 Opacity

An element can be made semi-transparent through the opacity attribute. Opacity is implemented differently in IE and Firefox. At one point, three CSS attributes had to be used simultaneously to cover most browsers:

IE: filter
Firefox: -moz-opacity
Opera: opacity

Firefox uses a naming convention for attributes that are proposed but not yet fully confirmed in the CSS standards. Before the final specification came out, the identifier -moz- was used to mark transitional, browser specific attributes.

Similarly, Safari and Chrome use the -webkit- identifier for some transitional features. This explains attributes like *-webkit-transform* and *-moz-border-radius*.

Both Safari and Chrome use the Webkit layout engine so you can expect similar rendering behavior in both browsers.

The *opacity* attribute is now fully standardized and supported by Firefox (Mozilla), Opera (Presto) and Chrome (WebKit). It takes a value from 0 to 1; 1 being fully opaque while 0 being fully transparent:

```
opacity:0.5 /* 50% transparency */
```

IE considers opacity to be one of the many filter modules that, in theory, infinitely extend the functionality of the browser. Microsoft provisioned a set of filter and transition effects such as alpha transparency, motion blur, rotation, mirror, gradient, etc., all implemented as internal filter plug-ins. This design is reflected in the *filter* attribute's syntax:

```
filter:alpha(opacity=50) /* 50% transparency */
```

Note the value is expressed in percentage without the percentage sign, ranging from 0 to 100.

Syntax is not the only difference – opacity may or may not be inherited.

If opacity is inherited, the effect is additive and cannot be reversed. In other words, if the parent has 50% opacity, all its children will look semi-transparent. If the child nodes have an opacity value of 100%, that's 100% of 50%, which is still 50%. If the child node opacity value is set to 50%, that's 50% of the original 50%, effectively 25% overall transparency.

In opacity is not inherited, only the opacity bearer (the element to which the opacity is assigned to) is affected.

Since the behavior of opacity inheritance is inconsistent across browsers and versions of browsers, we should not base our code on either assumption.

Opacity is commonly used to implement the transparent shadow behind a popup window, or the overall mask that dims the content page. Have the *div* blocks that are for mask, shadow and content declared independently from one another. We'll discuss more about pop ups and overlay effects in Chapter 5.2.2.

If you find yourself in the situation where IE seemingly ignores the opacity settings, even you use the *filter* attribute correctly, consider giving the element a "layout". The following web page details the concept of having a layout in IE:

http://www.satzansatz.de/cssd/onhavinglayout.html

Give the element an explicit width – any width other than "auto", and see if this fixes the problem.

```
<div style="filter:alpha(opacity=50);width:100%;">
Test
</div>
```

Realistically the element that needs to be transparent may already have a layout. It could be absolutely positioned or sharing horizontal space with other elements using float. The visual context the element is in requires it to have layout regardless, so in most cases, there's no need to add that 100% width.

The *opacity* attribute also has side effects on stacking context. Chapter 4.10 has discussed stacking orders in detail. In Firefox, assigning opacity to an element will automatically create a stacking order for this element. If you rely on Z-Index for certain visual effects, take extra caution when using transparency at the same time.

4.15.7 Inconsistent Default Values

Another source of layout inconsistency is default values. Browsers have different default values for margin and padding. This is mostly visible on the document body and form elements.

You can "reset" the defaults by clearing the white space:

```
<style>
body, form {margin:0; padding:0;}
</style>
```

Many other block elements also have inconsistent margin or padding values. For example, lists (*ul*, *ol*) and paragraphs (*p*).

You could download a master reset file that's released to the public domain:

http://meyerweb.com/eric/tools/css/reset/

Save the file as *reset.css*, and link it before linking your own style sheet.

```
<link rel="stylesheet" href="reset.css" type="text/css" />
```

The public reset file is an excellent baseline. Over time you may discover other inconsistencies or globally define your own preferences such as page color, font, etc.

There are other versions of reset files that are flowing around the Internet. Some may have side effects that you're not aware of. For instance, many of these reset files set the outline of active links to 0. As explained in Chapter 4.7, resetting outline styles without providing alternative visual cues makes the page less accessible.

Personally I prefer to set just the *body* tag. If I have a lot of forms on my web page, I'll reset the *form* tag too. As I encounter more and more inconsistent elements, I add them to the spreadsheet. This is clearly not the fastest way to get things done, but it has a few benefits.

First of all, without the false sense of perfection a reset file might give me, I'm more inclined to check for myself that every aspect of rendering is pixel perfect. When I introduce new tags other than the ones I have already normalized, I check again, and if they're displayed inconsistently, I look deeper into the cause and solutions. This process helps me, the developer, expand and refine my knowledge. Over time I become intimately familiar with the characteristics of each type of element. When I see a web page that's broken, I instantly know which tag is causing trouble.

Writing your own reset sheet is good for browser rendering performance, too. The reset file that I mentioned above is the "cleanest" and yet extensive enough one I can find. Even so, it unnecessarily reset the margin and padding for the *p* tag. Paragraphs, however, are supposed to have margin at their bottoms. Otherwise they don't look like paragraphs. So we'll have to reset the reset? When you write your own from ground up, you only reset it once. This is good not only for performance, but also simplifies code maintenance.

In addition to the margin and padding in paragraph elements, line height is also a source of inconsistency. From my painstaking debugging across all possible versions of browsers, I can tell you that pixel is the only unit that's interpreted consistently. If you font size is 12px, instead of setting the line height to 200% or 2em, use 24px. Be ready to be criticized for not being scalable, portable or adaptive, but also be ready to enjoy the rock solid, consistent result.

If you are also setting the font size for the entire document, set it for the *td* tag as well. Table cells do not otherwise inherit font settings from the document body.

```
body, table td {
    font-size:14px; font-family:arial;
}
```

4.15.8 Relative Positioning in Table Cells

The use of relative positioning is covered in Chapter 4.9. Remember that an absolutely positioned element needs to anchor on one of its parent elements. Either its immediate or indirect parent node needs to be relatively positioned.

The relative-absolute positioning combo allows total control over element placement. Test the following code in all your targeted browsers:

```
<table>
<tr><td>
   <div style="position:relative;">
   ABCD
   <div style="position:absolute;top:5px;left:0;">
   XYZ
   </div>
</td></tr>
<tr><td>
   <div style="position:relative;">
   ABCD
```

```
        <div style="position:absolute;top:5px;left:0;">
        XYZ
        </div>
</td></tr>
</table>
```

If you see two rows of ABCD, each covered by its own XYZ, then you may use absolute positioning inside a table cell. Some older versions of Firefox could not render the above code correctly.

Also do not assign *position:relative* to the *td* tag directly. Firefox, again, ignores the position attribute for table cells.

4.15.9 Full Table Width

Tables are suitable for displaying tabulated information. For example, a grid of numbers (spread sheet) or a submission form, where the form labels and fields need to align by columns, are typically implemented using tables.

In the past, tables have been misused and abused as a way of layout. But the opposite is also true – data grid and forms are where tables are supposed to be used, but they're often not.

By default, the table width adapts to the content width:

```
<table>
   <tr><td>A</td><td>B</td></tr>
   <tr><td>X</td><td>Y</td></tr>
</table>
```

There are times when you want the table to stretch the entire width. The following ways of setting widths are not equivalent.

```
<table width="100%">
<table style="width:100%;">
```

Experiment in several browsers. From my experience, the first method works better. Either case is problematic in IE because 100% is often ambiguously interpreted. If you notice that your table is taking up the full width of the document (i.e. too wide), consider confining the table in a div with explicit (and yet percentage-based) width:

```
<div style="width:100%;">
    <table width="100%">
        ...
    </table>
</div>
```

Once the 100% wide table is wrapped in a 100% wide div, it magically works – the magic of quirks mode!

4.15.10 Top Margin and Bottom Padding

There are times when margins and padding are visually equivalent. For example, a *div* container with no explicit width or height and no background image could use either top margin or top padding. If you are in this indifferent situation, use *padding-top* instead of *margin-top*, and *margin-bottom* instead of *padding-bottom* whenever you can.

The reasons is that there's a glitch in Firefox that sometimes collapses the parent container of a top-margined element.

```
<div style="background-color:red;">
  <div style="background-color:green;margin-top:10px;">
  Test
  </div>
</div>
```

The red background fails to render in Firefox because the container is "dragged down" by the green container. To fix this issue, we can move the gap to the parent container:

```
<div style="background-color:red;padding-top:10px;">
  <div style="background-color:green;margin-top:10px;">
  Test
  </div>
</div>
```

In IE, padding on a *table* is inherited by each cell or not at all recognized, depending on the context:

```
<table style="padding-bottom:10px;">
<tr><td>Line 1</td></tr>
<tr><td>Line 2</td></tr>
</table>
```

If you only need to create some clearance at the bottom of the table, use *margin-bottom* instead.

4.16 Media Query

This section is an addition to the original book because of the popularity and necessity of responsive designs. A web page is said to be responsive if the content layout adjusts to various screen sizes and devices, making the most of the screen real-estate. We will discuss the strategies and procedures for building responsive pages in Chapter 5. For now, let's look at a key element - CSS media query.

The first thing to know about media query is that it's not supported by all browsers. However, Firefox and Webkit browsers (Chrome, Safari), as well as more recent versions of IE support media query. Webkit support alone covers most of the mobile phone basis.

Also include the following tag in the HTML header:

```
<meta name="viewport" content="width=device-width" />
```

CSS media query can be simply described as "conditional CSS rules" based on media settings. For example, the following rule takes effect only when the browser window is narrower than 600 pixels:

```
@media screen and (max-width:600px){
    body{background:red;}
}
```

Although modern browsers support a large variety of media features such as screen orientation, pixel density (resolution), colour depth, etc., min-width and max-width are often enough to implement a fully responsive layout. In Chapter 5 we'll see how to use media query in a structured, manageable fashion.

This concludes our brief introduction to CSS. Keep on reading the next chapter on how to apply the knowledge of HTML, PHP and CSS to build static websites. Before you have mastered the concept and techniques discussed in this chapter, try not to confuse yourself with more "advanced" topics.

5.0 Skinning Websites

The process of converting a web page mockup into a real HTML page is called skinning. It is also called "templatizing" because traditionally the same HTML page template is used to implement all the pages of a website.

This chapter shows you the entire process of building static websites, also known as "brochure sites", starting with the first step – skinning.

5.1 Image Formats

The main image formats for the web are *.gif*, *.jpg* (or *.jpeg*) and *.png*. Also there is the icon format *.ico* for favicon. Let's look at the underling implementations of each format so that you understand their native capabilities and when to use which format.

5.1.1 Vector vs. Raster

Digital images are either vector or raster. Vector images are described as drawing instructions and are therefore scalable. Raster images are collections of grids of pixels. They are also called bitmap images.

The difference between vector and raster graphics can be exemplified by a red rectangle. Vector version of a rectangle would be described as "a rectangle starting at the location (200,120) with a dimension of 30x20 and filled with red". You could interpret the numbers with arbitrary units such as points, inches and centimeters. Any print unit described in Chapter 4.12 can be used. You can even apply transformations such as scaling, sheering or rotation without causing any quality degradation. Vector images are also called scalable images.

Raster images use a grid of colored pixels to represent information. For a rectangle that's 30 pixels wide and 20 pixels tall, 600 pixels are used. Each pixel carries the color red. Note this is only a logical representation, not necessarily how a bitmap image is stored in a file. A rectangle is a trivial case. Even raster images can be easily scaled up or down without losing details, because there's no detail to lose! We just *know* what a bigger rectangle should look like. But try scaling up a jpeg picture of a circle, or slanted rectangle. You'll see raster images are only suitable for display in fixed resolutions.

Websites embed mostly raster images because they're easier to render comparing to vector graphics. The process of converting a vector image to a raster image at *a specific resolution* is called "rasterization". Graphic designers commonly use tools like Adobe Illustrator to work with vector graphics, and then export, or "rasterize" the work to a PNG file at 72dpi; the file is further processed in Photoshop – a raster image editor.

5.1.2 Color Depth

We perceive color when light is beamed in our eyes, either directly or reflected from another surface. A white light is a composition of lights traveling in different wavelengths, covering the entire color spectrum. If we shine a white light through a prism, the light is split into a rainbow, revealing all its color components. Red has the least degree of refraction while purple has the most. Red and purple, or "violet", define the edge of the visible color spectrum. Any wavelength that's greater than red's is called "infrared", and wavelengths that are shorter than blue are called "ultraviolet".

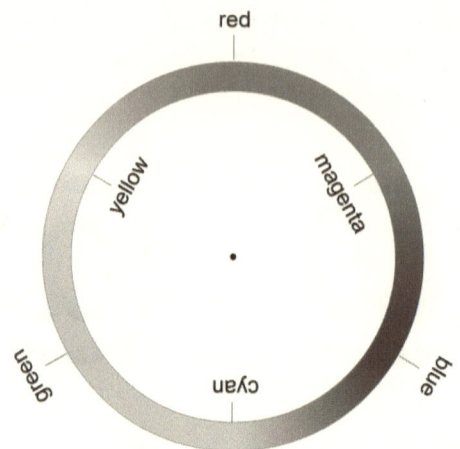

If we mix the longer waves (red) with shorter waves (violet) we get blue. The visible colors are usually arranged in a circle of continues colors – the color wheel. Red, Blue and Green are picked as "primary colors". When we add these primary colors together in different portions, we get other colors in the color wheel. The RGB color model is an additive model. The computer screen uses RGB because the monitor shines lights directly at us.

Printing, on the other hand, uses a subtractive color model because light is reflected from paper. Inks of different colors absorb the wavelengths that do not belong to the represented color. The color wheel shows that the compliments of Red, Green and Blue are Cyan, Magenta and Yellow respectively. This forms the CMY color model for process printing. Black ink is added to this process both for saving ink and alignment, or "keying", and hence the letter K, in CMYK.

Note that Red, Green and Blue are equally far apart from one another in the color wheel for mathematical convenience. The human eyes are not equally sensitive to each primary color. Other color models exist to more naturally describe how we perceive color. One example is Hue-Saturation-Brightness, or HSV, where V stands for "value". HSV is commonly used in motion pictures or statistical heat maps. Some video formats also exploit HSV to save bandwidth.

The hexadecimal format we use to describe color in HTML is RGB. Every two of the six letters represent a primary color component.

For example, #FFFF00 is R:255, G:255 and B:0, which is Yellow.

The reason the numeric of 0 to 255 is used is because it's exactly one byte. Remember hexadecimal (base-16) is just a short hand of writing binary (base-2). Instead of writing 1111 0001, we write F1. Every two hexadecimal digits represent a byte, or 8 bits.

With fewer bits, you can still express the entire color range, except that the transition from 0 to full intensity will not be smooth. Compare the color transitions between 16 values (4-bit) and 4 values (2-bit):

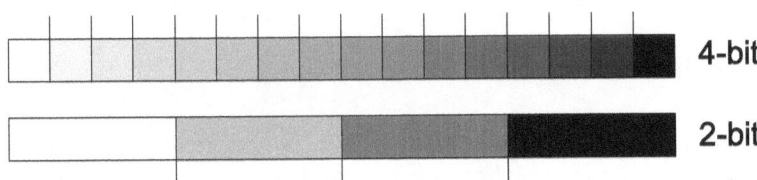

The number of bits allocated for describing color is called the "color depth" of an image. For each primary color component, having 256 intervals is granular enough. This is why grayscale images often have 256 colors. For color images, each component needs 256 colors, or 8-bits. Since there are 3 colors, a true color image has a depth of 24 bits. In the color settings for an old monitor in Windows, you've probably seen "High Color (16 bit)" and "True Color (24 bit)". Try to display a linear gradient fill from red to green in High Color (16bit) and you'll see the color bands similar to the ones illustrated in the above diagram.

In case you're wondering how you can divide up 16 bits by three, well you don't divide equally. The human eyes are more sensitive to shades of green, so the extra bit is given to green:

R	R	R	R	R	G	G	G	G	G	G	B	B	B	B	B

R	R	R	G	G	G	B	B

Similarly in 8-bit color, the blue has one fewer bit because the human eyes are least sensitive to shades of blue.

Keep in mind that different image formats pack the pixel colors differently. The Graphics Interchange Format (GIF), for example, supports 8 bits per pixel. This means that a .gif image cannot have more than 256 colors.

5.0 Skinning Websites

The palettes for the Portable Network Graphics (PNG) format support either 24-bit RGB or 32-bit RGBA. I'll explain what this means in the next section when we talk about transparency. In terms of color depth, a .png file supports at least 24 bits per pixel, or 8 bits per channel.

The color range in the JPEG (Joint Photographic Experts Group) format is equally non-restrictive. For web graphics, both .png and .jpg files support "enough colors". We'll discuss the major differences between .jpg and other formats in the Compression section.

5.1.3 Transparency

Both GIF and PNG support transparency. Transparent images are especially important for reusable icons where the background color changes according to design.

In GIF files, a pixel can be either opaque or transparent. This is sometimes called "binary transparency". Since all the transparent pixels have the same color of, well, transparent, it would be a waste of space to encode such info in every pixel. GIF uses a palette of 256 entries. One entry in this indexed palette can be designated as the transparent color.

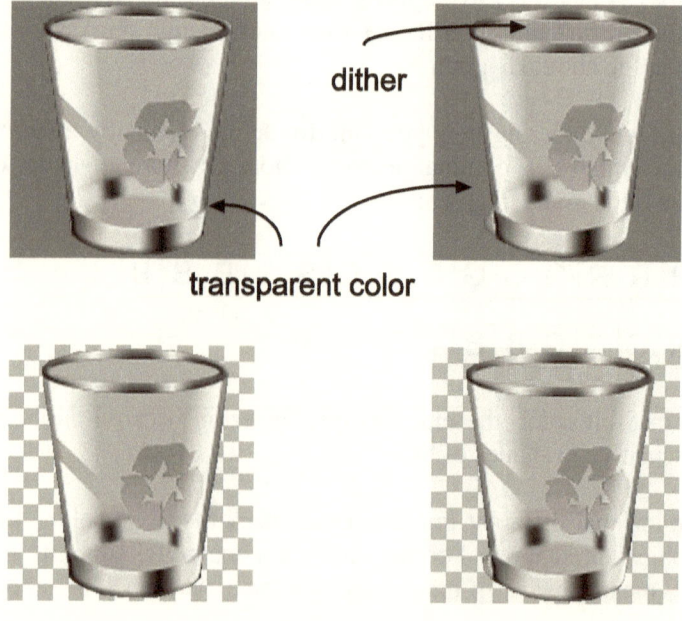

dither

transparent color

5.0 Skinning Websites

You could emulate semi-transparency by using patterned pixels that are in transparent color. This process is also known as "dithering". With proper hatching strokes, dithering emulation can achieve very artistic effects. The above diagram uses a simple grid of dots. When placed against a checkered background, the top of the recycle bin seems 50% transparent.

The PNG format uses an additional 8-bit channel to store the level of transparency in each pixel, extending the 24-bit pixel to 32-bit pixel. This transparency channel is called the Alpha channel. The color model of transparent PNG is therefore RGBA instead of just RGB.

As mentioned earlier, grayscale images are often stored in 8-bit pixels. The alpha channel in PNG works as a grayscale mask. White pixel tells the corresponding pixels in all other channels to be fully transparent; black pixels make them completely opaque. The shades in between make the pixels semi-transparent, with varying levels.

As shown in the following diagram, the image produced from RGB channels describes a recycle bin with background. The alpha channel masks out all the irrelevant information, making the bin look "clean". Pay special attention to the top of the bin as well as its shadow. The darker spot in the shadow in the alpha channel, combined with the white pixels in the RGB image, produces the effect of a "glow".

The transparency capability of the PNG format is quite promising. However, many older versions of IE do not support the alpha channel in PNG. There are CSS techniques that make PNG file work in both browsers, but the stunt tends to cause other layout issues in a more complex context.

There are times when transparency isn't really necessary. For example, if the background behind the bin is always the checkered pattern, then merge all the layers in the image and drop the alpha channel. It still looks like its transparent, and look is all we care about in a web page. Maybe this image indeed requires dynamic (or "real") transparency. Ask yourself whether binary transparency suffice. If not, can we dither it. Always use PNG's alpha transparency as the last resort.

5.1.4 Compression

Both GIF and PNG use lossless compression within their color space. This means that saving and displaying the image are reversible processes of each other.

JPEG compression, on the other hand, is lossy. Every time you save a JPEG file, some unnoticeable details get lost.

The compression scheme JPEG uses is a complex one, and it's suited for photographs where there's a lot of continuous tone. For example, the green on the leaves, the blue in the sky. JPEG achieves high compression ratio by encoding pixel blocks instead of individual pixels.

The above diagram illustrates the artifacts caused by JPEG compression. The line strokes in text and symbols are not as readily detected by the algorithm. Consequently "ghostly" pixels appear around edges.

Only use best quality JPEG for photographs and web-optimized images. Do not use JPEG to store or exchange raw design files. Every pixel counts, so use a lossless format. Since PNG has both the color depth and pixel fidelity, PNG *without Alpha channels* is an ideal format.

5.1.5 Resizing vs. Resampling

The term resizing and resampling tend to be used interchangeably. But there's a fundamental difference when it comes to image quality.

A raster image is distorted when it's displayed at a smaller or larger size. Since the image is an array of finite number of pixels, when it's squeezed into a smaller grid, some pixels have to be thrown out; when it's stretched, new pixels need to be made up to fill in the gap.

But which pixels to discard, and how are new pixels computed? When we resize an image, we simply delete or duplicate existing pixels. When we resample, "predictive" pixels are calculated to create a smoother result.

The above photograph is reduced to 1/3 of its original size using resizing, bi-linear resampling and bi-cubical resampling respectively. The left eye of the model is enlarged using the same three methods. As we can see, bi-linear resampling works nicely for reducing the image size; bi-cubical resampling is suitable for bloating the image size.

When we display an image on a webpage using the *img* tag, the width and height attributes should ideally match the exact width and height of the original image. If the image is resized on the browser, resampling may or may not occur, depending on the browser. The result is usually undesirable. Thumbnail images of larger photographs, therefore, are generated on the server using one of the more sophisticated resample algorithms.

In addition to the typical bi-linear and bi-cubical algorithms, there could be many other methods. As a web developer, or even a graphic designer, you don't have to worry about the exact implementation the web browser or Photoshop choose. It's important to understand, and *feel* the impact of scaling an image, so that you form the habit of pixel precision.

5.2 From Mockups to HTML&CSS

The design of a professional website usually begins by creating a set of wire frames on a "story board". These wire frames are further enhanced by graphic designers into a set of screenshots, or "mockups". As discussed in Chapter 5.1, these mockups are ideally stored as PNG files without alpha channels.

The job of a web developer is to convert these mockups to HTML pages, so that visual elements such as buttons and links can provide interactive feedback or navigational paths among pages. This encoding process is commonly, but mistakenly, viewed as a simple conversion process.

Coding web pages is not about expressing still images in HTML format. Consider the mockups to be snapshots of a living creature. Our job is to reconstruct this creature and bring it back to life.

Mockups describe what a web page should look like; they also hint how the page might behave. There are many missing details that need to be filled by the web developer. This is where skinning gets challenging, creative and fun.

5.2.1 Navigation Structure

When you get the set of screenshots from the graphic designer, make sure you examine all the files. Try to reconstruct the flow of the website and identify the entry point of the website, also known as the landing page, as well as one representative content page, from which you'll extract the common layout.

Most "brochure sites" use the same layout for most of its content pages. Two pages, however, tend not to share this layout. One is the home page; the other one is an optional splash page.

The exact definitions of home page, splash page and landing page might be different in other sources, if at all well defined. For consistency sake, let's define them as following:

A *splash page* is the cover of the website. It usually contains minimal content and prominent buttons or links to enter the main site. Generally speaking, there's no path that's link backed to the splash page. It's only seen once.

A *home page* also plays a similar role to a cover page, except that it provides far more information than a splash page. In terms of navigation structure, a home page is the default starting point that all other pages link back to. It's common practice to link the logo to the home page.

A *landing page* could be either a splash page or home page, or neither of them. A website might have multiple entry points. For example, if you feature one of the many products in an online ad, it's more effective to link the ad directly to the product page. Then the product page becomes a landing page. You may also want to cater to different audience by building additional splash pages that further link to main content. These splash pages are all landing pages to what're commonly called "micro sites".

The following diagram generalizes the layout of a typical website:

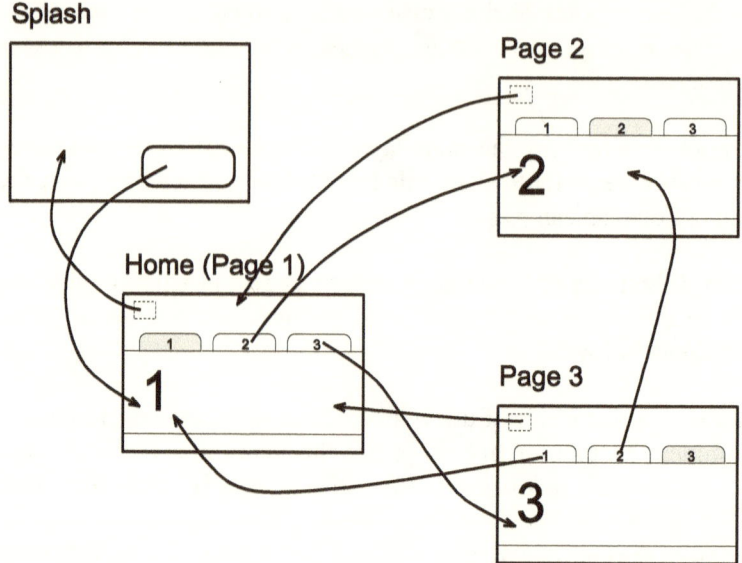

In the above example, all the content pages link to one another. In addition, the logos in Page 2 and 3 point to Page 1; this makes Page 1 a home page. The logo on Page 1 points back to the Splash Page, so that there's no dead path in site navigation.

Keep in mind the above diagram is not a formula. It's a mental model that helps you recognize the navigation pattern in many web sites.

Now take a break from reading, and go to 5 websites that you frequently visit. Sketch out their navigation diagram by identifying the transition points (links, buttons, images, etc.) on each page. Then categorize these pages by their navigation characteristics. In the above example, Page 2 and Page 3 have the same navigation structure, so they belong to the same group. The home page is another class, and the splash page is yet another. Since the home page and the other content pages share common header and footer, it makes sense to create a master template for both classes; then a more specialized template for Page 2 and Page 3. We'll take a closer look at the templating workflow in later chapters.

5.2.2 Page Layouts

Take a look at the websites you have examined in the previous chapter. Pay special attention to the relation between the content and the white space around it. Some websites have distinct background colors or images – make note of these too.

Change the browser window size and see how these websites adapt. Keep reducing the window and observe when the scroll bars occur; keep enlarging the window and see whether the content takes up more space accordingly, and whether it stops growing at some point. Is the content anchored on the left or staying in the center of the screen?

Now look at the mockups you are going to implement. Ask yourself and the graphic designer the same set of questions. A screenshot of a webpage only tells you how it looks like in one particular screen size. You have to provide an interpretation so that the website looks reasonable in most screens.

First let's define reasonable by pointing out the unreasonable scenarios you may want to avoid. You don't want the content to be too wide to fit in most windows; you also don't want to waste the available screen real estate by having too much white space. In addition, the content should be laid out in a comfortable-to-read fashion. We'll get to this later.

There are two general approaches to address the issue of different screen resolutions. One is to use a fixed width that's small enough to fit in the smallest, but yet contemporary screen sizes. At one point, websites needed to accommodate 800x600 screens. Then 1024x768 became the least common denominator. Looking at today's trend, 1280 might be the next minimal width.

The other approach is to use relative dimensions, so that the content grows with the screen. Adaptive layout, or commonly called "fluid layout", is good in theory. However it introduces many variables as you never know which screen the webpage will be displayed on. Adaptive layout is usually implemented with additional constraints, such as minimum and maximum content width.

Note that when we talk about page layout, we're only concerned with the relationship between the page and whatever stuff that's in the page. This abstraction is reflected by the following code:

```
<html>
<head>
<style>
```

```
body{background-color:black;}
#canvas{
   margin:10px;padding:10px 10px 200px 10px;
   background-color:white;
}
</style>
</head>
<body>
   <div id="canvas">
      Content
   </div>
</body>
</html>
```

In the above example, a white content area is placed on top of a black background. The content width scales with the screen.

Most page layouts fall into the following 5 categories:
1. fixed width, center positioned
2. adaptive width, center positioned
3. 2-column, side column fixed, content column adaptive
4. 3-column, side columns fixed, content column adaptive
5. custom panels

Now let's talk about the implementation of each layout.

Type I. Fixed Width Layout

This is the most popular layout not only because it's the easiest to code, but this is also how graphic designers prefer to think – they work with the mockup of a webpage like how they paint a picture. The canvas doesn't change its size, unlike a web browser window.

A fixed width web page can still have various content layouts, such as side bars, 3 column divisions, etc. The width of the content, or the div block with the "canvas" ID, is still fixed.

We have discussed in Chapter 4.15.2 on centering an element. Here we're going to center the canvas element, which has a fixed width of 900 pixels. This fits in 1024 screens or wider.

```
<body>
   <style>
```

```
body{
    margin:0;padding:0; /*reset*/
    background-color:#000000; /*black*/
    text-align:center;
}
#canvas{
    width:900px;
    margin:0 auto;
    text-align:left;
    background-color:#ffffff; /*white*/
    padding:10px; padding-bottom:200px;
}
</style>

<div id="canvas">
    Hello!
</div>
</body>
```

Many websites blend the background of the canvas into the background, so that the content width is perceived to be adaptive; other sites stylize the borders with visual effects such as soft shadows.

Proper white space handling is the key to making a fixed width layout aesthetically pleasing. Two common approaches are blending and framing.

In the above example, the width of the canvas is obviously fixed. When the page is displayed on a wide screen, it looks out of proportion and wasteful. A quick fix is to set the body background color to the same background color as the canvas. Google's home search page, for example, uses this tactic.

Another method to create the illusion that the content is utilizing the entire screen space is to use the same background image in both the content banner and the background.

The above diagram illustrates the relation between the content banner and the background image in the document body. The banner image doesn't have to be a solid color block, as long as the image can be extended on both sides.

```
<style>
body{
    margin:0; padding:0; text-align:center;
    background:transparent url(bodybg.png) repeat-x top left;
}

#canvas{
    width:900px; text-align:left; margin:0 auto;
}

#banner{
    background:transparent url(banner.png) no-repeat top left;
}
</style>
<div id="canvas">
    <div id="banner">
        ...
    </div><!-- banner -->
</div><!-- canvas -->
```

If you're not familiar with CSS background images, please review Chapter 4.13.

We'll be talking about building banners in greater details in later chapters, so don't worry about the banner component for now.

Some websites don't try to hide the fact that they're using fixed width for the content. On the contrary, they celebrate the separation of content from the background by framing the content. One example would be drop shadows. Note that using shadows or framing in general is not exclusive to fixed width layout.

The illusion of having both a left- and right-drop shadow can be achieved by one single tile background image:

Assuming the real content width is 980 pixels, and the shadow on each side is 8 pixels. The tile image is 996 pixels wide and 1 pixel tall.

```
body{
  margin:0;padding:0;
  text-align:center;
  background:transparent url(shadow.png) repeat-y top left;
}

#canvas{
  width:980px;
  text-align:left; margin:0 auto;
}
```

Drop shadow in adaptive layout has to be split into left and right side. We'll see its implementation in the next section.

Type II. Adaptive Single Column Layout

If the screen offers more space, the content should take full advantage of the real estate. This is the motivation behind adaptive layouts. The simplest form of an adaptive layout has only one column.

The width of the content is implied by the left and right margin settings. It's common to leave some breathing room on both side of the document:

```
body{margin:0; padding:0; text-align:center;}
#canvas{text-align:left;margin:0 20px;}
```

Note the 2-parameter shorthand, as discussed in Chapter 4.5, condenses the left and right margins into one parameter.

Similar to fixed layout, you can use various blending techniques to make the content seemingly stretch across the entire screen.

Drop shadow in adaptive layout is slightly more complicated. The single tile trick no longer works because the background image has a fixed width.

A natural but naïve approach is to divide the page in 3 columns: one for the left-side shadow, one for the main content and one for the right-side shadow.

In Chapter 4.15.4 we have talked about floating, which is essentially what you need for implementing columned layout. You should realize, however, that without knowing the height of the content, it's difficult to determine the heights of the side (shadow) columns. The following diagram illustrates a scenario you want to avoid:

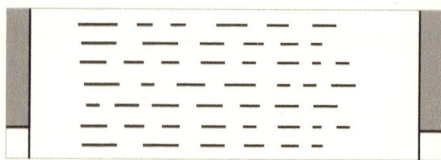

Notice how the content area outgrows the shadows on the side.

Another issue with the "three floating div" approach is that the horizontal alignment could be disrupted when the content column grows too wide. We'll talk about the detailed implementation of navigation tabs in later chapters, but it's important to see, at this point, how float-based layout could "snap". Many "old fashioned" developers would resort to using tables at this point. But there's a much more elegant way.

First let's review how background image works, as discussed in Chapter 4.13. Also have a close look at the Box Model diagram in Chapter 4.5 for a few seconds. Pay special attention to the shaded area and the content area.

Now create a background image that can be tiled as the left shadow. Something that looks like the following:

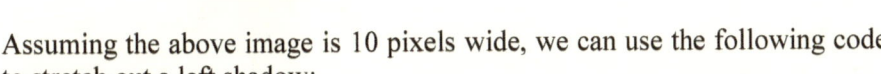

Assuming the above image is 10 pixels wide, we can use the following code to stretch out a left shadow:

```
<style>
#lshadow{
    padding-left:10px;
    background:transparent url(lshadow.png) repeat-y top left;
}
</style>
<div id="lshadow">
    <div id="content"> Main content here </div>
</div>
```

Add more lines to the content. See how the shadow grows with the content.

What about the right shadow? Well, the right shadow has nothing to do with the left shadow. Pretend that we don't need the left shadow; we can build the right shadow like this:

```
<style>
#rshadow{
    padding-right:10px;
    background:transparent url(rshadow.png) repeat-y top left;
}
</style>
<div id="rshadow">
    <div id="content">Main content here</div>
</div>
```

Now putting it all together:

5.0 Skinning Websites   157

```
<style>
#canvas{margin-left:20px; margin-right:20px;}
#lshadow{
   padding-left:10px;
   background:transparent url(lshadow.png) repeat-y top left;
}
#rshadow{
   padding-right:10px;
   background:transparent url(rshadow.png) repeat-y top left;
}
#content{
  padding:0 10px;
}
</style>
<div id="canvas">
   <div id="lshadow"><div id="rshadow">
      <div id="content">
         Main content here…
      </div>
   </div></div>
</div>
```

The following diagram illustrates the layering structure in the above code:

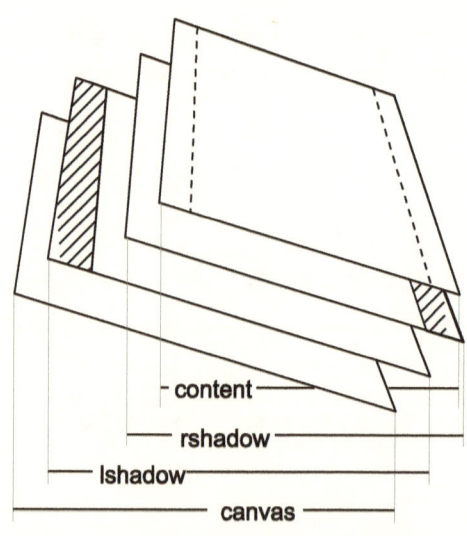

5.0 Skinning Websites

We should see beyond the above code and illustration, and fundamentally change the way we look at web layouts. Decompose a web page into layers where each layer takes care of one key aspect of the design. For example, the canvas layer uses the left- and right-margin to adjust its width; the left shadow layer only cares about the shadow image on the left side, leaving the right shadow to yet another layer. The content layer has its own padding so that the text within doesn't get too close to the shadows.

In other words, a web page is a projection of multiple layers on a single surface. Think 3D.

Type III. Adaptive 2-Column Layout

A typical adaptive 2-column layout consists of a fixed-width left column and a variable-width content column.

We cannot reuse the padding and background image trick as we did to making the shadows. The left column now has content. It's not just a background image. In this case, we'll have to use float.

In Chapter 4.8 we briefly talked about using floats to divide a fixed-width container into columns. For example:

```
<div style="width:600px;">
   <div style="width:290px;margin-right:20px;float:left;">
     Left Column
   </div>
   <div style="width:290px;float:left;">
    Right Column
   </div>
   <div style="clear:both;"></div>
</div>
```

When the width of the right (content) column is no longer fixed, things get tricky. Try removing the width attribute from the right column but give it a background color:

```
<div>
```

```
    <div style="width:200px; float:left;">
      Left Column
    </div>
    <div style="float:left;background-color:#848cf7;">
     Content Column
    </div>
    <div style="clear:both;"></div>
</div>
```

The background color makes it clear that the content column fails to utilize the entire remaining space.

By default, a div (block) element automatically occupies the entire width of its container. When it is absolutely positioned, or floating, its width will adapt to its content. This is a characteristic we'll find useful later, but in case of adaptive layout, it's in our way.

Now remove the left floating attribute from the content column, so that it expands to the full width:

```
...
<div style="background-color:#848cf7;">
    Line 1<br>
    Line 2<br>
    Line 3<br>
    Line 4<br>
    Line 5
</div>
...
```

Now that we added more lines to the content column, another layout bug got exposed: content from the right column wraps around the left column because the left column is much shorter.

Again this behavior is desirable in other situations, such as wrapping text around an image. To prevent wrapping, we confine the content column with either a left padding or left margin:

```
<div style="background-color:#848cf7;margin-left:200px;">
```

This approach works because the floating element overlaps the margin or padding of the content column.

Now let's add a background color to the main container, and a footer element outside the container, just to expose yet another issue:

```
<div style="background-color:#ffab00;">
   <div style="width:200px; float:left;">
     Left Column
   </div>
   <div style="margin-left:200px;background-color:#848cf7;">
     Line 1<br>
     Line 2<br>
    Line 3<br>
    Line 4
   </div>
   <div style="clear:both;"></div>
</div>
<div>Footer</div>
```

Test the above code in both Firefox and Internet Explorer.

In Internet Explorer, the footer is included by the column container, even though the footer is declared outside of it.

To fix this bug, we need to give the clearing div some invisible content such as a space. In addition, we need to make the div take up as little space as possible. Chapter 4.15.5 already mentioned a solution:

```
<div style="clear:both;font-size:1px;"> </div>
```

Usually the columns have different background colors, or have a divider in between. You may have noticed the challenge of variable column heights. Without setting explicit height, the two columns will almost certainly have different heights. This makes backgrounds look inconsistent and the dividing line potentially too short.

A handy technique is to use a y-repeating background image on the container level. You can be creative about the image. Here are some ideas:

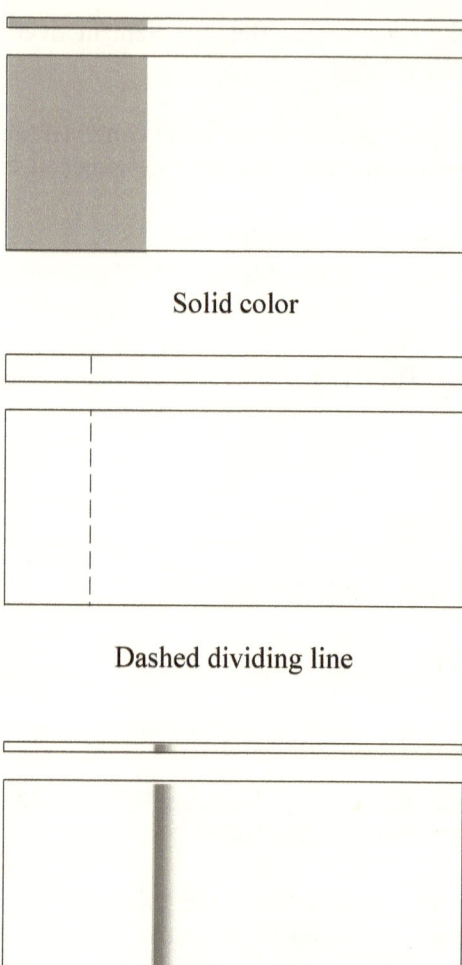

Solid color

Dashed dividing line

Drop shadow

Let's review all the features of a proper 2-column layout:

1. columns are displayed side by side;
2. the content column occupies the full width;
3. content doesn't wrap around the left column
4. footer is placed outside of columns
5. columns appear to have the same height

The following diagram labels the code fragments that are responsible for each of the above features:

```
<div style="background:transparent url(colbg.png) repeat-y top left;">
    <div style="width:200px; float:left;">
      Left Column
    </div>
    <div style="margin-left:200px;">
      Main Content
    </div>
    <div style="clear:both;font-size:1px;"> </div>
  </div>
```

(1) (5) (2) (3) (4)

Type VI. Adaptive 3-Column Layout

A 3-column layout can be viewed as a 2-column layout inside another 2-column layout.

First let's build a reverse 2-column layout where the right column is fixed and the content column to the left has adjustable width:

```
<div>
    <div style="width:200px;float:right;">
      Right column
    </div>
    <div style="margin-right:200px;">
      Main content
    </div>
    <div style="clear:both;font-size:1px;"> </div>
</div>
```

Note that the right column is declared before the content column. Otherwise it won't float correctly.

Now copy this code as the main content in the 2-column layout code from the previous section:

```
<div style="background:...;">
    <div style="width:200px; float:left;">
      Left Column
    </div>
```

```
   <div style="margin-left:200px;">
<div style="background:...;">
   <div style="width:200px;float:right;">
      Right column
   </div>
   <div style="margin-right:200px;">
      Main content
   </div>
   <div style="clear:both;font-size:1px;"> </div>
</div>
   </div>
   <div style="clear:both;font-size:1px;"> </div>
</div>
```

Remember to remove the redundant clearing div. The background trick needs to be played out in both layers. As long as the left (outer floating) column is shorter than the outer right (content and right column) column, the three columns will appear to have the same height.

Type V. Custom Panels

The layout of a web application can be far more complex than just a few columns. The web page could be conditionally divided into multiple panels. The existence, visibility and dimension of panels are affected by user interaction, browser window size and other factors.

We'll talk more about making custom panels after the introduction of JavaScript.

Regardless which layout is used, be it fixed, relative or JavaScript controlled, we should avoid explicit dimensions for the content. For example, do not specify *width:900px* inside a 900-pixel wide container.

Special: Full Bleed Single Column Layout

There's a special type of single column layout that's becoming popular among mobile-friendly websites. Content of a web site is laid out linearly (and vertically) on one page. Each section has its own background image so that the web page is nicely divided. The following diagram simplifies the model:

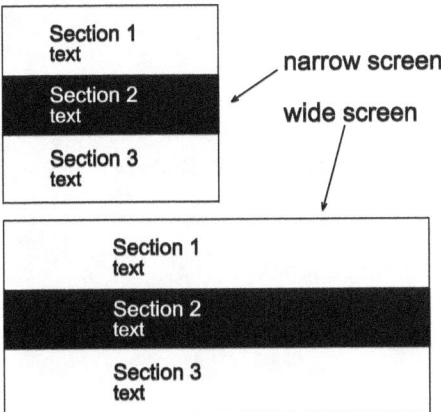

The main characteristic of this layout is that the background image occupies the entire screen space. The text in the content is centered in the screen.

Earlier in Type I – Fixed Width Layout we saw a technique of using overlapping background image to emulate a fully stretched header.

We could treat this layout as a special case of header stretching. Each section of the page is a fully stretched "header".

Unfortunately we cannot use the background image method because the document body can contain only one "shadow" background image. We need to build *real* full width components.

Consider the following first iteration:

```
<html>
<body style="padding:0;margin:0;text-align:center;">
<style>
.section,.dsection{
    width:1000px;text-align:left;margin:0 auto;
    padding:10px 0;
}
.dsection{color:#ffffff;}
</style>

<div class="section">
```

```
    <div class="sectioncontent">
        <h1>Section 1</h1>
        Text
    </div>
</div>


<div style="background-color:#000000;">

<div class="dsection">
    <div class="sectioncontent">
        <h1>Section 2</h1>
        Text
    </div>
</div>

</div>

<div class="section">
    <div class="sectioncontent">
        <h1>Section 3</h1>
        Text
    </div>
</div>

</body>
</html>
```

Pay extra attention to the bolded lines in the above code, especially the container for Section 2. We need to specify width for the content to center align, but any presence of width stops the background from stretching. Therefore the container that bears the background information should be *outside* the content container.

Load up the code in a browser. All seems well. The text stays in the center of the page; the background stretches to the edge of the screen. Now reduce the size of the browser window to half of the content width.

The first problem you'll notice is that there's no breathing space on the left of the text. This is an easy fix as long as we are aware of the issue. Add the following style:

```
.sectioncontent{padding:0 20px;}
```

Now scroll to the right side of the content. The background isn't stretched all the way!

It's important to understand that even though each section content container has fixed width, the containers do not stretch the document body. The background container is *under stretched*.

We cannot forcefully stretch the background container, but we can replicate the background in the content container.

```
<div style="background-color:#000000;">

<div class="dsection" style="background-color:#000000;">
   <div class="sectioncontent">
      <h1>Section 2</h1>
      Text
   </div>
</div>

</div>
```

Consider two scenarios: document body is wider than the content width; content width is wider than the screen, and subsequently the document body.

Either way, one of the backgrounds covers the screen.

Now we take out the inline styling, and rewrite the style block as following:

```
<style>
.section,.dsection{
   width:1000px;text-align:left;margin:0 auto;
   padding:10px 0;
}
.dsection{color:#ffffff;background-color:#000000;}
.sectioncontent{padding:0 20px;}
</style>
```

When building a full-bleed layout, watch out for elements that have fixed widths such as the content container in the above example. A "width-ed" element under stretches the background, so it requires a background double to cover up.

You may be thinking why should I care about small screens? If my content width is 980 pixels, which fit in most 1024x768 screens, shouldn't the document body always be wider than the content?

The twist is mobile devices such as the iPhone, iPad and Playbook that dynamically resizes the page. On these devices, a pixel is not a pixel. In fact there are two kinds of pixels. One is a hardware pixel – the smallest physical element that presents a composition of light on the screen. Then there's a logical pixel – what we *perceive*. A 600-pixel photograph can be displayed in a 300-pixel phone at a 2:1 ratio. Because the user is close to the phone screen, the content still "feels" as wide.

When we display a content that's 1000 pixels wide, the phone will squeeze it in the screen and represent the content in its entirety. However, the document body shrinks with the page. You will see the exact same two issues when viewing the page in a smaller window, namely the absence of margin and under stretching the background.

Again the implementation is simple: center the content, wrap the sections with padding and clone the background. It's more difficult to understand the problem and see why it matters.

Responsive Layout

When this book was first written in 2010, responsive web design wasn't as mainstream as it is today. Having a dedicated mobile domain, e.g. "m.abc.com" was still common practice.

The diversity of screen sizes and devices has made responsive layout necessary. Fortunately most of what we've learned previously still applies. With minimal modifications, we can make a web page progressively adaptive to its viewing media.

Bear in mind that certain designs cannot be made responsive. This is not because of technical limitations, but from a visual standpoint, the scale-down transformation just doesn't make sense.

For a design that can be made soundly responsive, the most common layout transformation is the "stacking effect".

When the screen is too narrow to accommodate side-by-side columns, the column number is reduced, and often collapsed to one.

The following code stacks the two columns when the screen is narrower than 300 pixels:

```
<style>
#left, #right{float:left;width:50%;}
.clear{clear:both;}

@media screen and (max-width:300px){
  #left, #right{float:none;width:auto;}
  #left{margin-bottom:10px;}
}
</style>
<div id="left">A</div>
<div id="right">B</div>
<div class="clear"></div>
```

Yes, column stacking is that simple. Make sure that the width of any element in a responsive layout is defined in percentage. Side-by-side layout is done through float. When we want to remove the columns, we simply clear the float. But be sure to clear the width while clearing floats. The bottom margin of the first stacking element is added to space out the column components.

The next example converts a 3-column layout into a stacking 2-column layout at the 600 pixel mark. The columns eventually collapse into a single file at 300 pixels:

```
<style>
#block_ab, #block_c, #block_a, #block_b{float:left;}
#block_ab{width:66%;}
#block_c{width:33%;}
#block_a, #block_b{width:50%;}

.clear{clear:both;}
```

```
@media screen and (max-width:600px){
  #block_ab, #block_c{float:none;width:auto;}
}

@media screen and (max-width:300px){
  #block_a, #block_b{float:none;width:auto;}
}
</style>

<div id="block_ab">
      <div id="block_a">A</div>
      <div id="block_b">B</div>
</div>
<div id="block_c">C</div>
<div class="clear"></div>
```

The above code shows a few techniques. The screen widths, at which the layout transformation is performed, are called breakpoints. The max-width condition is sufficient to implement multiple breakpoints as long as they are organized such that wider breakpoint blocks are declared before the narrower breakpoint blocks.

Also pay attention to the width calculation. The percentage width of an element is relative to its container if the container's width is explicitly set. Unlike other units in CSS, you *can* use fractions for percentages. But always double check with your target browser. When in doubt, "add under" rather than "add over".

Responsive Full-Width Tiles

Suppose we are building a grid of tiles. The grid has 3 columns when there's sufficient screen realestate. When the screen is wide enough for 2 columns, the tiles are arranged in 2 columns. The the screen gets even narrower, the layout breaks down to a single column.

The following code *almost* works:

```
<style>
.clear{clear:both;}
#grid{background:#dedede;}
.tile{
      float:left;width:32%;
```

```
        margin-right:1%;margin-bottom:20px;
        background:#ffab00; height:40px;
}

@media screen and (max-width:600px){
        .tile{width:48%;margin-right:2%;}
}

@media screen and (max-width:400px){
        .tile{
        width:auto;float:none;
        margin-left:0; margin-right:0;
        }
}

</style>

<div id="grid">
        <div class="tile"></div>
        <div class="tile"></div>
        <div class="tile"></div>
        <div class="tile"></div>
        <div class="tile"></div>
        <div class="tile"></div>
        <div class="clear"></div>
</div>
```

The problem is, in the 3-column and 2-column layouts, there's a gap on the last column.

We rewrite the code to give each tile to variate its class name. First we append its modulo 3 value, then modulo 2:

```
<div id="grid">
        <div class="tile_0_0"></div>
        <div class="tile_1_1"></div>
        <div class="tile_2_0"></div>
        <div class="tile_0_1"></div>
        <div class="tile_1_0"></div>
        <div class="tile_2_1"></div>
        <div class="clear"></div>
```

```
</div>
```

Note that this can be easily accomplished in PHP with the % operator.

Now the CSS is written to allow more precise column division:

```
.tile_0_0, .tile_1_0, .tile_2_0,
.tile_0_1, .tile_1_1, .tile_2_1{
    float:left;width:32%;
    margin-right:2%;margin-bottom:20px;
    background:#ffab00; height:40px;
}

.tile_2_0, .tile_2_1{margin-right:0;}

@media screen and (max-width:600px){
    .tile_0_0, .tile_1_0, .tile_2_0,
    .tile_0_1, .tile_1_1, .tile_2_1
    {width:49%;margin-right:2%;}

    .tile_0_1, .tile_1_1, .tile_2_1{margin-right:0;}
}

@media screen and (max-width:400px){
    .tile_0_0, .tile_1_0, .tile_2_0,
    .tile_0_1, .tile_1_1, .tile_2_1
    {width:auto;float:none;margin-left:0;margin-right:0;}

}
```

The above code may look tedious, but it's a one-time effort and it works well across browsers.

Responsive Images

In general, it's "easy" to make images scale. Put an image inside a container, and set the image width to 100%:

```
<style>
#container img{width:100%;}
```

```
</style>

<div id="container">
  <img src="logo.png">
</div>
```

A nice property of the image tag is that images resize in scale. Their aspect ratio is preserved if only one of width or height is defined while the other unconstrained.

Sometimes keeping the aspect ratio may not be what you want. A banner image, for instance, can scale down to a certain degree. But when the screen becomes too narrow, the image also becomes too short. This is especially troublesome if the banner image serves as a backdrop for a blob of text.

A solution is to lock the image height at certain width and clip off the sides:

```
<style>
#container img{width:100%;}
@media screen and (max-width:500px){
  #container{width:100%;overflow:hidden;}
  #container img{width:auto;height:100px;}
}
</style>

<div id="container">
  <img src="logo.png">
</div>
```

When a column becomes stacked, its width expands to the new, narrower screen width. This width may be wider than its original column width. In such cases, make sure the image is large enough; or it'll be stretched and appear blurry.

When possible, use the techniques that we discussed earlier for full bleed layout and tiling background. A graphic element could be an "image" image or a background image. There are tradeoffs in both. Picking the right implementation is a decision you'll have to make throughout the making of a responsive page.

The Big Monitor Problem

One of the main concerns of today's complex device landscape is small screens. Responsive design was primarily intended to fit more content into a narrow screen. However, the bigger headache with responsive design is what I call a "big monitor" problem.

When a full-width banner shrinks as the browser window, the end result is reasonable. But if the monitor grows larger and larger, should the banner grow as well?

It shouldn't, for two reasons. The banner's image source has limited resolution. Blowing it up makes the image blurry. Even a high definition image has a resolution limit. There is always a bigger monitor, but the image cannot grow indefinitely.

Another reason is the human scanning range. When a web page stretches from edge to edge on a large monitor, the user has to turn his head from left to right to read a line, and then turn to the left to read the beginning of the next line. Owners of large monitors don't typically fill up their desktop with one browser window. If they do, the web page should limit the content area to near the center of the screen in order to reduce "typewriter reading".

The following code grows the container to a limit of 600 pixels, with 20-pixel margin on each side. In practice use a larger number such as 1200.

```
<style>
.content{
width:600px; height:40px;
margin:0 auto;
background:red;
}

@media screen and (max-width:640px;){
  .content{width:auto; margin:0 20px;}
}
</style>

<div class="content"></div>
```

The default width is defined outside of a media query block. This width is understood by all browsers. Otherwise, the page will be too wide for some old IE browsers.

The margin is added to the content so that there's some room to breathe. It's a design decision, and you may implement the side gaps using a nested container. The breakpoint width should take this margin into consideration. Otherwise the content width will "jump" as you resize the window.

5.2.3 Page Components

A page from one web site may look drastically different from one from another website. But all pages in a structured web site share similar components. There are, of course, always exceptions, but even these outliers tend to have the functional components that are common in contemporary websites.

In general, every page in the same website has the same banner. This carries out a consistent image. The most prominent component in the banner is the logo. There could be other elements such as the location or language selectors, login bars, etc. The menu could be considered a banner component or on its own. The separation of banner and menu depends on visual design, and is often arbitrary.

You might have also heard of a "header" component. For now you treat the header as a collective term for the banner and menu. Later, we'll find out that it is more practical to see the header as a structural component. In the process of template extraction, any HTML code before the content body is encapsulated in the header component. Note this is looking at the code level, not the visual level.

The page footer usually contains textual links to other pages, for accessibility reasons. It also contains the copyright and sometimes contact info such as email addresses and phone numbers.

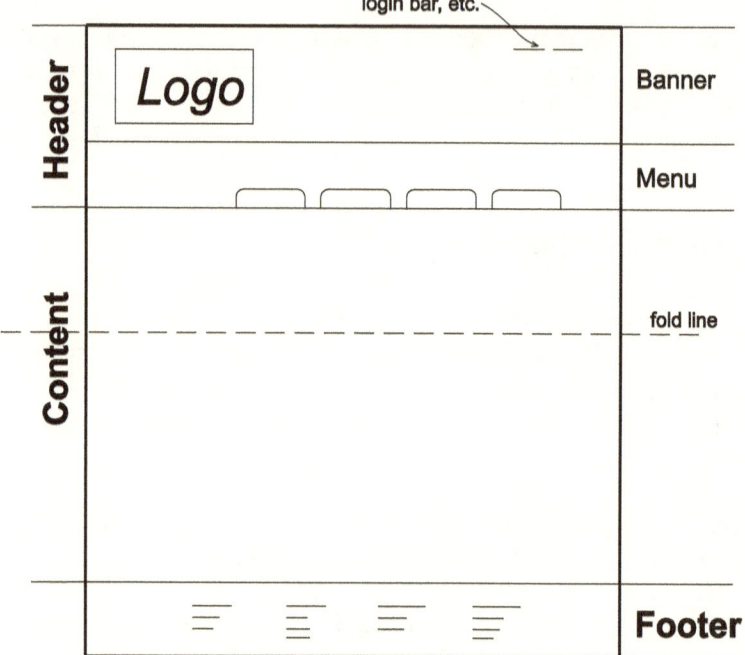

It makes sense for the header to have more bells and whistles than the footer. It's the first thing everyone sees. Nobody opens up a page and scrolls to the bottom of the page to read the footer. However, footer is not the only part of the page that's invisible. Nearly half of the page is scrolled out of the screen.

The imaginary line that cuts off the page is called a fold line. Important content should be arranged "above the fold". This is one of the many reasons why the banner in a content page tends to take less space than that in the home page or splash page. You won't find the fold line in the mockup, but always do a quick check and make sure the content fits in "short screens". The popularity of mobile screens and netbooks makes this check extra important.

5.2.3.1 Banners and Logos

In Chapter 5.2.1, you were asked to draw the flow diagram of 5 websites and identify their typical content pages. Now sketch the wireframes of these websites content pages. In addition, draw for another 3 websites. Make note of the fold line location in various screen resolutions.

After you've outlined the websites, focus on the top of each page, and look for patterns. You may notice that the header section of a typical web page contains a logo, a navigation menu and some links for login, social media, etc. The locations of these elements are also similar on each page. The logo tends to sit at the top left corner; the menu either overlaps the banner image on the right side, or takes up the entire horizontal space of its own; the login links and other buttons are usually located at the top right corner.

Let's implement the following header:

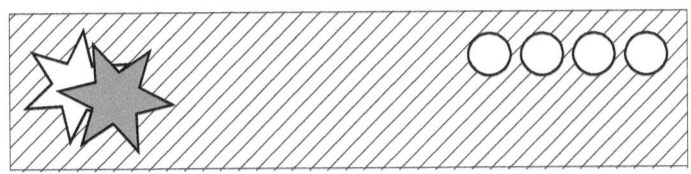

Measure the height of the banner image and create a container of the same height. Set the position of the container to be relative:

```
<style>
#banner{
height:120px;
position:relative;
}

#logo img{border:none;margin-top:10px;}
#logo a, #logo a:focus, #logo a:active{
outline:0;
}
</style>

<div id="banner">
    <div id="logo">
        <a href="index.php">
            <img src="logo.png">
        </a>
</div>
</div>
```

The logo element doesn't have to be absolutely positioned. It can occupy the banner's content space directly. It's a convention to link the banner image to the home page. When an image is wrapped around by a pair of anchors (the a-tag), its border appears. We overwrite this behavior in CSS. In addition, we also remove the dotted outline that shows up when clicking on the image. Try removing the outline line in CSS and compare the results.

Next we'll add two social media icons to the right of the banner:

```
<style>
...
#sociallinks{
position:absolute;
top:10px; right: 10px;
white-space:nowrap;
}
</style>

<div id="banner">
    <div id="logo">
    ...
    </div>
    <div id="sociallinks">
            <a href="...">Facebook</a>
            <a href="...">Twitter</a>
    </div>
</div>
```

You can continue to identify the rest of the elements that are positioned on top of the banner area. If the navigation menu overlaps the banner, create a menu container inside the banner container and set it to be absolutely positioned. Otherwise, place the banner container outside the banner like the following:

```
<div id="banner">
    ...
</div>
<div id="menu">

</div>
```

5.2.3.2 Menus

Next we'll build three types of navigation menus: vertical list, horizontal bar and sub menus.

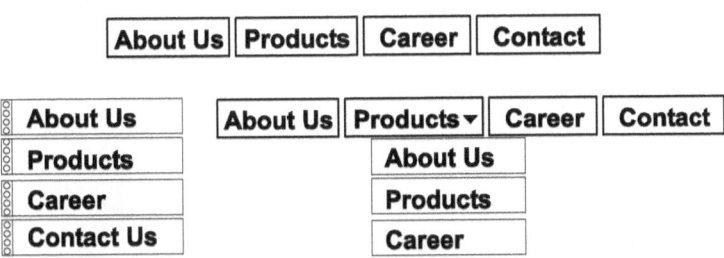

The vertical menu is straightforward to build. In fact we have already created on in Chapter 4.15.3.

Consider the following simplified implementation:

```
<style>
.menu{border:solid 1px #444444;width:100px;}
.menu a, .menu a:hover, .menu a:visited, .menu a:link{
    padding:10px;
    text-decoration:none;
    background-color:#ffffff;
    color:#000000;
    display:block;
}
.menu a:hover{background-color:#000000;color:#ffffff;}
</style>
<div class="menu">
    <a href="page1.php">Page 1</a>
    <a href="page2.php">Page 2</a>
    <a href="page3.php">Page 3</a>
</div>
```

If you look into the source code of Wordpress templates or code examples from other CSS tutorials, you may see something like this:

```
<style>
.menu{
```

```
      border:solid 1px #444444;width:300px;
list-style:none;padding:0;margin:0;
}
.menu a, .menu a:hover, .menu a:visited, .menu a:link{
      text-decoration:none;
      color:#000000;
}
.menu li{
      padding:0;margin:0;padding:10px;
      background-color:#ffffff;
}
.menu li:hover{background-color:#000000;}
.menu li:hover a{
      color:#ffffff;
}
</style>
<ul class="menu">
      <li><a href="page1.php">Page 1</a></li>
      <li><a href="page2.php">Page 2</a></li>
      <li><a href="page3.php">Page 3</a></li>
</ul>
```

Now run the above code in IE – it doesn't work. Add the following line to the top of the listing:

```
<!doctype html>
```

Reload the page. Now it works.

In Chapter 4.7 we talked about styling hyper links. The anchor tags are the only type of element that natively supports pseudo classes. If you really need to style another element differently when a mouse hovers over, you'll have to declare a doc type:

```
<!doctype html>
...
<style>
.test:hover{color:red;}
</style>
<div class="hover">Test</div>
```

Again, use <a> tags instead of other tags whenever you can. The hovering pseudo class is well understood by most browsers.

The code is now corrected below:

```
<style>
.menu{
    border:solid 1px #444444;width:300px;
    padding:0;margin:0;
    list-style:none;
}

.menu a{display:block;margin:0;width:100%;}
.menu a span{display:block;padding:10px;}

.menu a, .menu a:hover, .menu a:visited, .menu a:link{
        text-decoration:none;
        color:#000000;

}
.menu li{display:block;width:100%;}
.menu a:hover{
        color:#ffffff;
        background-color:#000000;
}
</style>
<ul class="menu">
        <li><a href="page1.php"><span>Page 1</span></a></li>
        <li><a href="page2.php"><span>Page 2</span></a></li>
        <li><a href="page3.php"><span>Page 3</span></a></li>
</ul>
```

The first fix is to move all the *:hover* related attributes from the list item tag to the anchor tag. Then we make the anchor tags *block* elements.

Each time an inline element is converted to a block element, check all its parent nodes and make sure they're block as well. For instance, the *a* tag is made to display block, but its *li* container is inline. Hence we set the *li* to display block as well. This effectively fixes many subtle bugs that are caused by containing block elements inside an inline container.

The menu now works in IE, but with some mysterious white margins. As mentioned in 4.15.6, specifying an explicit width gives an element a "layout" and thus fixes certain issues. We applied *width:100%* to both *a* and *li*. Note we can only do this because the outer container, *ul*, has an explicit width of 300 pixels. Also remember that we should never mix *width* and *padding* attributes in the same element. Therefore we created a nested element using the *span* tag.

Next we are going to build a horizontal menu bar:

```
<style>
.menu{border-bottom:solid 1px #444444;}
.menu a, .menu a:hover, .menu a:visited, .menu a:link{
    padding:10px; margin-right:20px;
    text-decoration:none;
    background-color:#ffffff;
    color:#000000;
display:block;
float:left;
}
.menu a:hover{background-color:#000000;color:#ffffff;}
</style>
<div class="menu">
    <a href="page1.php">Page 1</a>
    <a href="page2.php">Page 2</a>
<a href="page3.php">Page 3</a>
    <div style="clear:both;"></div>
</div>
```

The above code is nearly identical to the one for the vertical menu. We made all the menu items float to the left and added a clearing block. Each menu item also carries a right-margin of 20 pixels.

We can rewrite the above menu using an unordered list:

```
<style>
.menu{margin:0;padding:0;list-style:none;height:40px;}
.menu li{
    display:block;float:left;
    margin-right:20px;
```

```
    height:100%;
}
.menu a span{display:block;padding:10px;}
.menu a, .menu a:hover, .menu a:visited, .menu a:link{
    height:100%;
    text-decoration:none;
    background-color:#ffffff;
    color:#000000;
    display:block;
    float:left;
}
.menu a:hover{background-color:#000000;color:#ffffff;}
</style>
<body>
<div style="border-bottom:solid 1px #444444;">
<ul class="menu">
    <li><a href="page1.php"><span>Page 1</span></a></li>
    <li><a href="page2.php"><span>Page 2</span></a></li>
    <li><a href="page3.php"><span>Page 3</span></a></li>
</ul>
<div style="clear:both;"></div>
</div>
```

Again, we had to create additional layers to deal with the no-layout bug in IE. The good news is that you may not have to use these fixes when the menu code is embedded in a well defined header frame and content container. In a context of a "production" page, the menu will have a layout already.

So why are we going through trouble of writing the menu as a list when the menu is styled to look like nothing but a list?

The short answer is that an unordered list (or ordered list for that matter) of hyper links provides semantic organization of a web page, so that search bots and automated browsing agents alike can better understand the link structure of the page.

For example, a typical webpage can have many external links. How does a crawler understand that the links to Page 1, 2 and 3 logically belong to the same group? Tags such as *div* and *span* are semantically empty. This is a good thing when it comes to implementing pure visual. But when we intend to hint a search bot that these links are not just any other links, a *ul* tag works a lot better.

For the rest of the chapter, and for the most part of the book we'll build menus with plain *div*, *span* and *a* tags. That way, the code won't be sprayed with fixes that may or may not be necessary. Wait until the page is more or less done before converting to a list.

Now, moving on with building a horizontal menu.

It is common to place the menu items on the right side of the screen. This nicely balances out the logo in the header to the left. There are usually two ways to place the menu to the right.

One is to move the menu container itself to the right edge:

```
<style>
.header{position:relative;}
.menu{position:absolute;top:0;right:0;}
</style>
<div class="header">
<div class="menu">
...
</div>
</div>
```

Another approach is to float each element to the right:

```
.menu a, .menu a:hover, .menu a:visited, .menu a:link{
    ...
float:right;
}
```

If right-float is used, make sure the menu items are listed in reverse order. Otherwise they'll read as Page 3, Page 2 and Page 1 instead.

Next we'll add a sub menu to one of the horizontal menu items. This process takes only a few minor changes:

```
<!doctype html>
<style>
```

```
.menu{border-bottom:solid 1px #444444;}
.menu a, .menu a:hover, .menu a:visited, .menu a:link{
    padding:10px; margin-right:20px;
    text-decoration:none;
    background-color:#ffffff;
    color:#000000; display:block; float:left;
}

.menugroup{float:left;position:relative;}
.submenu{
    display:none;z-index:1000;
    position:absolute;top:39px;left:0;}
.menugroup:hover .submenu{display:block;}
.menugroup a{display:block;clear:both;white-space:nowrap;}

.menu a:hover{background-color:#000000;color:#ffffff;}
</style>
<div class="menu">
    <div class="menugroup">
        <a href="page1.php">Page 1</a>
        <div class="submenu">
            <a href="pagex.php">Page X</a>
            <a href="pagey.php">Page Y</a>
        </div><!-- submenu -->
    </div><!-- menugroup -->
    <a href="page2.php">Page 2</a>
    <a href="page3.php">Page 3</a>
    <div style="clear:both;"></div>
</div>
```

Let's take apart the above code and study each component thoroughly.

The most important element in a CSS menu is the hovering mechanism. The *hover* pseudo class is used to toggle the appearance of an element when it's under the mouse cursor.

```
<div class="menugroup">
    <a href="page1.php">Page 1</a>
    <div class="submenu">
```

```
    </div><!-- submenu -->
</div><!-- menugroup -->
```

It's crucial to understand that adding hovering to the <a> tag in the above snippet doesn't change the visibility of the submenu. That's why we need to toggle on the container, namely the menugroup class.

We've learned previously that without a doc type, the <div> element does not support pseudo CSS classes. Also we cannot use an anchor tag like the following:

```
<a href=# class="menugroup">
    <a href="page1.php">Page 1</a>
    <div class="submenu">
        <a href="pagex.php">Page X</a>
        <a href="pagey.php">Page Y</a>
    </div><!-- submenu -->
</a><!-- menugroup -->
```

Most modern browsers will render the above code as:

```
<a href=# class="menugroup"></a>
    <a href="page1.php">Page 1</a>
    <div class="submenu">
        <a href="pagex.php">Page X</a>
        <a href="pagey.php">Page Y</a>
    </div><!-- submenu -->
</a><!-- menugroup -->
```

There are two reasons for this. One is that a link inside another link is ambiguous. Also a block element is not supposed to be inside an inline element.

Since we have to trap the mouse hover on a <div> element, we'll have to add a doc type.

```
.submenu{display:none;}
.menugroup:hover .submenu{display:block;}
```

To position the submenu under the main menu item, we use the relative-absolute positioning combo:

```
.menugroup{position:relative;}
.submenu{display:none;position:absolute;top:39px;left:0;}
```

Remember the menugroup class is assigned to a <div> element. Make it left floating so that the main menu item looks just like any other items:

```
.menugroup{position:relative;float:left;}
```

The submenu has to lay over the content that's below the menu bar. In case the menu is blocked by other floating or absolutely positioned elements, we change its z-index value in order to bring it to the front:

```
.submenu{
    display:none; z-index:1000;
position:absolute;top:39px;left:0;
}
```

The *z-index* attribute modifies the stacking order of elements. You may refer to Chapter 4.10 for more information.

Note it's very important to put the sub menu right next to the main menu item. Otherwise, when the mouse moves away from the trigger, the sub menu becomes invisible. To illustrate the point, move the sub menu down by 30 pixels:

```
.submenu{display:none;position:absolute;top:69px;left:0;}
```

If the sub menu needs to appear to be disconnected from the main menu item, we can style it so that the "gap" is still part of the sub menu. In IE, invisible gaps such as margin-top won't work. Use background color that's closest to the content background or near-invisible border line to fill the gap with some "substance" so that the sub menu stays on.

Alternatively you may set the top position of the sub menu to 0, and clone the main menu item. This works well except that the sub menu may cover other adjacent main menu items.

5.2.3.3 Image+Text Combo

In static websites, the most common compositions of image and text are image and text side by side, and text overlayed on top of image. We'll explore ways to implement these compositions in this section.

The first and simplest scenario is text flowing around an image.

 There was little of pleasant interest in the next eighteen months of Jack's career. His share of the globe was a twenty-foot circle around a pole in the yard. The blue hills of the offing, the nearer pine grove, and even the ranch-house itself were fixed stars, far away and sending merely faint suggestions of their splendors to his not very bright eyes. Even the horses and men were outside his little sphere and related to him about as much as comets are to the earth. The very tricks that had made him valued were being forgotten as Jack grew up in chains.

```
<img src="..." style="
    float:left;
    margin-right:10px;
    margin-bottom:10px;
">
Some lengthy text that goes on and on until it flows around
the image...
```

If the text around the image is not sufficiently long, you'll have to manually terminate the floating:

```
<img src="..." style="..."
Some short text that is not enough to pass the image
<div style="clear:both;"></div>
```

There are times when the text should not flow and wrap under the image. The old fashioned way to ensure each element's territory is to use a table:

```
<table><tr><td>
<img src="...">
</td><td>
Some lengthy text that would otherwise wrap...
</td></tr>
</table>
```

The "modern" approach is to use CSS to implement the columns:

```
<div style="width:1000px;">
    <div style="width:80px;margin-right:20px;float:left;">
        <img src="...">
    </div>
    <div style="width:900px;float:left;">
    Some lengthy text that would otherwise wrap...
    </div>
</div>
```

But wait! Before you criticize the many flaws of the above code, we can abandon the above approach altogether! There is indeed a much better way.

Let's forget about building websites for a moment. Imagine you're holding a photograph in one hand, and a printed description of the photo on the other. Now you want to frame these two pieces of paper so that they *appear* to be side by side.

The obvious solution is to put them side by side. This, in web terms, is to use a 2-column layout. But what if the description paper is transparent, and that the text occupies only half of the page? Now you can put the photograph underneath the description. Each piece takes up the entire horizontal space and yet they look side by side.

In other words, when decomposing a page, always try to think in layers. **Don't slice; stack instead.**

The following example is similar to the one you've seen in Chapter 4.1.3:

```
<div style="
    background:transparent url(image.gif) no-repeat top left;
    padding-left:100px;
">
```

```
    Some lengthy text that would otherwise wrap...
</div>
```

Remember that the background image of an element is not confined by paddings. The text, on the other hand, flows within the remaining space.

Another thing to remember is that the background image does not take up space by itself. If the text stretches the container to, say, 40 pixels, and the image is 100 pixels tall, only the top 40 pixels of the image will be shown. In this case, either add bottom padding to the container, or make sure the text is long enough.

Besides the left-and-right layout, there's also the above-and-beneath layout, that is, text laying on top of the image.
We could use the relative and absolute positioning combo:

```
<div style="position:relative;">
    <img src="..." style="position:absolute;top:0;left:0;">
    <div style="position:absolute;top:10px;left:10px;">
    Overlaying text
    </div>
</div>
```

Again, we can use the background image trick instead of building the two layers:

```
<div style="height:100px;width:800px;
background-image:url(image.jpg);">
    <div style="padding-top:10px;padding-left:10px;">
        Overlaying text
    </div>
</div>
```

5.2.3.4 Columned Content

Sometimes we need to divide up the horizontal space and display content side by side as columns. This is not to be confused with columned page layout, which deals with the overall structure of the entire webpage.

Building columned content is a lot simpler comparing to columned layout. If you remember Chapter 4.8 "Using Float and Clear" and 4.15.4 "Floating", you already know how to create side-by-side content.

There are two reasons why we're talking about floating and columns for the third time. The first is that we've shifted our focus from CSS behavior in Chapter 4 to a slightly higher level of thinking in Chapter 5. Float, like many other CSS attributes, has its unique effects and subsequent uses. If CSS attributes were tools from a toolbox, we have learned the capability of the popular tools in Chapter 4. In Chapter 5 we look at what needs to be built first and summon the relevant tool or tools accordingly. It's important to realize the two different thought processes.

The second reason to bring up the topic of columns again is because columns are so common in today's web content. You'll have to develop muscle memory to build anything that's common.

Now we're going to look at one very specific setup: 3 equal-width columns taking up a space of 1200 pixels.

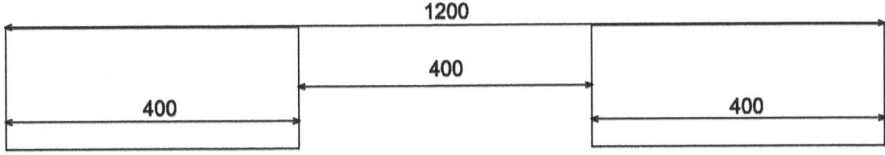

```
<style>
.col{width:400px;float:left;}
</style>

<div>
    <div class="col">Column 1</div>
    <div class="col">Column 2</div>
    <div class="col">Column 3</div>
    <div style="clear:both;"></div>
</div>
```

Remember to encapsulate the columns in a pair of div blocks and clear the float.

The issue with the above implementation is that there are no gaps between the columns. Next, we add some paddings to each column:

```
<style>
.col{width:400px;float:left;}
</style>

<div>
    <div class="col">
      <div style="padding:0 10px;">
        Column 1
      </div>
    </div>
    <div class="col">
      <div style="padding:0 10px;">
        Column 2
      </div>
    </div>
    <div class="col">
      <div style="padding:0 10px;">
        Column 3
      </div>
    </div>
    <div style="clear:both;"></div>
</div>
```

Interestingly, treating each column equally does *not* produce a balanced result, as we can see in the following illustration:

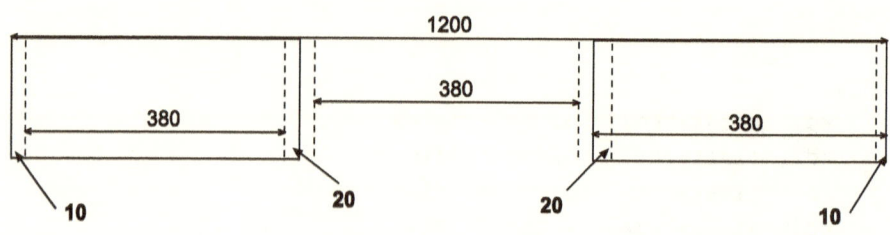

The padding between columns are added up to 20 pixels while the edge padding remain 10 pixels on each side. This layout is skewed. The gaps on the sides are also unnecessary.

Next, let's calculate the dimensions differently. Instead of allocating three columns, we budget the space for 2 gaps as well. The column widths are the same, and the gap widths are the same. All widths add up to 1200 pixels.

It takes a few trial and errs to find out a set of non-fraction numbers. There are multiple solutions but the following is one configuration:

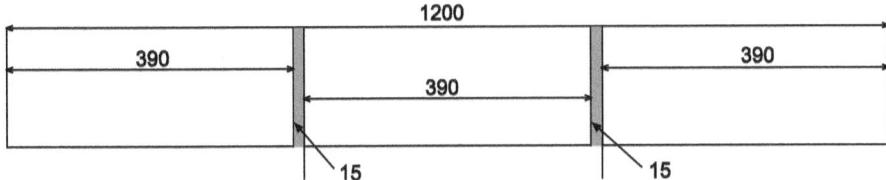

And the implementation is very simple:

```
<style>
.col{width:390px;float:left;margin-right:15px;}
</style>

<div>
    <div class="col">Column 1</div>
    <div class="col">Column 2</div>
    <div class="col" style="margin:0;">Column 3</div>
    <div style="clear:both;"></div>
</div>
```

It's important to zero out the margin in the last column. Otherwise the three columns will take up 405 pixels each, totaling 1215 pixels. The extra 15 pixels will wrap the last column to the next row, breaking the layout.

Again, the code for a *balanced* 3-column content division is very simple, as long as you perform the calculation beforehand. Do not simply divide the total width by 3.

```
Total = Width × 3 + Gap × 2
```

5.3 Creating Page Templates

A website is usually a collection of pages that share common elements. For example, the banner, navigation menu and footer look consistently across all pages.

We can better appreciate the benefits and necessity of page templates by first working without them. Consider the following set of pages:

Home Page:

```
<html>
<head><title>Home</title></head>
<body>
<div id="header">
   <a href="home.php"
      style="font-weight:bold;">Home</a>
   <a href="products.php">Products</a>
   <a href="about.php">About</a>
</div>
<div id="content">
   This is the home page content
</div>
<div id="footer">
   &copy; Some Random Corp.
</div>
</body>
</html>
```

Products Page:

```
<html>
<head><title>Products</title></head>
<body>
<div id="header">
   <a href="home.php">Home</a>
   <a href="products.php"
      style="font-weight:bold;">Products</a>
   <a href="about.php">About</a>
```

```
</div>
<div id="content">
   This is the product page content
</div>
<div id="footer">
   &copy; Some Random Corp.
</div>
</body>
</html>
```

About Page:

```
<html>
<head><title>About</title></head>
<body>
<div id="header">
   <a href="home.php">Home</a>
   <a href="products.php">Products</a>
   <a href="about.php"
      style="font-weight:bold;">About</a>
</div>
<div id="content">
   This is the about page content
</div>
<div id="footer">
   &copy; Some Random Corp.
</div>
</body>
</html>
```

Now, we need to add a new page, Services. We copy the above code and make some modifications:

```
<html>
<head><title>Service</title></head>
<body>
<div id="header">
   <a href="home.php">Home</a>
   <a href="products.php">Products</a>
   <a href="services.php"
```

```
          style="font-weight:bold;">Services</a>
   <a href="about.php">About</a>
</div>
<div id="content">
   This is the service page content
</div>
<div id="footer">
   &copy; Some Random Corp.
</div>
</body>
</html>
```

The issue of writing static pages in the above manner should now become obvious. When we add a new page, we'll need to change the navigation section in all of the other 3 pages. What if we need to change the order of menu items? Yes, we'll have to repeat the changes to all the other pages. What if we change the footer content? Yes, the same repetitive tasks need to be carried out.

5.3.1 Using Server-side Include

The idea behind server-side include is to define the common sections of a page in reusable PHP files. For example, the footer content can be stored in footer.php:

```
<div id="footer">
   &copy; Whatever Inc.
</div>
```

Then other pages can refer to this footer:

```
<html>
...
<body>
...
<?include 'footer.php'; ?>
</body>
</html>
```

We have already discussed about how server-side include works in Section 3.15.

Our focus now is on *how* to divide up a page most effectively.

First, let's look at the *wrong* way of extracting a template:

Home Page:

```
<html>
<head><title>Service</title></head>
<body>
<?include 'header.php';?>
<div id="content">
    This is the service page content
</div>
<?include 'footer.php';?>
</body>
</html>
```

Header:

```
<div id="header">
    <a href="home.php">Home</a>
    <a href="products.php">Products</a>
    <a href="services.php"
       style="font-weight:bold;">Services</a>
    <a href="about.php">About</a>
</div>
```

Footer:

```
<div id="footer">
    &copy; Some Random Corp.
</div>
```

If we templitize the pages like the above, we have already resolved some of the earlier mentioned issues. For instance, changing the footer information now requires modifying one file. The same is true with changing navigation items. However, what if we want to change the *structure* of the page? For example, we want to put the content container inside a canvas container:

```html
<html>
<head><title>Service</title></head>
<body>
<div id="canvas">
   <?include 'header.php';?>
   <div id="content">
      This is the service page content
   </div>
   <?include 'footer.php';?>
</div>
</body>
</html>
```

Again, we'll have to change each page - but we don't want that!

A better approach is to extract all the common elements, including tags, so that only pure content is left:

Header:

```html
<html>
<head><title>Service</title></head>
<body>
<div id="header">
   <a href="home.php">Home</a>
   <a href="products.php">Products</a>
   <a href="services.php"
      style="font-weight:bold;">Services</a>
   <a href="about.php">About</a>
</div>
<div id="content">
```

Footer:

```html
</div>
<div id="footer">
   &copy; Some Random Corp.
```

```
</div>
</body>
</html>
```

Home Page:

```
<?include 'header.php';?>
   This is the home page content
<?include 'footer.php';?>
```

Now, *all* the changes are centralized in two files. Pay special attention to the opening, but unclosed tag in the header, and the closing tag in the footer that has no matching opening tag.

5.3.2 Personalize Each Page

So far we have extracted the common elements into reusable server-side include files. These components, however, do not always look exactly the same on different pages. For example, each page may have a different banner image. The page titles should reflect the content on each page. The navigation menu should indicate which page is currently being displayed.

We can use PHP global variables to give server-side include files personalized behaviour.

Here's *header.php* again, with some modification:

```
<html>
<head><title><?echo $pagetitle;?></title></head>
<body>
<div id="header">
   <a href="home.php">Home</a>
   <a href="products.php">Products</a>
   <a href="services.php"
      style="font-weight:bold;">Services</a>
   <a href="about.php">About</a>
</div>
<div id="content">
```

Now, to use this file, we define the page title as a global variable right before we include the header.

Home Page:

```
<?
$pagetitle="Welcome";
include 'header.php';
?>
    This is the home page content
<?include 'footer.php';?>
```

About Page:

```
<?
$pagetitle="About Us";
include 'header.php';
?>
    This is the about us page
<?include 'footer.php';?>
```

Next we set the menu item for the current page to bold. Look at the header file again:

```
<style>
.cur{font-weight:bold;}
</style>
<html>
<head><title><?echo $pagetitle;?></title></head>
<body>
<div id="header">
    <a href="home.php"
    <?if ($page=='home') echo 'class="cur"';?>
    >Home</a>
    <a href="products.php"
    <?if ($page=='products') echo 'class="cur"';?>
    >Products</a>
    <a href="services.php"
    <?if ($page=='service') echo 'class="cur"';?>
```

```
   >Services</a>
   <a href="about.php"
   <?if ($page=='about') echo 'class="cur"';?>
   >About</a>
</div>
<div id="content">
```

In each page, set the value of the *page* variable, so that the header bolds the proper heading. For example, the Service Page:

```
<?
$pagetitle="About Us";
$page='service';

include 'header.php';
?>
   Our Services
<?include 'footer.php';?>
```

The naming of the page identifier is arbitrary. You can even use numeric values if you want. Identifiers are also case sensitive. So if *page* is compared to "service", the service page should set it to "service" instead of "Service".

Setting paging identifier in each page may seem like a lot of work, especially comparing to the practice of using the page filename as the identifier. However, separating the logical page from the physical file allows superior flexibility and hence maintainability. For example, multiple pages can share the same identifier and trigger the same navigation item. This is cumbersome using the filename-based approach.

Another point to bear in mind is that the landing page of a web site is not usually representative of the typical structure of the entire site. You may either use a different set of header and footer for the "special" pages, or use additional shared components for content pages. Regardless how you extract the template, the goal should be consolidating changes. For example, when a new navigation item is added to the site, only one file should be changed instead of multiple files.

5.3.3 Skin, Slice, Templatize

If you are in any sense confused by what you've read so far in Chapter 5, do not worry. We will work through a real-world example, so that you can see how the principles are applied to a live project.

We will be following the procedure of skin, slice and templatize. The stage of skinning converts static graphics files to HTML and CSS code. The slicing stage is not to be confused with slicing images. It's for extracting common components to shared include files. The last step, templatising, adapts the reusable components to page contexts.

The example we are using here is The Food Network (www.foodnetwork.ca).

I, or this book is not affiliated with The Food Network. The reason I picked the site is because it is typical both in terms of design and organization of content. The topic of food is also non-political. Who doesn't enjoy a nice meal?

For clearer illustration, I'm going to simplify the site to the following set of pages:

Main Landing Page:

Recipes & Menus Sub Landing Page:

Guides & Articles Sub Landing Page:

Other Static Pages:

There are many other pages on the Food Network website. Our goal is not to replicate their website. Instead, we'll be creating stub pages for the "On TV", "Video" and "Sign In" pages so that the site navigation is complete.

Back in Chapter 5.2.1 we discussed about navigation structure. The screen shots from foodnetwork.ca, shown above, roughly capture the structure of the Food Network.

The master landing page has two menus. The horizontal one contains links to the "Recipe & Menus" page as well as the "Guides and Articles" page. The master landing page also has a vertical menu that points directly to pages in the sub landing pages.

The vertical sub menu items are more extensive in specific sections. For example, under the "Guides and Articles" heading on the main landing page, there are 9 items. On the "Guides and Articles" page the sub menu has 23 items.

Analyzing the structure, commonality and differences among the pages helps us form an implementation strategy. We will derive 3 template variations to build a clone of foodnetwork.ca.

Next we'll examine the page layout. You may refer to Chapter 5.2.2 to brush up your memory.

Pick one page from foodnetwork.ca. View the page in different browser window sizes and observe how the page structure reacts.

Food Network uses a fixed width layout (Type I). In addition, there are three columns. The left column is used for the vertical menu. It uses up 150 pixels of horizontal space. The main content occupies 480 pixels. The right column is for "side content" or "related articles". It uses 300 pixels.

The gap between the first two columns is 10 pixels wide. The gap between the main content and the right column is 20 pixels. Ideally the gap space should be balanced, but we are simply replicating a website so let's stay true to the original design.

The total content width adds up to 960 pixels.

$150 + 10 + 480 + 20 + 300 = 960$

Let's start with a simple HTML page:

```
<html>
<head>
    <title>Food Network</title>
    <style>
body{margin:0;padding:0;text-align:center;}
#canvas{width:960px;margin:0 auto;text-align:left;}
    </style>
</head>
<body>
    <div id="canvas">
    Some Text
    </div>
</body>
</html>
```

Then we tile some background image:

```
body{
...
background:transparent url(bubbles.png)
    repeat-x top left;
}

#canvas{
...
padding-bottom:600px;
}
```

We added the padding to canvas so that the content is "tall enough" to stretch the container. This is only temporary.

The red menu bar stretches across the screen instead of staying within the confinement of the 960-pixel-wide content space. This changes how we build the site.

A straight forward solution is rather complicated:

```
<div id="canvas">
...
</div><!-- escaping canvas -->

<div style="background:transparent url(menu.png)
    repeat-x top left;">
<!-- entering a replica of canvas -->
<div style="width:960px;margin:0 auto;text-align:left;">
    <div style="background:transparent url(menu.png) repeat-x
top left;">
        Menu
    </div>
</div>
</div>
```

If you're puzzled why we have to break out of the canvas container and re-enter with a redundant background image, review the section about Full-Bleed Layout.

A much simpler and elegant solution is to play tricks on the background image itself. Instead of having bubbles and the line, we can combine them into a single image file, bubbleline.png:

```
body{
...
```

```
background:transparent url(bubbleline.png)
    repeat-x top center;
}
```

Reload the web page. It already looks a lot better.

Next we're adding a footer section. The background image of the footer is also stretching to the edge of the screen:

In order to make the footer background stretch, we need to place the footer outside of the canvas container.

```
...
<style>
...
#footer{
height:101px;
background:transparent url(footer.png) repeat-x top left;
margin:0 auto;
}

</style>
...
<body>
<div id="canvas">
...
</div><!-- canvas -->

<div id="footer">
Footer Text
</div>
```

Reload the screen. The footer may seem fine to you. Now shrink the browser screen until a horizontal scroll bar shows up. We set the canvas width to 960 pixels, so a window narrower than 960px would trigger the scroll bar.

Scroll to the bottom of the page where you can see the footer background. Then scroll to the right. The footer image does not cover the right side! This is a classic case of under stretching. We have discussed about under stretching in Full Bleed Layout.

The solution is to protect the content space with explicit width:

```
<style>
#footer{
height:101px;
background:transparent url(footer.png) repeat-x top center;
margin:0 auto;
}

#footercontent{
height:101px;
width:960px;
background:transparent url(footer.png) repeat-x top center;
}
</style>
...
<div id="footer">
   <div id="footercontent">
      Footer
   </div>
</div>
```

Note that the background image position is now "center" instead of "left". This is because the footer is center aligned, and overlaying two identical images that's also center aligned creates one, seamless background image.

Next we decompose the header:

If you download the logo file directly from foodnetwork.ca, you'll see the logo is a transparent PNG. We know, from Chapter 5.1.3, that GIF enjoys wider browser support, and that if we can make GIF transparency work the result will be consistent in all browsers.

The PNG file has a alpha channel that acts as a mask. Anything beyond the mask is purely transparent:

If we used the same mask to clip the GIF image, the edge around the transparent area would be harsh. So instead, we include the anti-aliased pixels around the edge.

The darker background color in the bottom image is set as transparent color. The image looks weird by itself but overlays perfectly on the menu bar.

The bubbles repeat in the background and there happens to be a gap behind the logo, so we don't really need to trim the upper corners of the logo image.

As a matter of fact, we don't really need transparency at all, given the context of the website. The logo on the bottom right has the transparency shadow pre-pressed into the background. Sure we won't be able to use the image elsewhere, but it works well for this location and works on every browser.

By now you may have noticed that decomposing the screenshot of a website can be quite different from taking image resource directly from a graphic designer. In an ideal world, that transparent PNG from the logo layer in the Photoshop file should just work when inserted directly in a website. Modern browsers are getting closer to that ideal. Graphic designers are also more likely to produce web-friendly artworks. After all, many of them are also building websites.

This is not to say, however, that smart image pre-processing is not important. By merging logical layers into a single, directly consumable image, we can greatly simplify web coding as well as enhancing compatibility.

Since the header has a fixed height, we can use the relative-absolute position combination to place the elements (logo, menu, search box, etc.). You may want to review Chapter 4.9 and 5.2.3.1.
`<style>`

```
...
#header{position:relative;}
#header #logo{position:absolute;top:65px;left:0;}
</style>
...
<div id="canvas">
   <div id="header">
      <div id="logo">
         <img src="logo.gif">
      </div>
   </div>
</div>
...
```

You may fine tune the logo position based on how you slice your logo image.
The top of the web page should look like the following:

Using the same technique, we'll place a menu:

```
<style>
...
#menu{
position:absolute;  top:146px; left:180px;
font-size:18px;  font-family:arial,sans-serif;
}
#menu a{
display:block;padding:6px 18px;
float:left;
border-left:solid 1px #FF3B39;
border-right:solid 1px #D81816;
}
#menu a, #menu a:link, #menu a:hover, #menu a:visited{
color:#ffffff;text-decoration:none;
}
#menu a:hover{
background:transparent url(menu_on.png) repeat-x top left;
```

```
}
</style>
...

<div id="canvas">
   <div id="header">
      <div id="logo"><img src=" logo.gif"></div>
      <div id="menu">
          <a href="recipes.php">Recipes & Menus</a>
          <a href="guides.php">Guides & Articles</a>
          <a href="ontv.php">On TV</a>
          <a href="video.php">Video</a>
          <div style="clear:both;"></div>
      </div>
   </div>
</div>
...
```

Let's read through the above code.

First, the menu container is absolutely positioned. Its parent container, "header", has relative positioning and serves as an anchor.

Then we override the display type of anchor tags inside the menu container from inline to block. This gives these hyper links proper box model so that we can add padding. Padding is important for the hover effect we'll see very soon.

Block elements break the line. That's why we add float:left to each link, and a clearing block in the end.

The padding of links and the exact position of the menu container are determined by a few trials and errors.

The link style is set by setting all its pseudo classes (e.g. hover, link, visited).

When the link is hovered upon, the following background image is used:

Since the image is tiling on the x-axis, we can make it only 1 pixel wide.

Finally, the dividers between menu items are simulated by 2 lines, coloured in #FF3B39 and #D81816, respectively. If you take a screenshot of the website and zoom in the divider, you'll see the 3D looking divider is exactly those two lines.
Conveniently, the two lines are implemented by the right border of a link and the left border of its following link.

Be aware that the widths of these links are not perfectly consistent in all browsers. The 18-pixel padding expands the links on both sides. Borders take up another 2 pixels. These 2 pixels only add to the total width in non-IE browsers. Since the exact width of the menu item is not critical or noticeable, we can accept such compromise.

If you really need exact widths, however, you can use a pair of *span* tags around the links and give them the borders instead.

With the mouse hovering a menu item, the header looks like the following:

Next we'll add a little search box:

```
<style>
...
#searchbox{
position:absolute;  top:90px;left:140px;
background-image:url(search.gif);
width:624px;  height:47px;
}

#search{
```

```
position:absolute; top:12px; left:15px;
font-size:20px;
color:#B0B0B0;
width:425px;
border:none;
background-color:transparent;
}
</style>
...
   <div id="header">
      ...
      <div id="searchbox">
         <input id="search">
      </div>
   </div>
...
```

We hide the real border of the input box and give it a proper font size so that its height fills up the search box image. The search container is absolutely positioned inside the header container, so the header container is the anchor of the search container. The search container, in turn, is the anchor for the search input box because the search input box is also absolutely positioned.

Remember that in Firefox absolutely positioned elements do not take up space in their containers. The width and height of the search container has to be explicitly set. Otherwise you won't see the search image at all.

The search input box is not as wide as the background because the right side is reserved for adding the dropdown menu and the search icon. The interaction and functionality of these elements are discussed in later chapters.

At this point we have built a frame that's common to all the pages. Before we build the content for each page, let's break the following page into reusable components:

```
<html>
<head>
   <title>Food Network</title>
<style>
body{
margin:0;padding:0;
```

```css
text-align:center;
background:transparent url(bubbleline.png) repeat-x top left;
}

#canvas{
width:960px;margin:0 auto;
text-align:left;
padding-bottom:600px;
}

#footer{
height:101px;
background:transparent url(footer.png) repeat-x top center;
}

#footercontent{
height:101px;
width:960px;
margin:0 auto;
background:transparent url(footer.png) repeat-x top center;
}

#header{position:relative;}
#header #logo{position:absolute;top:65px;left:0;}
#menu{
position:absolute;top:146px;left:180px;
font-size:18px;
font-family:arial,sans-serif;
}
#menu a{
display:block;padding:6px 18px;
float:left;
border-left:solid 1px #FF3B39;
border-right:solid 1px #D81816;
}
#menu a, #menu a:link, #menu a:hover, #menu a:visited{
color:#ffffff;
text-decoration:none;
}
#menu a:hover{
background:transparent url(menu_on.png) repeat-x top left;
```

```
}
#searchbox{
position:absolute;
top:90px;left:140px;
background-image:url(search.gif);
width:624px;height:47px;
}
#search{
position:absolute;
top:12px;left:15px;
font-size:20px;
color:#B0B0B0;
width:425px;border:none;
background-color:transparent;
}
</style>
</head>
<body>
    <div id="canvas">
    <div id="header">
        <div id="logo"><img src="logo.gif"></div>
        <div id="menu">
            <a href="recipes.php">Recipes & Menus</a>
            <a href="guides.php">Guides & Articles</a>
            <a href="ontv.php">On TV</a>
            <a href="video.php">Video</a>
            <div style="clear:both;"></div>
        </div>
        <div id="searchbox"><input id="search"></div>
    </div><!-- header -->

</div><!-- canvas -->

<div id="footer">
    <div id="footercontent">
        Footer
    </div>
</div>

</body>
</html>
```

First move all the text in the *style* block to an external file *food.css*.

```
<html>
<head>
   <title>Food Network</title>
   <link rel="stylesheet" href="food.css" type="text/css" />
   ...
```

Then we slice the page into server include files.

Header (header.php):

```
<html>
<head>
   <title><?echo $pagetitle;?></title>
   <link rel="stylesheet" href="food.css" type="text/css" />
</head>
<body>
   <div id="canvas">
   <div id="header">
      <div id="logo"><img src="logo.gif"></div>
      <div id="menu">
         <a href="recipes.php">Recipes & Menus</a>
         <a href="guides.php">Guides & Articles</a>
         <a href="ontv.php">On TV</a>
         <a href="video.php">Video</a>
         <div style="clear:both;"></div>
      </div>
      <div id="searchbox"><input id="search"></div>
   </div><!-- header -->
```

Footer (footer.php):

```
</div><!-- canvas -->

<div id="footer">
   <div id="footercontent">
      Footer
   </div>
</div>
```

```
</body>
</html>
```

Note how the canvas container closes in the footer instead of the header.

Next we use the above components to build the pages:

Landing page (index.php):

```
<?php
$page='home';
$pagetitle='Food Network Canada';
include 'header.php';
?>
Home Page Content
<?
include 'footer.php';
```

Other pages are built the similar way. But here's one more trick.
An observant reader may have noticed that the background image on the website changes from page to page. We can use block styles inside each page to override the global default.

For example, the Guides and Articles page uses the following graphic:

Remember how we combined the red bar with the bubbles? We can take the same approach and change the background to a single tiling background:

Guides & Articles (guides.php):

```php
<?php
$page='guides';
$pagetitle='Guides & Articles';
include 'header.php';
?>
<style>
body{background-image:url(bubble-wave.png);}
</style>

Guides & Articles Content
<?
include 'footer.php';
```

If you'd like to proceed building the rest of the pages, keep in mind that Food Network's website is a bit too complex for a beginner project. In addition, I believe the design of certain content pages lacks consistency and coherence. Having said that, however, you can still go ahead and implement the pages using the process we just discussed. The Articles & Guides page can be viewed as a landing page for a sub site, or "micro site". Examine the common elements between the sub landing page and its content pages. We see that the vertical menu is present in all the pages, so we can start from there.

6.0 MySQL

Now we are going to change the gear and look into a very different area of web programming. If the web skinning project from the last chapter is still lingering in your mind, give it a rest for now. Using include files to build reusable components is effective for small static websites. When you get closer to building the content, or "real substance" of a functional website, however, this include-file trick simply won't be enough. Before we can draw the line between static web pages and dynamic web site, we need to study how to build a dynamic one. This, in turn, requires better command and more elegant use of a server-side scripting language such as PHP. Although we have covered the basics of PHP in Chapter 3, we did so without the presence of a database.

In this chapter, we'll cover the essentials of MySQL database in the context of a database-driven dynamic website. With a database, you'll see the "need" and patterns of using PHP. Many topics that are covered in Chapter 3 will make more sense to you by the end of this chapter.

6.1 Relational Databases

Before we explain what databases are and how they work, let's look at the role a database plays in a web application.

Remember that the rendering of a PHP page is "pass through". Any variables that are manipulated by the PHP script will no longer exist by the end of the page cycle. An application, on the other hand, remembers its state of execution. For example, when a checkbox is clicked, the box should stay checked even when the user navigates away from the current web page. A contact that's added to a phonebook application should not disappear the next time the website is visited. The data is said to be *persistent*. There are several ways to persist data. Cookie, files, database and shared memory are just a few examples.

Conceptually, any mechanism that allows information storage and retrieval is a database. For example, a text file could be considered a database storage:

```
Fred Flintstone, 203-212-1322
```

```
Barney Rubble, 203-212-0749
Joe Rockhead, 102-853-1021
```

A file alone cannot be a database. It's just storage. We have to define how to access the information. The following code reads the text file into a PHP array:

```
$f=fopen('numbers.txt','rt');
$names=array();
while (!feof($f)){
   $line=trim(fgets($f));
   if ($line=='') continue;
   $parts=explode(',',$line);
   $name=trim($parts[0]); $number=trim($parts[1]);
   array_push($names,
       array('name'=>$name, 'number'=>$number)
   );
}
```

We'll talk more about file operations later. If you see a function you don't know in the above code, look it up on php.net. Also review PHP Arrays in Chapter 3.

The above code defines a process (or algorithm) for reading the text file. The text file follows a specific format (or protocol), namely each contact record ends with a line break, and that the sub fields of a contact, name and phone number, are separated by a comma. This is the format of a Comma-Separated-Value (CSV) file.

The code reads each line, parses the fields and stores the extracted information in an array. This algorithm converts the data structure that's used by, and stored on a file to a more accessible PHP object that stays in memory for further processing.

Niklaus Wirth, a legend in computer science, published a book titled

Algorithms + Data Structures = Programs

The book title captures the two parts of a database: storage and access.

So far we have only implemented an algorithm that reads from a text file. The file, along with the code, is said to be a "filed-based read-only database".

Clearly this primitive "database" is far from a web application's typical needs. Text files are storage-inefficient. It's also difficult to quickly locate specific records or modify existing entries. This is the very reason database products were invented. Instead of burdening the programmers with complex data structures and advanced search algorithms, a Database Management System (DBMS) offers transparent storage and retrieval capability. A PHP programmer does not need to know how MySQL writes to its binary files or how a record is manipulated physically on the disk. The focus of an application program is to describe to the database his logical requirements.

MySQL is one of the many products that belong to a specific kind of database - a *relational* database, or RDBMS.

Relational database share some common characteristics. The underlying implementation of MySQL, Microsoft SQL Server, PostgreSQL are all drastically different, but their data presentation model and retrieval interface are more or less the same. That's why things you learn about MySQL from this book are largely reusable when you pick up another database product.

The first commonality is that relational databases describe information in tables. We already saw the clumsy attempt to separate the name and number fields in the text file. Excel spreadsheet is another example of tabulated storage:

contactid	fname	lname	phone
2	Fred	Flintstone	203-212-1322
5	Barney	Rubble	203-212-0749
6	Joe	Rockhead	102-853-1021

Tables in relational databases are very similar to spreadsheets. In the above example, each contact record has an unique identifier. This is the *Primary Key* of the table. The IDs do not have to be sequential but they have to be unique.

The IDs are convenient to describe and locate a specific record. This is useful to establish relationships between records in various tables.

For example, we can store the phone numbers in a separate table and reference to the contact table:

phoneid	contactid	phone	Phonetype

1	2	203-212-1322	home
4	2	917-184-2932	office
5	6	102-853-1021	home

Now we can drop the Phone column in the main Contact table.

The Phone table also has a primary key "phoneid" that uniquely identifies each record. Note that although a primary key is not required to create a table, it serves performance and functional purposes as we'll see later.

The "contactid" field in the Phone table refers to the primary key in the main Contact table. The field names do not technically have to be the same in the two tables; however, having the same indicates a logical connection. The "contactid" field is often called a *foreign key*. Depending on the database product and its setup, the linkage between logically connected tables may or may not be enforced. The database may not even be aware of such affiliation. We can see that if we delete a record in the Contact table without removing his related phone records, the entries in the Phone table will point to a non-existing record. If the database is set to protect against such corruption by automatically deleting related records, the database is said to support *referential integrity*.

By cross referencing the two tables we can see that Fred has two phone numbers, Barney has no phones, and Joe only has one house number. Unlike the primary key, we can have duplicated values in a foreign key. This is how we express a *one-to-many relationship*, or "1-N".

Many real-life scenarios are 1-N relationships. For example, a couple can have zero, one or multiple children. A tree may have multiple apples. However, each child can have only one biological mother (assuming no crazy genetic science involved), and an apple that belongs to one tree cannot belong to another. If this is the case, the "-to-many" table (e.g. Children, Apples) needs only one foreign key column to express the 1-N relationship.

There are also *many-to-many relationships*. For example, a movie has multiple actors, but an actor can be in multiple movies. In this case, we cannot use a foreign key in either the Actors- or Movies table because neither table is subordinate to another.

We create tables for Movies and Actors separately:

movieid	title	year	director

1	Shawshank Redemption	1994	Frank Darabont
2	Legends of the Fall	1994	Edward Zwick
3	Forrest Gump	1994	Robert Zemeckis
4	Top Gun	1986	Tony Scott
5	Sleepless in Seattle	1993	Nora Ephron
6	You've Got Mail	1998	Nora Ephron
7	Meet Joe Black	1998	Martin Brest

And the actors:

actorid	name	birthyear
1	Tim Robbins	1958
2	Tom Hanks	1956
3	Tom Cruise	1962
4	Meg Ryan	1961
5	Morgan Freeman	1937
6	Brad Pitt	1963
7	Anthony Hopkins	1937

Now we create a table to bridge the actors and movies. In addition to merely describing the N-N relationship, we are also storing the role an actor plays in a specific movie.

amid	movieid	actorid	role
1	1	1	Andy Dufresne
2	1	5	"Red"
3	2	6	Tristan Ludlow
4	2	7	William Ludlow
5	3	2	Forrest Gump
6	5	2	Sam Baldwin
7	6	2	Joe Fox
8	5	4	Annie Reed
9	6	4	Kathleen Kelly
10	4	3	Maverick
11	4	1	Merlin
12	7	6	Joe Black
13	7	7	William Parrish

First of all, don't be overwhelmed by these tables. They might look intimidating but they store information very efficiently. The relationships between movies and actors are captured without having duplicate information. If you are a heavy Excel user, you'll need to get used to reading pure reference numbers in the bridging table.

These three tables can answer all sorts of questions. For example:

What are the main actors in The Shawkshank Redemption?
What movie has the presence of both Tim Robbins and Tom Cruise?
What movies were made in 1993?

Relational databases have a standard communication protocol for you to ask the above questions, namely, the Structured Query Language (SQL).

For example, to list out all the 1993 movies in the database, we execute the following query:

```
select * from movies where year='1993';
```

Or if you want to find out all the actors in Shawshank:

```
select actors.* from movies,actors,actormovies
where movies.movieid=actormovies.movieid
and actors.actorid=actormovies.actorid
and movies.title like 'Shawshank Redemption';
```

The result of the above queries can be expressed also as tables:

actorid	name	birthyear
1	Tim Robbins	1958
5	Morgan Freeman	1937

Don't worry about the syntax just yet. We'll discuss about query writing and table structure design in great details in later chapters. For now, it's important to start thinking in tables and get familiar with the RDBMS related concepts.

6.2 Setting Up MySQL

Installing MySQL can be a straight forward process. Simply download the software and follow the instructions for your target operating system.

A typical question I get with MySQL setup is:
"MySQL is successfully installed. Now What?"

Remember that at the end of Apache installation, you might have asked yourself a similar question? Except that when Apache is up and running, you can see it by viewing the default web page on a browser.
How can I see that MySQL is really running? Or in other words, how do I "use" MySQL?

To answer these questions, we can, again, draw comparisons from Apache. As a web server (HTTPd), Apache listens on Port 80 and reponds to requests that are from either the same computer or a remote location. How the requests are transmitted is transparent to Apache, as this is handled by the networking layer. HTTP requests originate from web browsers. Therefore, browsers are called the "clients" and Apache the "server".

MySQL also uses a client-server architecture. In a typical setup, the MySQL server listens on a default Port 3306. Requests to the server are sent by MySQL clients. Think these clients as special browsers that send requests in proprietary binary format instead of plain text HTTP. The clients can be either a MySQL command line prompt program or a PHP extension. Regardless of the form, MySQL clients provide us a human understandable interface, and in particular, SQL.

For the sake of completeness, I'd like to point out that the client-server setup over TCP/IP, as we discussed above, is only one way to communicate with MySQL. In Unix like systems, MySQL can also be configured to use sockets. The Windows counterpart of a Unix socket is a named pipe. These are alternative connection methods to set up a same-host database. You may read more about sockets and named pipes to expand your knowledge horizon, but to put simply, they are special types of files that enable inter-program communication and they only work if the client and server are on the same computer.

In order to verify that MySQL is up and running, the following components need to be fully functional:
1. a running MySQL server instance
2. a client that has access to the MySQL server
3. a sample database for testing
4. a user that can access the sample database

The MySQL installer will guide you through the process of Step 1. You'll also be prompted to set a root password. The root user has unlimited access to the entire database system.

In addition to user names, MySQL applies different security policies to their connecting origins. For example, a user can be granted full access only if it's connected from the localhost. If you are new to MySQL, a locally connected root user is sufficient to get the system up and running. We'll revisit user setup in a later chapter.

Once you have Part 1 and 4 running, you can use the MySQL commandline client to test the database. Assuming the root password is "1234", go to the command prompt and issue the following command:

```
mysql -uroot -p
```

Run the above line in the MySQL executable folder. In Windows it would be the "bin" sub folder. In Linux, the path to the client program is already set, so you can just run the above command anywhere.

When prompt to enter the password, type in "1234".

Note that there's no space between the letter u and the user name root. It is a shorthand of writing the following command:

```
mysql --user root --password
```

When the password is omitted in the commandline, it is entered interactively. Do not ever write the password directly because the password is visible and is saved in terminal command history.

Upon successful connection you'll see the MySQL client prompt:

. . .

```
Type 'help;' or '\h' for help. Type '\c' to clear the current
input statement.

mysql>
```

A MySQL server instance runs several databases. The following databases
are pre-installed:

```
mysql> show databases;
+--------------------+
| Database           |
+--------------------+
| information_schema |
| mysql              |
| performance_schema |
| test               |
+--------------------+
4 rows in set (0.00 sec)
```

Having a MySQL server up and running is only half of the work. Next we'll
put this database server in our web ecosystem.

At the beginning of Chapter 3 we discussed the relationship betweeh PHP
and the Apache server. Apache is configured to handle both static and
dynamic contents. If the requested resource is a PHP script, the PHP
extension is summoned to process the script. The result of the script is then
returned to Apache and eventually the browser. How exactly does PHP treat
the script is none of Apache's concern. The use of PHP is also transparent to
the browser, besides some signatures in the response header.

A database layer is often used as the "3rd Tier":

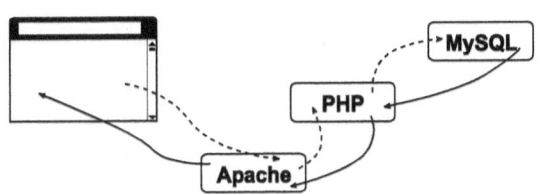

In the above diagram, the dashed lines are requests; solid lines are responses.

The relationship between PHP and MySQL is similar to that between Apache and PHP. A PHP script can use either "hard coded" values or "live data" from the database. Previously we modified *httpd.conf*, the configuration file for Apache so that Apache knows how to call PHP. Now we'll change the PHP settings so that PHP can connect to the MySQL server through a *MySQL client interface for PHP*, or a *MySQL connector*.

PHP extends its functionality by loading dynamic extension modules. This is, again, similar to how Apache extends itself. Older versions of PHP have a built-in MySQL connector. Then the connector became a separate module due to licensing restrictions. After all, a MySQL connector is a MySQL product, and needs to be supplied by its original vendor. In more recent versions of PHP, the connector is conveniently bundled in the PHP extension directory.

To enable the MySQL connector for PHP, we need to locate the config file and add (or uncomment) the following line:

```
extension=php_mysql.dll
```

In Linux, the following line may be indirectly included by the main config file:

```
extension=php_mysql.so
```

And of course you have to supply these binary connector files. In Windows, the extension files are in the *ext* folder. Keep in mind *php_mysql.dll* may be one of a few files you need to make available. For example, *libmysql.dll* is a dependency for php_mysql.dll.

If you are using a Debian/Ubuntu flavor of Linux, MySQL connector can be enabled by simply running:

```
sudo apt-get install php5-mysql
```

When we just installed PHP we created a test file with the following content:

```
<?php
phpinfo();
```

The output of this file helps locate the config file, *php.ini*:

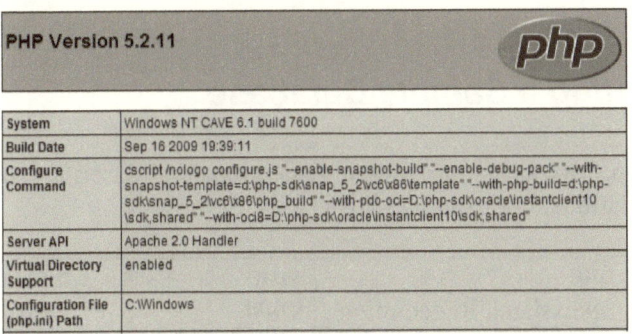

System	Windows NT CAVE 6.1 build 7600
Build Date	Sep 16 2009 19:39:11
Configure Command	cscript /nologo configure.js "--enable-snapshot-build" "--enable-debug-pack" "--with-snapshot-template=d:\php-sdk\snap_5_2\vc6\x86\template" "--with-php-build=d:\php-sdk\snap_5_2\vc6\x86\php_build" "--with-pdo-oci=D:\php-sdk\oracle\instantclient10\sdk,shared" "--with-oci8=D:\php-sdk\oracle\instantclient10\sdk,shared"
Server API	Apache 2.0 Handler
Virtual Directory Support	enabled
Configuration File (php.ini) Path	C:\Windows

Scroll down the page and see the module info for MySQL:

mysql

MySQL Support	enabled
Active Persistent Links	0
Active Links	0
Client API version	5.0.51a

Directive	Local Value	Master Value

Just to paint a more complete picture, this is the error message you'll get for **not** installing the MySQL extension when running a script that depends on MySQL functionality:

```
Fatal error: Call to undefined function mysql_connect in ...
```

All the PHP functions that begin with *mysql_* rely on the MySQL connector extension.

At this point you have an Apache server up and running, handling HTTP requests from web browsers. You also have a MySQL database server running. Apache is extended to intepret PHP scripts. And the PHP extension is further set up to communicate with the MySQL server.

Now take a moment to reflect on this setup. Refer to the diagram that shows the linkage between Apache, PHP and MySQL. Look at the Trace diagram at the beginning of this book. Convert these diagrams to a mental image and let it sink in.

6.3 Creating a Sample Database

In Chapter 6.1 we saw some sample data tables that describe movies, actors and their relations. For example, this is a list of movies:

movieid	title	year	director
1	Shawshank Redemption	1994	Frank Darabont
2	Legends of the Fall	1994	Edward Zwick
...	...	...	...

Each MySQL server instance contains several databases. Each database contains a few tables. Once we have the tables set up we can insert records. With a sample database and some test data it's a lot easier to discuss concepts such as querying, data binding, etc.

To create a database, we can use any MySQL client to send the server the command. A MySQL client can be the command-prompt client program, a GUI program or a PHP script. Let's do it the "hard way" by using the command prompt program for now. In Windows, the MySQL client is located at *C:\mysql\bin\mysql.exe*. You may want to replace the path with your own install path.

```
> mysql -uroot -p
Enter password:
```

Once the root password is entered at the prompt you'll see the MySQL prompt:

```
mysql> show databases;
+--------------------+
| Database           |
+--------------------+
| information_schema |
| mysql              |
| performance_schema |
| test               |
```

6.0 MySQL

```
+--------------------+
4 rows in set (0.00 sec)
```

Now let's create a new database:

```
mysql> create database imdb;
Query OK, 1 row affected (0.01 sec)
```

Make sure you end a command with a semi-colon. Otherwise the prompt will wait for more input until the delimiter (;) is hit.

Check that the database is created:

```
mysql> show databases;
+--------------------+
| Database           |
+--------------------+
| imdb               |
| information_schema |
| mysql              |
| performance_schema |
| test               |
+--------------------+
5 rows in set (0.00 sec)
```

Next we'll switch the current database context to the newly created database:

```
mysql> use imdb;
Database changed
```

A new database has no tables to begin with:

```
mysql> show tables;
```

Note the following two lines:

```
mysql> use mysql;
Database changed

mysql> show tables;
```

gives the same result as:

```
mysql> show tables in mysql;
```

However, the former approach changes the current database whereas the latter does not.
Switch the current database to imdb again just in case you moved away.

```
mysql> use imdb;
```

Now we create a table by describing its structure:

```
mysql> create table movies (
        movieid int unsigned not null auto_increment,
        title varchar(255) not null,
        movieyear varchar(4) not null,
        director varchar(255) not null,
        primary key(movieid)
        );
Query OK, 0 rows affected (0.02 sec)
```

When you type in multiple lines in the client program, the exact output looks like the following:

```
mysql> create table movies (
    -> movieid int unsigned not null auto_increment,
    -> title varchar(255) not null,
    -> movieyear varchar(4) not null,
    -> director varchar(255) not null,
    -> primary key(movieid)
    -> );
Query OK, 0 rows affected (0.02 sec)
```

The arrow indicates the line continues from the previous line. Do not type the arrows. To avoid confusion, the line-continuing arrows are omitted in future examples.

Similarly we can create a table of actors:

```
mysql> create table actors (
        actorid int unsigned not null auto_increment,
```

```
        name varchar(255) not null,
        birthyear varchar(4) not null,
        primary key(actorid)
        );
Query OK, 0 rows affected (0.02 sec)
```

Check that we have both tables:

```
mysql> show tables;
+----------------+
| Tables_in_imdb |
+----------------+
| actors         |
| movies         |
+----------------+
2 rows in set (0.01 sec)
```

We can further inspect the structure of a table by issuing the *describe* command:

```
mysql> describe actors;
+-----------+--------------------+------+-----+---------+----------------+
| Field     | Type               | Null | Key | Default | Extra          |
+-----------+--------------------+------+-----+---------+----------------+
| actorid   | int(10) unsigned   | NO   | PRI | NULL    | auto_increment |
| name      | varchar(255)       | NO   |     | NULL    |                |
| birthyear | varchar(4)         | NO   |     | NULL    |                |
+-----------+--------------------+------+-----+---------+----------------+
3 rows in set (0.00 sec)
```

As we can see, the columns (or fields) of a table are also defined by a table. Each field carries the following attributes:

Field name: Try to use all lower case names without any spaces. Also avoid using MySQL keywords as field names. The *year* column is named as *movieyear* in the *movies* table for this very reason.

Type: A field may store either string, numeric value, date or even advanced data types such as native geo coordinates. MySQL needs to know the exact type for storing data so that it can utilize the storage and execute queries effectively. We'll discuss more about data types soon.

Nullable: Whether the value of the field in question can be empty. It's important to know that an empty string and a null value are not the same even though they often have the same presentation. Not all fields can be null. For example, the primary key field cannot be null.

Index Type: We'll look at index types in greater details later. For now, just get yourself acquainted with the major types of indexes: *Primary Key*, *Unique Key* and *Index*. There can be only one primary key in a table.

Default Value: If the default value of a field is specified AND a new recorded is created without providing the field value, such default value will be used.

Extra: This column in the table structure table is mostly used to store the "auto_increment" status of a field. Only the primary key field can be set to auto increment. Auto increment is crucial to generate unique IDs.

Before we dive into the technical details of data types, do this exercise first: create a table called "movieactors". Upon calling

```
mysql> describe movieactors;
```

you should see:

```
+-----------+-------------------+------+-----+---------+-------
---------+
| Field     | Type              | Null | Key | Default | Extra
|
+-----------+-------------------+------+-----+---------+-------
---------+
| amid      | int(10) unsigned  | NO   | PRI | NULL    |
auto_increment |
```

```
| actorid   | int(10) unsigned | NO   |      | NULL    |
|
| movieid   | int(10) unsigned | NO   |      | NULL    |
|
| role      | varchar(255)     | NO   |      | NULL    |
|
+-----------+------------------+------+-----+---------+-------
---------+
3 rows in set (0.00 sec)
```

If you need more help, here's a template to follow. Fill in the blanks:

```
mysql> create table _____ (
          ____ int unsigned not null auto_increment,
          _____ int unsigned not null,
          _____ ___ _____ not null,
          ____ varchar(255) not null,
          primary key(____)
       );
```

MySQL offers a large variety of data types that can be put in the following categories: *numeric, string* and *date/time*. In addition, MySQL support spatial extensions that allow native handling of geo-spatial data types.

For the maximum storage efficiency you should pick the type that's just enough to accomodate the data range. For example, a column in a sales database that tracks sales stages can be storaged using *unsigned tinyint*, as this stores 0-255.

Before you dig in the manual and learn about all the differences between data types, let's reduce our options to the following types:

tinyint - small range, suitable for tracking states, modes, etc.
int - good enough for most integer storage cases
bigint - when *int* doesn't have enough range
decimal(5,2) - money; 5-digit precision and 2 decimal places
double - for storaging other fraction types
varchar(255) - strings and text that are under 255 characters
longtext - long blobs of text
datetime - date/time; varchar(20) is often used instead to store UNIX timestamp. We'll discuss date/time handling in later chapters.

6.0 MySQL   235

As you build more applications you'll develop an intuition of what exact type to use. You'll also become more precise. For example, you'll know to use *binary(20)* in combination of the *unhex* function to store a fixed 40-digit SHA1 password hash instead of wasting space with *varchar(40)*.

Again, space efficiency is not a big deal comparing to two other constraints: range and precision. Use numeric types to store numbers and string types to store strings. Always have enough length to accomodate the data range and if precision is important, use *decimal* instead of *double* or *float*.

Understanding the technical characteristics of different data types is a matter of research. The biggest challenge is not about finding the right type for a specific use, but anticipating what the use case will be. Take water-coloured painting for example. You can pick and mix any colour you want. More skillful painters can get the exact colour faster but this is just technicality. Knowing *what* colour goes *where* to make a painting look good and meaningful is the real challenge.

Now, if you are still itching to know (as I'm itching to tell) the difference between *decimal* and *double*, or that between fixed- and floating- point calculation in general, here's a quick explanation:

0.0001 is treated as an exact value when stored in decimal. Storing the same number in *double* introduces floating-point errors. Summing 0.0001 10,000 times will produce exactly 1 in *decimal*. In double, however, the result is approximate. It could be 1.00001, 1.0000, 0.9999, etc.

At this point you may have formed an impression that floating point is less accurate than fixed point. Quite on the contrary, floating point is more precise for describing real numbers where the digits just don't end. Computers have finite (and descreete) number of storage units so fractions are always described with some loss, be it *decimal* or *double*. However, in money handling, we know the exact number of decimal points. 1 cent is exactly 1 cent. Adding 100 pennies should give us exactly a dollar. Therefore using *decimal* is more suitable in this case.

Again, I can't stress enough, despite my length technical explanation above, that at this stage of learning, knowing too much of the technical stuff is only distracting. As long as you don't use varchar(255) to store everything, it doesn't really matter much if you use *float*, or *double* or *decimal*. And you absolutely should not optimize for storage at this stage. Later on you'll see that storage is indeed important even though disk storage is so cheap thesedays. The more records you can stuff in the same chunk of memory (or "page") the better. We'll get to that when you're comfortable with other aspects of MySQL, especially building functional applications with MySQL.

6.4 Basic CRUD Operations

In the previous chapter we created our first database *imdb* and two data tables *movies* and *actors*. If you did your exercise there should be a *movieactors* table as well.

Seeing these tables as spreadsheets in Excel, we can perform the following operations:

Create - add records to the table
Retrieve - fetch records from the table
Update - modify existing records
Delete - remove a record

Some quick examples:

Adding a movie:

```
mysql> insert into movies (title,movieyear,director)
       values('Shawshank','1994','Frank Darabont');
Query OK, 1 row affected (0.17 sec)
```

Finding a movie that's made in 1994:

```
mysql> select * from movies where movieyear='1994';
+---------+-----------+-----------+----------------+
| movieid | title     | movieyear | director       |
+---------+-----------+-----------+----------------+
|       1 | Shawshank | 1994      | Frank Darabont |
+---------+-----------+-----------+----------------+
1 row in set (0.03 sec)
```

Change the movie title from "Shawshank" to "Shawshank Redemption":

```
mysql> update movies set title='Shawshank Redemption'
       where movieid=1;
Query OK, 0 rows affected (0.04 sec)
Rows matched: 1  Changed: 0  Warnings: 0
```

Delete all movies in 1994:

```
mysql> delete from movies where movieyear='1994';
Query OK, 1 row affected (0.03 sec)
```

In a web application, interfaces for creating, retrieving, updating and deleting database records are created as wrappers for statements like the above.

6.5 Query, Bind and Render

Before we dive into SQL syntax, let's put what we have just learned in the context of a web app.

Using the MySQL commandline tool, we can connect to a database server, pick a database and fetch records from a data table.

```
> mysql -uroot -p
Enter password: ******

mysql> use imdb;
Database changed

mysql> select * from movies;
```

Now we'll do exactly the same in PHP. Our goal is to have a web page that shows all the movie titles in the database:

```
1  <?php

2  $db=mysqli_connect('localhost','root','******','imdb');

3  $query="select * from movies";
```

```
4  $rs=mysqli_query($db,$query);

5  while ($myrow=mysqli_fetch_assoc($rs)){
6      $movieid=$myrow['movieid'];
7      $title=$myrow['title'];
   ?>
8  <div>#<?echo $movieid;?> <?echo $title;?></div>
   <?
9  }//while
```

Line 2 in the above listing connects to the database server and selects the imdb database. Line 3 and 4 send a query. The remaining code loops through the results and prints the output in HTML.

In a typical data-driven web page, the database connection is established only once, at the beginning of the script.

Line 3-9 perform the query-bind-render routine. The query is sent in Line 3. Then we enter the loop that fetches each record as an associative array. One instance of *$myrow* may look like this:

```
Array
(
    [movieid]=>1
    [title] => Shawshank Redemption
    [year] => 1994
    [director]=>Frank Darabont
)
```

Inside the loop, we bind the values we need later from *$myrow* into local variables. (Line 6, 7)

Since we just need to print out the movie titles without further processing, we can render the HTML code right away. (Line 8)

If you're new to database programming, the syntax and flow in the above code will take some to get used to. The bind and render pattern is nothing new. Consider the array below:

```
$movies=array(
   array('movieid'=>1, 'title'=>'Shawshank Redemption'),
   array('movieid'=>2,'title'=>'Legends of the Fall'),
   array('movieid'=>3,'title'=>'Top Gun')
);
```

We can render the above array:

```
foreach ($movies as $myrow){
   $movieid=$myrow['movieid'];
   $title=$myrow['title'];
?>
<div>#<?echo $movieid;?> <?echo $title;?></div>
<?
}
```

The code inside the loop is identical to the database routine!

Now the question is, why can't the *mysqli_query* function simply return an array, like the one we hard-coded in the above example? The code would then be a lot more intuitive to read, right?

The nature of *mysqli_query*'s return type is a pointer. The result of a database query can be potentially huge. So instead of returning the whole array at once, we use the *$rs* to store a reference point. Imagine the IMDB database is a library and the movies table is a bookshelf. Matching results to the query are all on one book. *mysqli_query* walks to the bookshelf, grabs the book and put it on your desk. *$rs* is a bookmark that's placed on the first page of the book.

Each time you turn the page, you have to call the *mysqli_fetch_assoc* function. When you reach the end of the book, the function will return null and effectively terminates the loop.

It's important to know that if your result set has thousands of records, all of them will be downloaded from the database to the web server even though *$rs* points to just one of them. There is a mode that downloads the data asynchronously, but the use of this mode is beyond the scope of this book.

There's another set of MySQL functions that have nearly identical syntax:

```
mysql_connect, mysql_query, mysql_fetch_assoc
```

Starting PHP 5.5.0, all the functions in the MySQL extension will be removed. The Improved MySQL extension (MySQLi) should be used instead.

Note that the argument order is different between *mysqli_query* and *mysql_query*.

```
mysqli_query($db,$query);
mysql_query($query,$db);
```

PHP offers extensions to many other database products. Their functions are quite inconsistent. It's highly recommended that you create wrapper functions to unify the calls. For example:

```
<?php
//mysqli version
function sql_connect($host,$database,$user,$pass){
    $db=mysqli_connect($host,$user,$pass,$database);
    return $db;
}
function sql_query($query,$db){
    $rs=mysqli_query($db,$query);
    return $rs;
}
```

And MySQL version:

```
<?php
//mysql version
function sql_connect($host,$database,$user,$pass){
    $db=mysql_connect($host,$user,$pass);
    mysql_select_db($database,$db);
    return $db;
}

function sql_query($query,$db){
    $rs=mysql_query($query,$db);
    return $rs;
}
```

Then in your main script, include the appropriate database function file and use the cross platform *sql_* functions.

By far, we've learned how to execute a "select" query from PHP and render its results. That covers the R in CRUD. Insertion, deletion and updating don't return records from the database, so executing their queries is quite simple. For example:

```
<?php
$query="delete from movies where year='1994';
mysqli_query($db,$query);
```

You can also find out how many records were deleted in the previous statement:

```
<?php
$query="delete from movies where year='1994';
mysqli_query($db,$query);
$count=mysqli_affected_rows($db);
```

Now take a break from reading and get your hands dirty. With the knowledge you possess at this point, you can already create considerable damage. So harness the power before moving on.

Exercise 1: Set up the IMDB database and replicate all the above scripts. Make them run on your local machine without generating any errors.

Exercise 2: Rewrite the movie listing page with *mysql_* functions instead of *mysqli_*.

Exercise 3: Write wrapper functions and modify the main script so that the database can be switched easily

Exercise 4: Install some open source web apps (Wordpress, Joomla for example) and connect *directly* to their databases. Create a webpage that prints out contents in one of the tables. For example, a page of all the blog post titles.

Exercise 5: Install a database server other than MySQL. For example, Microsoft SQL Server Express is freely available. Create the IMDB tables and sample data in MSSQL; setup the PHP extensions for MSSQL; write wrapper functions so that your script in Exercise 3 works with minimal changes.

6.6 Join Queries

At the beginning of Chapter 6.1 we explored the relationships between data tables, namely 1-1, 1-to-many (1-N) and many-to-many (N-N).

We can use the references (or foreign keys) in tables to construct a complete view of a logical record.
For example, the *movieactors* table contains the pointers to both movis and actors, but none of their details. We can tell, that Movie #1 and Actor #5 are related. By joining the *movieactors* table and the *actors* table, we then see that Morgen Freeman plays a role in Movie #1:

```
select * from movieactors,actors
where movieactors.actorid=actors.actorid and actors.actorid=5
```

In order to see a complete record of both the movie and actor, we can connect all three tables:

```
select * from movieactors,actors,movies
where movieactors.actorid=actors.actorid
and movieactors.movieid=movies.movieid
and actors.actorid=5;
```

The above query returns all the movies Morgan Freeman is in.

We can also pull all the actors in Shawshank Redemption, or Movie #1:

```
select * from movieactors,actors,movies
where movieactors.actorid=actors.actorid
and movieactors.movieid=movies.movieid
and movies.movieid=1;
```

6.6.1 Inner Join

All the query join examples we've seen so far are inner joins. Writing inner joins is easily done by the following steps:

1. list the table names after the "from" keyword
2. pick the desirable column names after "select"
3. connect the bridging IDs in the "where" clause
4. add any additional constraints in the "where" clause

Now let's put the above steps to test:

```
select __[2]__ from __[1]__ where __[3]__ and __[4]__
```

Movie and actor information is spread across 3 tables. In step one, we add *movies*, *actors* and *movieactors* in the from clause.

```
select __[2]__ from movies, actors, movieactors where __[3]__
and __[4]__
```

Step 2 for now can be as simple as using a wildcard symbol * to get all the fields. This is not an issue if the tables don't have many columns. Later we'll see that when writing nested queries, the columns cannot have duplicate names, so we'll need to hand pick the fields. For demonstration's sake, let's pick only movie titles and actor names:

```
select title, name from movies, actors, movieactors where
__[3]__ and __[4]__
```

If multiple tables have the same field name, use the table name to distinquish them. For example, *movieid* is common in both *movieactors* and *movies*.

```
select movies.movieid, title, name from movies, actors,
movieactors where __[3]__ and __[4]__
```

Next, in Step 3, we connect all the tables:

```
select movies.movieid, title, name from movies, actors,
movieactors where
movies.movieid=movieactors.movieid
and movieactors.actorid=actors.actorid
and __[4]__
```

Make sure, I mean, be absolutely certain, that no tables in the *from* clause is left out in the "bridges" in the *where* clause.

Just to illustrate by using a counter example, run the query without a where clause:

```
select * from movies, actors, movieactors
```

The results are a list of all possible combinations of the three tables. If there are 7 films, 7 actors and 13 movie-actor pairings, you'll see 637 records.

```
7 x 7 x 13 = 637
```

The conditions in Step 3 weed out the mathematically probable but logically incorrect combinations.

The last step is to add any additional constraints. For example, we only need to fetch the films in 1994:

```
select movies.movieid, title, name
from movies, actors, movieactors where
movies.movieid=movieactors.movieid
and movieactors.actorid=actors.actorid
and movieyear='1994';
```

6.6.2 Left Join

Let's begin this chapter by adding a film to the *movies* table:

```
insert into movies (title,movieyear,director)
values ('The Lion King','1994','Roger Allers');
```

Then we use an inner join to list out all the movies:

```
select movies.movieid, title, name
from movies, actors, movieactors where
movies.movieid=movieactors.movieid
and movieactors.actorid=actors.actorid
```

Hmm, the movie we just added is not showing in the list. What's going on?

Now run this query instead:

```
select * from movies
left join movieactors on movies.movieid=movieactors.movieid
left join actors on movieactors.actorid=actors.actorid
```

The Lion King now shows in the query result. Since we don't have associated records for this film in either *movieactors* or *actors* table, columns from those tables are null.

Here's a pragmatic explanation of a left join: it works just like an inner join except that if corresponding records in joined tables are missing, null values are used to pad the records in the "main table". And the "main table" is described before the "left join" keyword.

The reason why an orphan record is omitted in an inner join is because inner join returns the intersect of sets. We can use a Venn diagram to visualize an inner join:

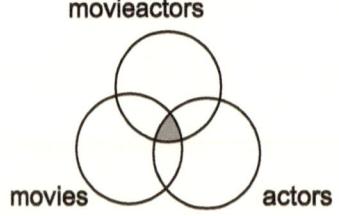

An outer join is equivalent to a set union:

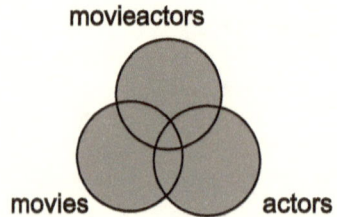

Assuming we have an orphone movie record, The Lion King, and an orphan actor, Jack Black. Results of an outer join query look like the records below:

movies.title	movieactors.amid	actors.name
The Lion King	*null*	*null*

| Forest Gump | 5 | Tom Hanks |
| *Null* | *null* | Jack Black |

A left join is a partial outer join. It returns all the records that match the criteria on the main table:

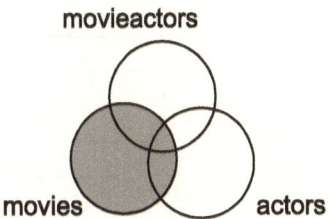

A right join is just like a left join, except that it takes the opposite direction to null-fill records. In the above table, the row for Jack Black is the result of the *movies* table right joining on the *actors* table via the *moviesactors* table.

In practice we don't see right joins often because they can be expressed as left joins. Also, full outer joins are very uncommon. In fact, there's no native keyword in MySQL that performes a full outer join. Full outer joins can, however, be emulated by taking the union of left- and right-joins.

6.7 Group By (Aggregate) Functions

Aggregate functions use the input from multiple rows to calculate single values. They are commonly used in conjunction with the Group By clause, where rows that share common values are lumped into smaller set of rows.

To best explain the concept of an aggregate function, let's first add a new column in our *movies* table:

```
alter table movies
add running time int unsigned not null;
```

Then we update existing records with the running time data.
For example:

```
update movies set runningtime=89
where title like 'The Lion King';
```

For your convenience, here's a list of running times for the sample movie database:

movieid	Title	year	runningtime
1	Shawshank Redemption	1994	142
2	Legends of the Fall	1994	133
3	Forrest Gump	1994	142
4	Top Gun	1986	110
5	Sleepless in Seattle	1993	105
6	You've Got Mail	1998	119
7	Meet Joe Black	1998	178
8	The Lion King	1994	89

Now we can find out the average running time of all the movies in the database:

```
select avg(runningtime) from movies;
```

The query returns one row that contains a single value 127.25

We can also break down the result by year:

```
select avg(runningtime) from movies group by movieyear;
```

Since the database contains movies from 4 distinct years, we got 4 rows in the result:

```
+------------------+
| avg(runningtime) |
+------------------+
|         110.0000 |
|         105.0000 |
|         126.5000 |
|         148.5000 |
+------------------+
```

We can't really see which year has which average running time, so we add the year to the *select* clause:

```
select movieyear, avg(runningtime) from movies
group by movieyear;
```

```
+-----------+------------------+
| movieyear | avg(runningtime) |
+-----------+------------------+
| 1986      |         110.0000 |
| 1993      |         105.0000 |
| 1994      |         126.5000 |
| 1998      |         148.5000 |
+-----------+------------------+
```

We can rename the column title by assigning an alias using the "as" keyword.
This is important when binding the results to associative arrays in PHP:

```
select movieyear, avg(runningtime) as rt from movies
group by movieyear;
```

```
+-----------+----------+
| movieyear | rt       |
+-----------+----------+
| 1986      | 110.0000 |
| 1993      | 105.0000 |
| 1994      | 126.5000 |
| 1998      | 148.5000 |
+-----------+----------+
```

Another very useful aggregate function is *count()*.

```
select movieyear, avg(runningtime) as rt,
count(movieid) as c from movies
group by movieyear;
```

```
+-----------+----------+---+
| movieyear | rt       | c |
+-----------+----------+---+
| 1986      | 110.0000 | 1 |
| 1993      | 105.0000 | 1 |
| 1994      | 126.5000 | 4 |
```

```
| 1998        | 148.5000 | 2 |
+-------------+----------+---+
```

The above result gives us a clear overview on the distribution of our data and the trend of movie running times over the years.

The *group by* clause is also often used to eliminate duplicate rows that are caused by a *join* statement:

select title from movies, movieactors
where movies.movieid=movieactors.movieid;

Now use *group by* to "roll up" the unique films:

```
+----------------------+
| title                |
+----------------------+
| Shawshank Redemption |
| Legends of the Fall  |
| Forrest Gump         |
| Top Gun              |
| Sleepless in Seattle |
| You've Got Mail      |
| Meet Joe Black       |
+----------------------+
```

When multiple rows are clustered into one, we lose some information. In this case, the Actor IDs. We can still have a sense of the size of each group by using the *count* function.

```
select title, count(movies.movieid) as c
from movies,movieactors
where movies.movieid=movieactors.movieid
group by movies.movieid;
```

Note that every mention of "movieid" is written as "movies.movieid" to disambiguate.

```
+----------------------+---+
| title                | c |
```

```
+----------------------+---+
| Shawshank Redemption | 2 |
| Legends of the Fall  | 2 |
| Forrest Gump         | 1 |
| Top Gun              | 2 |
| Sleepless in Seattle | 2 |
| You've Got Mail      | 2 |
| Meet Joe Black       | 2 |
+----------------------+---+
```

Aggregates and group-by's are expensive. They should perform on indexed columns. We'll learn more about indexing in Chapter 6.10.

When writing a web application, there are many situations where a group-by may seem suitable even though it's not. Consider a web page that generates the following output:

1986
   Top Gun
1993
   Sleepless in Seattle
1994
   Forrest Gump
   Legends of the Fall
   Shawshank Redemption
   The Lion King
1998
   Meet Joe Black
   You've Got Mail

First let's do this the straight-forward but inefficient way. We use a group-by to find out the unique years. Then we retrieve the movies within each year:

```
$query="select movieyear from movies group by movieyear
    order by movieyear";
$rs=sql_query($query,$db);
while ($myrow=sql_fetch_array($rs)){
    $movieyear=$myrow['movieyear'];
    echo "<b>$movieyear</b><br>";
    $query="select title from movies
        where movieyear='$movieyear' order by title";
```

```
    $rs2=sql_query($query,$db);
    while ($myrow2=sql_fetch_array($rs)){
        $title=$myrow2['title'];
        echo "    $title<br>";
    }//inner while
}//outer while
```

Remember, group-by's are expensive, round-trips to the SQL server are expensive, nested loops are expensive. The above code is, therefore, quite costly to run.

The first query the script sends is to get the unique years. In the worst case, each movie year is different. In the case of our sample database, there are 4 unique years, so 4 additional queries are sent. The number of queries being sent depends on the situation of the data. In a database of 1000 records, we are looking at a worst case of 1000x1000=100,000 iterations!

Now the improved code:

```
$lastyear='';
$query="select movieyear,title from movies
    order by movieyear, title";
$rs=sql_query($query,$db);
while ($myrow=sql_fetch_array($rs)){
    $movieyear=$myrow['movieyear'];
    $title=$myrow['title'];
    if ($lastyear!=$movieyear){
        $lastyear=$movieyear;
        echo "<b>$movieyear</b><br>";
    }//if
    echo "    $title<br>";
}
```

Only one query is ever sent to the database. The records are scanned only once. The number of loop iterations is the same as the number of records. Since there's no additional query traffic, going through 1000 records in this code is a lot faster than going through 1000 records in the previous code.

Apart from the coding techniques, we can learn a few things from the above example:

- What seems to be a group-by may not need a group-by
- SQL results don't have to immediately meet the final requirement
- PHP post-processing could greatly optimize the routine

6.8 Pagination

A database table can contain more records than a human can consume at a time. Even 100 records is too much to read. In this chapter we'll look at the syntax of retrieving partial results. Later we'll build a paging interface using PHP, and even later we'll build an AJAX record pager so that the user can browse through segments of records without navigating to a new web page.

In MySQL, the syntax of getting the top N records is quite simple. For example, the top 3 longest movies in our database:

```
select * from movies order by runningtime desc limit 3;
```

Pay attention to the placement of the *limit* clause - it's after the *order by* clause.

If we want to display all the records, 3 at a time, here's how we get to the second chunk of 3 records:

```
select * from movies order by runningtime desc limit 3,3;
```

and Record 6-9:

```
select * from movies order by runningtime desc limit 6,3;
```

In fact, the top 3, or the first segment of 3, can be written as:

```
select * from movies order by runningtime desc limit 0,3;
```

When the *limit* clause is provided with two parameters, the first one is the record offset, and the second one is number of records. The following snippet makes it very easy to remember the order and calculation of the *limit* parameters. We'll see the code again in later chapters:

```
$perpage=3;
$page=2; //getting the 3rd page. first page is Page 0
$start=$page*$perpage;
$query="select * from movies order by runningtime desc
        limit $start,$perpage";
```

The above code pulls Records 6-9.

When using *limit*, it's a good idea to have an *order by*. Otherwise the records may be sorted unpredictably, yielding inconsistent results.

The SQL queries we saw in previous chapters are compatible on most database products. Yes, there are some wacky Microsoft ways of writing inner joins that are not acceptable by MySQL, but what we've see so far are the least common denominators.

6.8.1 Syntax Differences

Paging through records is, quite unfortunately, not standardized. For instance, in PostgreSQL the syntax goes:

```
select * from movies order by runningtime desc
        limit [perpage], [offset];
```

The paramater sequence is just the opposite of MySQL.

In MS SQLServer the situation is worse. Getting the top N results is achieved by the *top* keyword:

select **top 3** * from movies order by runningtime desc;

The *top* syntax doesn't support an offset. For SQLServer 2005 (don't laugh at its age. There's still a lot of SQLServer 2000 running out there), we can temporarily create a column that assign each row a unique sequence number. Then use the *between* clause. Here's how we get Records 6-9:

with *recs* **as** (
select movies.*,
row_number() over (order by runningtime desc) as *rownumber*
from movies
) select * from *recs* **where** *rownumber* **between 6 and 9**;

Apparently the Oracle DB uses something similar.

You don't have to fully understand the above syntax. My point is, different database products offer various syntax, and some can be a bit cumbersome or plain inefficient. Some database APIs attempt to abstract away all the differences but this would incur significant overhead. When you write an database application, have a specific target in mind first. If you have to port it to a different database system later, start with queries that involve pagination.

Learning a new database is a lot like picking up a second, or even third foreign language. You already know what to look for so the process can be a lot quicker. You may come across a database that's not even a relational database, but the principle stays: a reasonal interface has to offer a way to return a subset of the records and an option to specify an offset. Now you know what questions to ask.

6.8.2 Full Table Scan

There are times when each record in a database table should be processed. For example, sending daily updates to every subscribed user, or downloading the latest price info from a database of Amazon product URLs.

Picture a database of 5 million records. (The GeoIP database in the public domain has about 4,000,000 records in its IP range table.)

We certainly do not want to run the following query without paging:

```
select * from geo_ip order by geoipid
```

Even if the database can scan all of the 4 million records swiftly, transferring the entire result set is a total waste of memory, if the memory is at all sufficient.

We could break down the data into smaller ranges:

```php
<?php
$page=0;
$perpage=30;
do {
    $start=$page*$perpage;
```

```
$query="select * from geo_ip order by geoipid
    limit $start,$perpage";
$rs=sql_query($query,$db);
if (sql_affected_rows($db,$rs)<=0) break;
while ($myrow=sql_fetch_array($rs)){
    //process each record within the set here
}
$page++;
} while(1);
```

The above script runs on a small database just fine.

But just try to execute the following query directly on MySQL:

```
select * from geo_ip order by geoipid limit 3000000,30;
```

The query takes over a second to run! In terms of functionality and complexity, fetching the 3 millionth page offers no more benefit than getting the first page. But as we dig deeper, the query takes longer to run. Comparing to the mere dozens of milliseconds, 1 second of query time is unacceptably long.

The reason for the slow query is because internally, MySQL retrieves all of the 3,000,030 records and discarded the first 3,000,000.

Now look at the following code:

```
<?php
$lastid=0;
do{
    $query="select * from geo_ip where geoipid>$lastid
        order by geoipid limit 30";
    $rs=sql_query($query,$db);
    if (sql_affected_rows($db,$rs)<=0) break;
    while ($myrow=sql_fetch_array($rs)){
        //process the record here

        $lastid=$myrow['geoipid'];
    }
} while (1);
```

Before trying out the script, let's test the query itself:

```
select * from geo_ip where geoipid>3000000
        order by geoipid limit 30
```

This query runs a whole lot faster. Moreover, as we get to higher record IDs, the running time doesn't grow as much. This query is said to "scale well".

Paging through the entire data table via record IDs relays on two ingredients:

1. we're sorting on *geoipid*, the primary key, which is fast
2. we're sorting on *geoipid*, the primary key, which is unique

A primary key is a special type of index. We'll find out how, and how much, indexing can speed up information lookup.

Because every record has a different ID, we can sort the records in ascending order, and use the last record's ID as the lower bound for the new chunk. As we comb through the records, we update the last record's ID accordingly.

What if we want to page through the records on a different column that has duplicate values? For example, a pricing table:

productid	price
1	12.00
2	15.00
3	15.00
4	15.00
...	...
100	15.00
101	22

The above script would get trapped in an infinite loop because the last ID stays on 15.

In fact we have already seen a solution to this problem. Well, sorta. Look at the paging syntax for Microsoft SQL Server. What the query does is basically assigning a temporary row ID to each result, and sort by the synthethized ID.

Crafting a query that works efficiently on this principle is a challenging task. The good news, why would we ever want to step through a database on a non-primary key? Sorting on primary key works well, though the records may not be in any logical sequence. But logical order is for human consumption. Why would you expect a human user to see the 1000000th record through a web interface? Even 10,000 records is too much in most cases. If the web application fails to trim down the data to a human consumable size, we have some design issue to work out first.

6.9 Nested Queries

Nested queries are expressive and powerful. I'm almost hesitant to write about them, fearing that they'll be misused and abused. In this chapter, let's look at a few typical scenarios where nested queries are suitable... or not.

So far we have learned that **aggregates are expensive**, and that *limit* **clauses with high offsets are expensive**.

Now you're finding out that nested queries can also potentially choke the database when used carelessly.

An example of a nested query:

```
select * from actors,(
    select movies.*,movieactors.actorid
    from movieactors, movies
    where movieactors.movieid=movies.movieid
)t where actors.actorid=t.actorid
```

The functional equivalence of the above query can be written with a join:

```
select actors.*, movies.*
from movies,movieactors,actors
where movies.movieid=movieactors.movieid
and actors.actorid=movieactors.actorid
```

As the database grows larger, the non-nested query will run significantly faster.

We can use the *explain* keyword to look into each query:

```
explain select * from actors,(
    select movies.*,movieactors.actorid
    from movieactors, movies
    where movieactors.movieid=movies.movieid
)t where actors.actorid=t.actorid
```

In the *table* column, we see that MySQL created a temporary table called
<derived2>. The creation of temp tables requires extra resource.

Use joins instead of subqueries whenever you can.

Temp table is also the key reason why *group-by*'s are expensive:

```
explain select * from movies group by movieyear;
```

Look at the *Extra* column:"Using temporary; Using filesort".

Of course we can't always dodge expensive queries. There are two typical
scenarios where nested queries (or subqueries) are effective solutions.

The first case is checking existance. Say, we want to find all the movies that
have related actor records:

```
select movies.* from movies,movieactors,actors
where movies.movieid=movieactors.movieid
and movieactors.actorid=actors.actorid;
```

For certain movies we have multiple actors. Therefore we end up with
duplicates. We could use a *group-by* to trim the data:

```
select movies.* from movies,movieactors,actors
where movies.movieid=movieactors.movieid
and movieactors.actorid=actors.actorid
group by movies.movieid;
```

If on average, each movie has 5 actors, we're discarding 80% of the records
in the group-by.

Here's a subquery alternative:

```
```

```
select movies.* from movies where exists (
    select * from movieactors,actors
    where movieactors.actorid=actors.actorid
    and movies.movieid=movieactors.movieid
);
```

There has been much debate on which query is more efficient. In theory, subqueries are more expensive, but so is group-by. Many SQL products are smart enough to optimize the above query. The *exists* syntax seems more intuitive to some programmers. So, pick your medicine.

Another nested query scenario can be described as "sort before group". For example, what are the latest movies each actor is in?

The following query returns incorrect result:

```
select name, title, movieyear
from actors, movieactors, movies
where actors.actorid=movieactors.actorid
and movieactors.movieid=movies.movieid
group by actors.actorid
order by movieyear desc
```

According to our sample database, the latest movie Tom Hanks was in is "You've Got Mail", not "Forrest Gump".

We need a subquery to sort first, and then group up:

```
select * from (
    select actors.actorid, name, title, movieyear
    from actors, movieactors, movies
    where actors.actorid=movieactors.actorid
    and movieactors.movieid=movies.movieid
    order by movieyear desc) t
group by t.actorid
```

The *explain* result, or "query execution plan" certainly looks nasty for the above query. We should be as restrictive as possible for the inner query, so that the temporary table doesn't have too many records.

Imagine there's a *gender* column in the *actors* table. And we're pulling the latest movies of all the male actors. Compare the two queries:

```
select * from (
    select actors.actorid, name, title, movieyear, gender
    from actors, movieactors, movies
    where actors.actorid=movieactors.actorid
    and movieactors.movieid=movies.movieid
    order by movieyear desc) t
where t.gender=0
group by t.actorid
```

and

```
select * from (
    select actors.actorid, name, title, movieyear
    from actors, movieactors, movies
    where actors.actorid=movieactors.actorid
    and movieactors.movieid=movies.movieid
    and gender=0
    order by movieyear desc) t
group by t.actorid
```

The second query is a lot more efficient.

6.10 Creating Indexes

Adding indexes to a data table can drastically improve lookup performance.

The following query adds an index to the *movieid* column in *movieactors*:

```
alter table movieactors add index (movieid);
```

While we're at it, let's index the *actorid* field as well:

```
alter table movieactors add index (actorid);
```

All the joins in the previous examples will run much faster now.

The way indexes work is very similar to indexing tabs in a phone book. Instead of going through every page to find a "George", we first jump to the G tab. If the second letter is also indexed, we can also avoid scanning Ga, Gb, Gc and Gd.

In theory, without an index, working with 10,000 records may take 1000 times longer than with 10 records. An index reduces the search space to a logrithmic growth. So instead of 1000 times longer, it's only 4 times longer!

The exact numbers are different in practice, but you get the sense of scale.

A special type of index is the primary key. Each table can have only one primary key. Operating on the primary key is often the fastest.

Another special type of index is the "unique" index. Say, you don't want any name collision in the *actors* table:

```
alter table actors add unique (name);
```

In most storage engines, the constraint of having a distinct value doesn't apply to *null* values.

If indexes are so great, why don't we index every column?

Well, indexes take up space. Not every column can benefit from an index, so we're wasting space for nothing. Also as we modify, delete or update records, the indexes are rebuilt on the fly. Sometimes adding a single record changes MySQL's decision on the best strategy on indexing, which in turn, triggers substantial disk I/O. The read performance we gain from indexing can be viewed as a trade off from the write performance.

Which columns should we create index for?

Any fields in the *where* clause, *order* clause and aggregates.

If a query is running for too long, use the *explain* keyword to gain some insight. The result often points to a table with some missing indexes.

7.0 Building Dynamic Websites

In Chapter 5 we had our first blend of HTML, CSS and some minimal use of PHP. Now with the knowledge of MySQL, we're ready for the second round of blend - building database-driven websites!

The objective of this chapter is simple - to build a movie database website that allows the user to browse and modify film and actor information. We'll be using the same sample database that's created in Chapter 6.

The key difference between a web application and a loose collection of scripts is that a web application has a structure. In Chapter 5.2.1 we were introduced the process of defining the navigation structure when skinning a static website. The same process applies here.

For our movie database app, we'll build the following pages:

- a movie listing page (movies.php)
- an actor listing page (actors.php)
- movie details page (movie.php)
- actor details page (actor.php)

Additional pages might be created to perform auxillary functions. We'll deal with them as we go.

As an exercise, you're asked to perform the tasks below:

- create a header, footer and main menu so that the user can easily navigate to movie listings (movies.php) and actor listings (actors.php)

- templatize the site so that you have header.php and footer.php to include

- create a static landing page; it may have no content besides the header, footer and menu for now; the landing page is just a place holder for the sake of completeness

Our movie listing (movies.php) is based on the sample code in Chapter 6.5:

```php
<?php
```

```
include 'header.php';
?>
<h1>Movies</h1>
<table>
<tr>
    <td><b>Title</b></td><td><b>Year</b></td>
</tr>
<?
$query="select * from movies order by title,movieyear";
$rs=mysqli_query($db,$query);
while ($myrow=mysqli_fetch_assoc($rs)){
    $title=$myrow['title'];
    $movieyear=$myrow['movieyear'];
?>
<tr>
    <td><?echo $title;?></td>
    <td><?echo $movieyear;?></td>
</tr>
<?
}//while
?>
</table>
<?
include 'footer.php';
```

Remember to connect to the database in header.php, so that we can access the database via the *$db* handle anywhere in the script.

Now you can build actors.php in a similar fashion.

7.1 Adding URL Parameters

Next, let's add a link to each movie record:

```
<?php
include 'header.php';
?>
<h1>Movies</h1>
```

```
<table>
<tr>
    <td><b>Title</b></td><td><b>Year</b></td>
    <td></td>
</tr>
<?
$query="select * from movies order by title";
$rs=mysqli_query($db,$query);
while ($myrow=mysqli_fetch_assoc($rs)){
    $movieid=$myrow['movieid'];
    $title=$myrow['title'];
    $movieyear=$myrow['movieyear'];
?>
<tr>
    <td><?echo $title;?></td>
    <td><?echo $movieyear;?></td>
    <td>
        <a href="movie.php?movieid=<?echo $movieid;?>">
        view
        </a>
    </td>
</tr>
<?
}//while
?>
</table>
<?
include 'footer.php';
```

Load the page again, and hover your mouse over each "view" link. You'll see that the record ID of each movie is included in the link.

If you're unfamiliar with how query parameter works, review Chapter 3.14.

Next we work on *movie.php* to display more details about the movie:

```
<?php
$movieid=$_GET['movieid']+0;
if (!$movieid) {
    header('Location: movies.php');
    die();
```

```
}

include 'header.php';

$query="select * from movies where movieid=$movieid";
$rs=sql_query($query,$db);


...

include 'footer.php';
```

The above script sends the database different queries based on the value of the *movieid* parameter. The query is said to be "parameterized".

Whenever we make our script incorporate values that are supplied by the user we have to be extremely careful. The URL request string can be tempered against our system. The first few lines in the script ensures that the *movieid* parameter is present and numeric. If the argument has a faulty format, the user is redirected to the main listings page as a fallback.

On the movie details page we can display all the information about the film:

```
$query="select * from movies where movieid=$movieid";
$rs=mysqli_query($db,$query);
$myrow=mysqli_fetch_assoc($rs);
$title=$myrow['title'];
$movieyear=$myrow['movieyear'];
$director=$myrow['director'];
?>
<div>
"<?echo $title;?>" was created in <?echo $movieyear;?>. <br>
It was directed by <?echo $director;?>.
</div>
<?
```

You can format and style the info text however you want. More importantly we can display all the associated actors:

```
$query="select * from movieactors,actors where
    movieactors.movieid=$movieid
    and movieactors.actorid=actors.actorid order by name";
```

```
$rs=mysqli_query($db,$query);
while ($myrow=mysqli_fetch_assoc($rs)){
    $actorid=$myrow['actorid'];
    $name=$myrow['name'];
    $role=$myrow['role'];

?>
<div>
<a href="actor.php?actorid=<?echo $actorid;?>">
  <?echo $name;?> as <?echo $role;?>
</a>
</div>
<?

}//while
```

The above code is a classic example of URL parameterization. It uses *movieid* in the query string to generate actor listing that's specific to the requested movie. The script then further propagates links to actor detail pages by parameterizing the *actorid* argument.

Now it's your turn to build *actor.php*. It should guard against bad requests, display basic actor info, and lists out all the movies this actor has been in.

For your convenient, the query for this exercise is prepared below:

```
select * from movieactors, movies where
movieactors.actorid=$actorid
and movieactors.movieid=movies.movieid
```

7.2 Handling Paging

In Chapter 6.8 we were shown how to retrieve records from a specific page. Now we'll add a web interface so that the user can simply page through the records by clicking on the "Prev" and "Next" links.

In movies.php:

```
1    $page=$_GET['page']+0;
2    $query="select * from movies ";
3    $rs=mysqli_query($db,$query);
4    $count=mysqli_affected_rows($db);

5    $perpage=3;
6    $maxpage=ceil($count/$perpage)-1;
7    if ($maxpage<0) $maxpage=0;
8    if ($page<0) $page=0;
9    if ($page>$maxpage) $page=$maxpage;
10   $start=$page*$perpage;

11   $query.=" order by title limit $start,$perpage";
12   $rs=mysqli_query($db,$query);
```

Compare the code above to the non-paging version from the last chapter. The orginal query is split and modified in Line 2 and 11. The database is pulled twice. The first query asks for all the records, so that we can get a record count. The second query adds a page limiter to the first query.

Line 5 defines the number of records we wish to see on each page. Setting it to a small number makes debugging easier.

Line 6 calculates the maximum page number. The ceiling function ensures there are enough pages, even if the last page is partially filled. Since page numbers are zero-based, the page count is substracted by 1.

Line 7-9 perform boundary checks so that page numbers are within range.

Next we can add paging links only if there are more than one pages:

```
if ($maxpage>0){
?>
Page <?echo $page+1;?> of <?echo $maxpage+1;?>
   
<a href="movies.php?page=<?echo $page-1;?>">
&laquo; Prev
</a>
 | 
<a href="movies.php?page=<?echo $page+1;?>">
```

```
Next &raquo;
</a>
<?
}
```

Note that we increased the display values of page and max page by one, so that the reading is more logical to a human user. Internally we still use zero-based indexes to simplify calculation.

You may add additional conditions so that the previous page link is hidden if it's already on the first page. Similarly the link to the next page is hidden on the last (max) page. On a public-facing website this is important as it reduces duplicate content.

If the listing page carry other parameters in the URL, make sure to forward them to paging links. It is a common mistake to miss these additional parameters.

Making Tie-Breaking Consistent

When the sort fields contain the same value, MySQL will break the tie in an arbitrary, i.e. inconsistent fashion. Inconsistent tie-breaking could cause the same record being displayed in multiple pages, as the sorting is not guaranteed. To make tie-breaking consistent, use the table's primary ID as a secondary sort field. Line 11 in the previous example can be written as:

```
$query.=" order by title, movieid limit $start,$perpage";
```

7.3 Form Posts

At the beginning of the book we were introduced some form controls. For instance:

<input> for entering a single line of text;
<textarea> for a blob of text;
<input type="radio"> picks one out of several options in the same group;
<input type="checkbox"> allows multiple options to be picked

And the list goes on.

These form controls are often nested in a pair of *form* tags:

```
<form method="POST" ...>
...
</form>
```

Many programmers found forms intimidating to work with when they got started not only because of the variety of control syntax and the notion of the POST method (why does it matter anyway, right?), but also because the new mental model forms have introduced.

So far we are exposed to several programming models:

HTML/CSS are declarative. The markups are interpreted and rendered by web browsers.

PHP is procedural programming. There's a flow to the execution of the script. It runs from the top, branches upon conditional statements, and enters loops here and there but eventually exits.

SQL is a query language. In a sence it's declarative but more structured. The way you think when writing SQL queries is definitely different than writing CSS.

The switch from static HTML coding to PHP is straightforward, thanks to the templating nature of PHP. When necessary, PHP code also summons MySQL, but the output is still HTML. So far we're pushing content from the server to the browser.

Web forms change this direction; they offer a mechanism of gathering and submitting information back to the server. It is an input method, just like the URL query parameters.

The form itself doesn't perform any sort of magic beyond that. The script that handles the form data does.

Let's look at a simple example for calculating the sum of two values:

```
<!-- sum.html -->
<form method="GET" action="add.php">
    <input name="a">
```

```
    +
    <input name="b">
     
    <input type="submit" value="Go">
</form>
```

Then in *add.php*:

```php
<?php
$a=$_GET['a'];
$b=$_GET['b'];

echo "$a + $b = ".($a+$b);
```

Now when you submit the form in sum.html, values of the two input fields are sent to *add.php*. It's up to *add.php* to decide what to do with the form data.

The names of the input fields are mapped to the key values of the GET array. Take a look at the URL field in your browser. You can see that when a form is posted using the GET method, field data is appended as query parameters.

There are several reasons why GET is not commonly used for transmitting form data.

First of all, submitting form data using GET is the same as dumping all the form fields as query string directly in the browser URL field. Web browser will remember this form submission and will even allow bookmarking the page. If this form happens to be a credit card purchase, your credit card will be processed each time you load the page!

When we use POST to submit the form, browsers recognize the potential unwanted side effect and warns the user of resubmitting data during a page refresh. Most search engines use GET to transmit the search term, so that their users can simply reload the page without the warning. You can see the search parameters in the URL bar.

Another reason why POST is often referred instead of GET, especially during server-to-server requests and AJAX requests, which we'll see later, is that POST can carry much more data. The URL string in a GET request has a character limit. Older browsers can carry less than 300 characters; modern browsers have increased the limit but not by a lot. URL litering aside, submitting a 5-page agreement via GET isn't just feasible.

"POST is a special kind of GET"

As far as the server side (PHP) is concerned, a form field is accessed through either the $_POST or $_GET array. A POST request, however, may still contain GET parameters.

Just like GET, a POST is an HTTP request that's transmitted in plain text:

```
POST /defaultsearch.php?lang=de HTTP/1.1
Host: www.some-website.com
User-Agent: Mozilla/5.0
Accept: text/html
Content-Type: application/x-www-form-urlencoded
Content-Length: 15

searchterm=test
```

Now let's take a look at what makes a POST request a POST. The first verb in an HTTP request indicates the method. Other than this first verb, the content type and length fields, and the POST data, the request looks just like a GET request because it really is. The "lang" query parameter is still accessed via $_GET in PHP despite a POST request.

When a form is submitted, the browser automatically encode it with the x-www-form-urlencoded encoding scheme. The Content-Length field marks the number of characters in the POST data before encoding. This length field is not only useful for validating a correct transmission, but also helps the network figure out when should the transfer terminate, because a large form submission make break a request into smaller chunks.

The POST data starts after an extra line break (CRLF). This is part of the HTTP protocol that differentiates data from another request header field.

Another way to look at this: a GET is like the subject line in an email, and a POST is an email with a body. A POST request carries extra information and should be seen as an extended GET.

Next let's get back to the calculator example. Change from GET to POST in the form method and remove the action attribute:

```
<form method="POST" action="add.php">
    <input name="a">
    +
    <input name="b">
     
    <input type="submit" value="Go">
</form>
```

When a form tag is missing the action attribute, the form is posted back to the same page. This allows us to merge sum.html and add.php into one script, say, calc.php:

```
<?
$sum='';
$a=$_POST['a'];
$b=$_POST['b'];
if (is_numeric($a)&&is_numeric($b)){
        $sum=$a+$b;
}
?>
<form method="POST">
        <input name="a" value="<?echo $a;?>">
        +
        <input name="b" value="<?echo $b;?>">
        =
        <input name="c" value="<?echo $sum;?>">
        <input type="submit" value="Go">
</form>
```

The above script behaves differently during initial page load and a form submission. When the form's posted, the values a and b are numeric; the script then calculates the sum and populates the form fields with the sum and the original input values. This flow creates a sense of continuity.

7.4 Form Validation

We have to be always careful when processing input data from the end user. A form has to be validated before it's submitted. The server side script has to check each input value again.

Server-side validation is necessary and has to be implemented before client-side validation for a couple of reasons. First, client-side validation is not to be trusted. Browsers that do not run JavaScript also bypass the client-side.

Depending on the context, validating user input data can be very complex. For example, we may want ensure that a phone number is all digits; but we would also want them to have a valid length, and follow certain grouping convention. Ideally, a phone number should be an existing number.

The question really is how far you'd like to go. In most cases, some basic data cleansing is enough to protect the database from injections and the overall application from malfunctioning. The common checks are "non-empty", "all numeric" and "no spacing". In addition, the inputs are encoded so that special characters don't mess up the database.

```
<?
$sum='';
$a=$_POST['a'];
$b=$_POST['b'];
if (is_numeric($a)&&is_numeric($b)){
        $sum=$a+$b;
} else {
?>
<div style="color:#ab0200;">
Both operands must be numeric!
</div>
<?
}
?>
<form method="POST">
        <input name="a" value="<?echo $a;?>">
        +
        <input name="b" value="<?echo $b;?>">
        =
```

```
        <input name="sum" value="<?echo $sum;?>">
        <input type="submit" value="Go">
</form>
```

Client-side validation relies on JavaScript to intercept the form submission. It prevents the page from being reloaded and therefore offers improved usability.

The mechanics of blocking a form post is simple but often misunderstood.

```
<form ... onsubmit="return false;">
```

Now let's use the calculator example:

```
<?
$sum='';
$a=$_POST['a'];
$b=$_POST['b'];
if (is_numeric($a)&&is_numeric($b)){
      $sum=$a+$b;
} else {
?>
<div style="color:#ab0200;">
Both operands must be numeric!
</div>
<?
}
?>
<form method="POST" onsubmit="return checkform();">
        <input name="a" value="<?echo $a;?>">
        +
        <input name="b" value="<?echo $b;?>">
        =
        <input name="sum" value="<?echo $sum;?>">
        <input type="submit" value="Go">
</form>
<script>
function checkform(){
        var a=document.getElementById('a');
        var b=document.getElementById('b');
        if (parseInt(a,10)!=a||parseInt(b,10)!=b){
```

```
        alert('Invalid input values');
        return false;
    }
    return true;
}
</script>
```

You may ignore the details of the JavaScript function if you aren't yet familiar with JavaScript. The gist of the function is to return true or false based on whether the input values are acceptable. Here's a common mistake:

Correct:

```
<form method="POST" onsubmit="return checkform();">
```

Wrong:

```
<form method="POST" onsubmit="checkform();">
```

Later in the event handling section we will talk about Event Bubbling. One way to block an event is to "return false". For example you can disable a link by using:

```
<a href="http://www.test.com/" onclick="return false;">
```

7.5 Character Encoding

In the header of an HTML page the character encoding is specified:

```
<meta http-equiv="Content-Type"
    content="text/html; charset=utf-8" />
```

And on some websites you might see other encodings, such as "iso-8859-1".

Web pages that are in foreign languages may use a locale-specific encoding. For example, typical Russian encodings are koi8-r and cp1251. Chinese encodings are gb2312 and big-5 for simplified and traditional respectively.

Why are there so many encodings while Unicode (utf-8) is supposed to unify all of them?

Let's look at how computers use digits to represent readable characters. In most computing systems the smallest storage unit is a byte. A byte is 8 bits. In Chapter 5.1.2 we showed how a byte is used to express colours.

The 8 bits in a byte gives it a numeric range of 0 to 255. The ASCII table defines how a character is interpreted.

```
Code            Char
32-47           (symbols)
48-57           0-9
58-64           (symbols)
65-90           A-Z
91-96           (symbols)
97-122          a-z
```

Some language-specific encodings take advantage of the extended code range. For example, KOI8-R fits most of the Cyrillic alphabet in the 192-255 range.

Certain languages have more alphabets, and the 255 code spaces is not enough. The Chinese encoding GB2312, for instance, uses two bytes to denote one Chinese character. The value of the first byte is from 161-247. The value of the second byte is from 161-254. This design allows a degree of ASCII compatibility. When both bytes fall in their designated ranges, the two characters are interpreted as a Chinese character. The two bytes in this case are called "code points".

Unicode was introduced to, as its name suggests, unify all the code pages. Unicode allows multiple languages display on the same web page without confusion. More importantly, it allows the programmers not to worry about the inherent differences between language encoding.

UTF-8 is an encoding that can represent every character in the Unicode character set. UTF-8 has variable width characters. Some languages take 2 code points for each character; some take 3. The leading byte contains information about the overall length of the character. How Unicode reads the variable-length character stream is beyond the scope of this chapter. However, it's important to know that Unicode is ASCII compatible, meaning that characters that can be expressed in ASCII take up only one byte.

When creating web pages, make sure to use UTF-8. This requires a header tag that tells the browser to use Unicode:

```
<html>
  <head>
    <meta http-equiv="Content-Type"
      content="text/html; charset=utf-8" />
  </head>
```

We should also make sure that the content in the page is indeed UTF-8 encoded. For example, the Euro sign should be coded as three bytes (E2 82 AC).

The communication between PHP and MySQL doesn't have to be in Unicode. The data storage can also use ISO-8859-1 (Latin-1). This is recommended because a single-character encoding system can store Unicode as well as other character encodings.

Some PHP string functions are not safe with Unicode characters. For example, the strlen of the Euro sign is 3, but the muti-byte function mb_strlen returns the correct, logical length of the Euro symbol, which is 1:

```
$len = mb_strlen('€', 'utf-8');
```

Although the Euro sign can be coded with the HTML entity €, it is not the same as directly encoding the UTF-8 code point stream. When handling user input, it's recommended not to convert the data into HTML entities.

7.6 File Operations

A complex web application doesn't just read and write to a database. Sometimes it accesses the disk files too. Some PHP functions create files implicitly, such as the ones that saves image objects to files, or ones that opens a zip archive into arrays of file handles and strings.

Sometimes we want to have direct control over the bytes that are read from, or written to a specific file. Here we're going to learn some classic C-style file operations.

This is a routine that prints every line in a text file:

```
<?
$f=fopen('test.txt', 'rt');
while (!feof($f)){
    $line=trim(fgets($f));
    echo $line."\r\n";
}
fclose($f);
```

Let's examine each line in the above code. The *fopen* function takes two parameters: the name of the file, and the mode in which the file is open. For example, "rt" means "Read as Text". We'll delve more into file modes later.

The *fopen* function returns a handle for accessing the file. We have assigned the handle to variable $f. The *fgets* function fetches a line and advances the file cursor until *feof* returns true. Upon termination of the read loop, the handle to the file is closed.

Although the entire file content can be mapped into one string, it is not recommended for scalability reasons. For example, fitting a 1Gigabyte file in one shot could crash the server.

When a file is opened in text mode, the *fgets* function reads in the file until it hits an end-of-line (EOL) symbol. The returned value contains the new line character (LF). If CR-LF is used to delimit the lines, CR-LF is returned by the *fgets* function.

To read the file in binary mode, we can use "rb" as the second *fopen* parameter. Line break and carriage return characters are just like any other bytes in binary mode. The function *fread* is used to read X number of bytes each time, until the end of file (EOF) is hit.

A text file is like a book. Each time there's an EOL, a page is flipped. A binary file on the other hand is more like a scroll of film. When to stop viewing the film is up to the viewer and the underlying content. The chunk size for a binary read is somewhat arbitrary.

The following routine writes "Hello, World" to a file:

```
$f=fopen('test.txt', 'wt');
```

```
fwrite($f, 'Hello, World');
fclose($f);
```

If the file test.txt does not exist, it'll be created upon opening. The content of an existing test.txt will be truncated.

Sometimes we need to write to the end of a file. For example, logging debug messages in a file. For this we use the "a" mode, for "append":

```
$f=fopen('test.txt', 'at');
```

So far we've only scratch the surface of PHP's file handling capabilities. Nevertheless, you'll be surprised to see that what we've covered can already be put in many practical scenarios. Many interchange file formats are text based. More specifically, these files are line-based, meaning that each line contains a record.

7.7 Handling File Uploads

Uploading a file in PHP takes several steps:

1. displaying the upload form
2. validating the uploaded file
3. processing the uploaded file

By now we should know that user input can be gathered in a web form and transmitted to the server through POST. An input field can be set to various types to implement difference interfaces. For example, radio buttons, checkboxes, masked passwords. When the type of an input field is set to "file", it works as a file selector.

```
<input name="myfile" type="file">
```

The above line alone is not sufficient to make the file upload work because an uploaded file has multiple components: file name, file type, file size and the file content.

By default, a form submission uses the application/x-www-form-urlencoded encoding. All the characters are encoded before sent, and special characters are converted to ASCII hex values.

For the file upload to work, we need multipart/form-data encoding where characters are transmitted as is, and different parts of the file are divided by a magical string separator. The generation and parsing of this separator follow the RFC-2388 standard. We don't worry about the implementation details, as the browser and PHP handle the intricate internals for us. All we need is the multipart/form-data encoding:

```
<form enctype="multipart/form-data" method="POST">
    <input name="myfile" type="file">
    <input type="submit" value="Upload">
</form>
```

On the server side, the uploaded file can be retrieved in the $_FILES, just like the way we use $_GET and $_POST.

The $_FILES array is shown as following using print_r:

```
Array
(
    [myfile] => Array
        (
            [name] => index.php
            [type] => application/octet-stream
            [tmp_name] => C:\Windows\Temp\php447E.tmp
            [error] => 0
            [size] => 53
        )

)
```

When a file is uploaded it is stored in a temporary folder that's specified in PHP configuration. A temporary name is also assigned to the uploaded file.

Technically we can use standard file operations on the temporary file. We have the full path of the file name, so what stops us to open and read the file?

Remember that user input is not to be trusted. At this point we need to make sure that this file is indeed uploaded through an HTTP POST. You may ask, how can it not be uploaded? Isn't that what we just did to make the upload work?

The multipart/form-data encoded data is still a form POST, which is part of an HTTP request transmitted in plain text. A malicious user can modify the request so that the file name in the FILES array carries a special string that further points to a sensitive file in the operating system. For example, a file that contains passwords. Further details of this attack is not disclosed here as it's out of the book's scope. We just need to know this is a type of file upload attack, which can be possibly detected by either is_uploaded_file() or move_uploaded_file() function.

```
<?
$dir='/var/www/uploads/';
if (isset($_FILES['myfile'])){
    $target=$dir.$_FILES['myfile']['name'];
    if (move_uploaded_file(
      $_FILES['myfile']['tmp_name'], $target)){
        //process uploaded file here
    }
}
```

In a web application where files are uploaded by end users, the actual file name should not be their original name. For example, one user may upload "my-cat.jpg", and another user may have the same file. It's recommended to use a database to store the logical file names but use the auto increment ID as part of the file name. We'll see in Chapter 7.6 how this logical filename is restored during file download.

Similar to the array notation in regular POST fields, multiple file uploads are achieved the same way:

```
<input name="myfiles[]" type="file"><br>
<input name="myfiles[]" type="file"><br>
```

The FILES array is not organized by file, but rather by merged attributes. Instead of this:

```
Array
(
```

```
[myfiles] => Array
    (
        [0] => Array
            (
                [name] => import.php
                [type] => application/octet-stream
                [tmp_name] => C:\Windows\Temp\phpA79C.tmp
                [error] => 0
                [size] => 180
            )
        [1] => Array
            (
                [name] => index.php
                [type] => application/octet-stream
                [tmp_name] => C:\Windows\Temp\phpA79D.tmp
                [error] => 0
                [size] => 53
            )
    )
)
```

The array is stored this way:

```
Array
(
    [myfile] => Array
        (
            [name] => Array
                (
                    [0] => import.php
                    [1] => index.php
                )

            [type] => Array
                (
                    [0] => application/octet-stream
                    [1] => application/octet-stream
                )

            [tmp_name] => Array
                (
```

```
                [0] => C:\Windows\Temp\phpA79C.tmp
                [1] => C:\Windows\Temp\phpA79D.tmp
            )

        [error] => Array
            (
                [0] => 0
                [1] => 0

    )

        [size] => Array
            (
                [0] => 180
                [1] => 53
    )
    )
)
```

The following code displays the file name and size of each file:

```
foreach ($_FILES['myfile']['name'] as $idx=>$filename){
    $filesize=$_FILES['myfile']['size'][$idx];
    echo "$filename $filesize<br>";
}
```

Some browsers allow a single file picker to select multiple files:

```
<input name="myfiles[]" type="file" multiple>
```

The array notation is required for PHP to populate the FILES object correctly.

The multiple attribute is not supported in lower versions of Internet Explorer. Sometimes it is acceptable to punish IE users by allowing them to upload one file at a time (as there's only one file selector), and improve the user experience in browsers that support multiple file selection. In other cases it's probably a good idea to use multiple single file pickers.

We have to be mindful of a few resource limits when handling file uploads:

- Transfer time
- POST size
- File size
- File count
- Memory limit

The web server has a limit on how long the upload process can run before it times out. Make sure the upload is not halted by this limit.

The uploaded file size is part of the overall POST size. When increasing the limit of *upload_max_filesize* in PHP settings, remember to also increase *post_max_size*.

Starting PHP 5.2.12, the *max_file_uploads* limits the number of files for each upload. Make sure this value is large enough for your application needs.

It is also necessary to ensure that the memory limit is large enough to handle the upload overhead.

Last, we need to make sure that the upload target directory has write permission. Otherwise we'll see permission denied error.

7.8 Response Headers

PHP has a simple function that generates output in the response header. For example:

```
header('Content-Type: image/png');
```

The above code is used to force the browser to treat the server response as an PNG file even though the request path is something like thumbnail.php.

The header function is also used to perform a server-side redirect:

```
header('Location: another.php');
```

The header function takes two additional optional parameters: "replace" and "http_response_code".

For example, when the Location field is present in the HTTP response header, the server software (Apache) will automatically set the response code to 302 - temporary redirect.

We can use the http_response_code parameter to set the redirect type to 301 - permanent redirect:

```
header('Location: another.php', true, 301);
```

In practice we terminate the script right after the header redirect:

```
header('Location: another.php');
die();
```

The default value of the "replace" parameter is true, meaning if a header of the same type is set again, only the later value is used. For example:

```
header('X-Test: 1');
header('X-Test: 2');
```

The second line will nullify the first line. The final output has only one X-Test header, with a value of 2.

Some protocols require multiple values of the same header field. We can set the replace field to false, so that all the headers are in the response:

```
header('X-Test: 1', false);
header('X-Test: 2', false);
```

The header functions have to be called before any other output is produced. Knowing the HTTP protocol this makes sense.

Consider the HTTP response of the following code:

```
echo "Hello";
header('Location: another.php');
```

The response header will look like this:

```
Content-Type: text/html
Content-Length:
Server: Apache/2.2.22

Hello
Location: another.php
```

The location directive is now part of the content. PHP will generate a warning if *header* is called when any other output is sent.

The header function allows us to describe precisely how we'd like the returned content to be treated. For example, we can indicate that the file returns an image, AND that we'd like the force download the image instead of viewing it directly:

```
header('Content-Type: image/png ');
header("Content-disposition: attachment; filename=logo.png");
```

In Chapter 7.7 we suggested save the uploaded filenames in a database and issue physical filenames by using a stem and unique database IDs. Now we can download the files using the above code and specify a logical filename other than the names they are actually stored as.

Another nifty trick is to open an HTML table as an Excel spreadsheet:

```
header("Content-Type: application/vnd-ms-excel");
header('Content-Disposition: attachment; filename=test.xls');
?>
<table>
<tr><td>Name</td><td>Age</td></tr>
<tr><td>Bob</td><td>42</td></tr>
</table>
```

Newer versions of Excel will issue a warning message because the content of the above page isn't really in Excel format. Nevertheless Excel will map each column in the above table to a spreadsheet.

7.9 HTTP Cookie

An HTTP cookie is a mechanism for web sites to remember stateful information. Since HTTP is a stateless protocol, a cookie works by accepting a small piece of data from the server and store such data on the browser. All subsequent requests to the server carry the cookie data in the HTTP request header.

Cookies are used to remember user preferences and, more importantly, authentication states. Without cookie, we'd be entering our user name and password each time we reload the page.

PHP provides ways to issue and retrieve cookies. We can view cookies as a miniature file system. Setting a cookie is like writing to a file:

```
setcookie('test', 123);
```

In another page, we can load the test cookie's value:

```
echo $_COOKIE['test'];
```

It's important to understand the difference between a cookie and a file. The following code won't work correctly:

```
setcookie('test', 123);
echo $_COOKIE['test'];
```

You may clear the browser cookie and run the above code. The output is not "123". Once the page is loaded again, the output becomes "123".

Let's look at how HTTP protocol implements browser cookies.

The *setcookie* function adds to the response header:
```
Set-Cookie: test=123
```

Once the cookie is accepted by the browser, all *future* requests will carry this cookie in the request header:

```
GET /test.php HTTP/1.1
Host: test.com
Cookie: test=123
```

PHP populates the $_COOKIE variable with the request header. When we read the cookie immediately after setting the cookie, we won't read the actual cookie value because the new request hasn't been sent yet. The COOKIE variable still carries the cookie information of the *current* request.

Because *setcookie* writes to the response header, it has to be called before any other output is sent; just like the *header* function.

In addition to reading and setting cookies, there's another important operation that clears a cookie:

```
setcookie('test', NULL, time()-3600);
```

The 3rd parameter in the *setcookie* function specify the expiry. When it's set to a past time, the browser removes the cookie.

When the expiry parameter is left empty, the cookie is removed only when the browser is closed. This is called a "session cookie".

The following example shows how to use cookies to authenticate a user. Keep in mind this is for illustration purpose only, and the system is by no means secure without additional measures.

First we create a form that asks for user's email and password. In the same file we test whether a form has been posted. If the posted email and password are set to test@test.com and test123 respectively we authenticate the user and redirect the user to index.php. Note that cookie and redirect are both in the HTTP response header. They can be communicated to the browser in a single response.

```php
//login.php
if ($_POST['email']=='test@test.com'
     &&$_POST['password']='test123'){

    setcookie('signedin', 1);
    header('Location: index.php');
    die();
} else {?>
<form method="POST">
    <input name="email" type="email"><br>
    <input name="password" type="password"><br>
```

```
    <input type="submit" value="Sign in">
</form>
<?
}
```

In index.php, we can redirect the user to the login page if the "signedin" cookie is missing:

```
if (!$_COOKIE['signedin']){
    header('Location: login.php');
    die();
}
```

We can also sign the user off by clearing the cookie. A convenient place to clear the cookie is the login screen:

```
if (!_POST['email']) setcookie('signedin', NULL, time()-3600);
```

Although building a proper cookie-based authentication system is beyond the scope of the book, we can briefly point out how the above rudimentary system can be improved.

First of all, cookie values can be easily changed by the end user, especially with the help of the built-in developer tool or Firebug. This means that the authentication system can be effortlessly bypassed. A countermeasure is to place another cookie variable that verifies the integrity of the first cookie. This is done through a hash digest such as MD5:

```
setcookie('check',md5('mysecretkey'.'1'));
```

When we check the cookies, we can compare the hashes:

```
$check_=md5('mysecretkey').$_COOKIE['signedin'];
$check=$_COOKIE['check'];

if ($check==$check_&&$_COOKIE['signedin']){
  //allow access
} else {
  //send to login screen
}
```

A hash digest function has several useful properties. MD5, for example, converts a string into a 32-digit hexadecimal number. The hash value of two different strings should be different. This is the **Collision Resistent** feature of a hash. Looking at the hash, one should not be able to work out the original value - this makes a hash function a **One-Way** function. In the above code we added some secret message to the original message. This process is called **Salting** a hash. Salting makes hashes much harder to crack.

Although the cookie value of "signedin" is validated by the "check" cookie, our system is still vulnerable to a replay attack. A malicious user can observe the value of "check", and use it on another machine at another location, at a different time, regardless the content of the check cookie. The attacker simply has to copy and paste. Our second line of defense makes the check cookie less predictable. The method is simple - hash on more than just a simple boolean value. Instead the hash is computed on multiple components, such as the IP address of the machine, the current date, the user's ID - the more specific the hash is, the hard it is to reuse. For example:

```
$ip=$_SERVER['REMOTE_ADDR'];
$check=md5('mysecret'.$ip.$userid);
setcookie('check',$check);
```

As you can see, the mechanics of an HTTP cookie is quite simple. Using cookies to implement systems requires more skills and experience. What's more challenging, however, is to recognize *when* cookies should be used. Ask questions like "Should we persist data on the client-side or server side?" or "how long should the application state last?" When the concept of a "session" is involved, a cookie is often called for. In other cases, cookies may not be a good idea.

7.10 Working with Date and Time

Date and Time is a very complex subject to work with. This chapter will explore a few key concepts, as well as equip you with a handful of tactics that will get you out of trouble most of the times when it comes to date and time.

First, time is continuous. We talk about the Date and the Time as if they were different components. We also describe time in hour, minute and second. These components complicates time processing. It would be great if there was one number that presents all components in a moment - its year, month, day, hour, minute and second.

There is such number. It is the Unix Epoch Time, or Unix Time Stamp, which defines the number of seconds that have elapsed since the beginning of January 1st, 1970, UTC.

The second prior, namely 23:59:59 December 31th, 1969, is "-1" in Unix Time.

PHP has a function that converts data/time components into Unix time stamp:

```
mktime( hour, minute, second, day, month, year )
```

For example, the time stamp for 10:25:17pm on January 10th, 2012:

```
$stamp = mktime(22, 25, 17, 1, 10, 2012);
```

Remember to use the 24-hour format.

The next important concept is Timezone. Toronto is in Eastern Standard Time, or EST. Without daylight saving, it is 5 hours behind the Universal Time and therefore +5. Berlin sees midnight an hour before London, so their timezone is -1. When North America is observing daylight saving, however, the east coast is only 4 hours behind.

To avoid confusion and establish consistency, we should explicitly specify the timezone in which the application is built for:

```
date_default_timezone_set('UTC');
echo mktime(0, 0, 0, 1, 1, 1970).'<br>'; // 0

date_default_timezone_set('America/Toronto');
echo mktime(0, 0, 0, 1, 1, 1970).'<br>';  // 18000 (5 hours)
```

Timezone is easy to understand and fairly simple to calculate. But we should be mindful of timezone differences and make it a habit to always look at a timestamp in the context of a timezone.

To convert a timestamp into a human readable date, we use the *date* function, which takes a format string as its first parameter, and an optional, second, timestamp parameter:

```
date_default_timezone_set('America/Toronto');
echo date('F j, Y g:ia', 0);
//prints "December 31, 1969 7:00pm"
```

It's important that if two Unix timestamps are the same, they mean the exact moment. A timestamp is defined as the seconds elapsed from a specific time *in a specific timezone*. The reason *mktime* returns different values according to timezone settings is because the input parameters, namely, the "logical time", are open to intepretation.

When the *date* function is called without a second parameter, it formats the current time. You can also obtain the current timestamp by calling the time function:

```
$now = time();
```

8.0 JavaScript Essentials

JavaScript is a versatile and dynamic language that is used for client-side scripting, among other places. Although the syntax of JavaScript is simple, the extensible nature of the language allows JavaScript codes to be potentially very complex and even cryptic at times. Conversely it is also possible to build advanced interactive features using just a few simple elegant lines of code.

In this chapter we'll learn the JavaScript syntax, its interaction with the DOM, and strategies to simplify programming.

8.1 Basic Syntax

The syntax of JavaScript is similar to that of PHP. As a procedural language, JavaScript has the same ways of describing loops, branching conditions, assigning variables and calling functions.

Unlike PHP, a JavaScript variable isn't denoted by a leading dollar sign ($). A JavaScript object can hold many types of data. For example:

```
var size=20; // a number
var name='Bob'; // a string
var colors=['red', 'green', 'blue']; // an array
var person={firstname:'Bob', lastname:'Carson'}; // an object
var callback=function(){alert('Hi');}; // a function
```

String literals in JavaScript are marked with either paired single quotes or double quotes. Strings are concatenated with the plus sign (+):

```
var firstname='John', lastname='Smith';
var name=firstname+' '+lastname;
```

JavaScript is a case-sensitive language. We recommend using all lowercase variables to avoid confusion. Many DOM objects and JavaScript commands have mixed letter casings. We must remember them correctly.

The *var* statement declares a variable and limits the scope of the variable to the current execution context. To understand scoping and execution context we must first understand how JavaScript is executed in an HTML document. JavaScript code is marked by the script block. Technically a script block may be inserted anywhere in an HTML page. The moment a browser sees an open script tag it blocks the rendering process and executes the code in the script block line by line.

Because the execution of JavaScript prevents the browser from loading image resources or rendering the document in parallel, it is highly recommended that all script blocks are declared at the end of the document, right before closing the "body" tag. This is also where the DOM elements are ready to be referenced by JavaScript.

The following code shows the effect of referencing a DOM node too early:

```
<html>
<body>
<script>
document.getElementById('test').value='test';
</script>
<input id="test">
</body>
</html>
```

The browser will throw an error because when the JavaScript is executed, the rest of the document hasn't been parsed, and there's no element named "test" at the time of execution. The above code should be corrected as following:

```
<html>
<body>
<input id="test">
<script>
document.getElementById('test').value='test';
</script>
</body>
</html>
```

If there is a syntax error in JavaScript such as unclosed script tag, unpaired quotation marks, etc., the entire script block is ignored with an error message in the browser's debug console. If there's a run-time error, usually caused by referencing a null pointer or an uninitialized variable, the remaining of the script will not execute.

When a variable is declared outside of a function its execution context is global. Different script blocks do not form separate execution contexts. Assigning value to an undeclared variable will automatically create a global variable.

Compare the following examples:

Example 1:

```
var a=12;

function test(){
        a=0;
}

test();
alert(a);
```

Example 2:

```
var a=12;

function test(){
        var a=0;
}

test();
alert(a);
```

Variable "a" in the first example is in the global scope. Changing the value of this variable changes its global value.

In the second example the variable "a" is declared as local. It is only visible to its containing function. Changing the variable value will not affect the global variable "a".

We can see that JavaScript handles scoping opposite to PHP. In PHP, variables inside functions are local unless they are explicitly declared as global. In JavaScript, the var statement is used to mark a local variable.

When writing JavaScript in an HTML page, it is advised to always declare local variables inside functions and avoid using global variables. Later we'll see techniques for implementing global variables without using variables in the global scope.

In PHP there is no syntax difference between a regular array (list of items) or an object (a key-value dictionary, or a hash map).

The following array object defines a list of objects; each object contains an array.

```php
$cars=array(
    array(
        'make'=>'Ford',
        'model'=>'Escape',
        'colors'=>array('Red', 'Silver')
    ),
    array(
        'make'=>'Honda',
        'model'=>'CR-V',
        'colors'=>array('Green', 'Black')
    )
);
```

JavaScript objects are marked in curly brackets; arrays are denoted with square brackets. The above example in JavaScript is written as follows:

```javascript
var cars=[
  {make:'Ford', model:'Escape', colors:['Red', 'Silver']},
  {make:'Honda', model:'CR-V', colors:['Green', 'Black']}
];
```

Now we can access the first array element using the index notation:

```javascript
var ford = cars[0];
```

We can also get and set the attribute values of an object:

```
var model = ford.model;
```

The following syntax is equivalent to the above line:

```
var model = ford['model'];
```

The advantage of using squared bracket syntax is that sometimes the key of an object may contain special characters such as spaces and dashes. Compare the following notations:

```
var firstname=person.first-name; // read: person.first - name
var firstname=person['first-name']; // correct
```

The length of a JavaScript array can be accessed by the length attribute:

```
for (var i=0; i<cars.length; i++){
  console.log(cars[i].make+' '+cars[i].model);
}
```

Unlike PHP, there is no foreach statement in JavaScript. We can traverse each key-value pair using the following syntax:

```
for (key in car){
 var value=car[key];
 console.log(key, value);
}
```

The above code is similar to the following PHP code:

```
foreach ($car as $key=>$value){
  echo "$key $value";
}
```

Attributes are automatically created when assigned new values. For example:

```
var obj={name:'Test'}
obj.color='red';
```

The content of the obj is now

```
{name:'Test', color:'red'}
```

The value of a non-existing attribute is "undefined". Accessing this value doesn't give an error. Trying to retrieve the child attribute of a undefined attribute, however, generates a run-time error:

```
var test = obj.asdf; // test is "undefined"
var test2 = obj.asdf.color; // null-pointer error
```

In later chapters we will see that JavaScript's ability to dynamically create object attributes is crucial to many coding techniques.

8.2 DOM Interaction

When a browser reads an HTML page it parses the document to a tree of nodes. We have seen in Chapter 4 how this tree is used for CSS to apply cascading rules. The same DOM tree is accessible to JavaScript:

```
<div id="node_a">
  <div id="node_a1"></div>
  <div id="node_a2"></div>
</div>
<div id="node_b"></div>
<div id="node_c"></div>
```

In the above example, Nodes A, B and C are on the same level. Node A1 and A2 are child nodes of A, and Node A is the parent node of A1 and A2.

In JavaScript we use document.getElementById to obtain the handle of a node directly by referencing its ID:

```
var a1=document.getElementById('node_a1');
```

For the sake of illustration, we can also get the handle to Node A by its relationship with A1, in addition to getElementById('node_a'):

```
var a=a1.parentNode;
```

The DOM tree is mapped to a JavaScript presentation that is almost identical to the document. The attributes, value and children of each node are accessible to JavaScript. Based on practical use cases, some of the most important "attributes" are style, value and innerHTML.

```
<div id="test">Hello, there!</div>
<input id="test2">

<script>
var test=document.getElementById('test');
var test2=document.getElementById('test2');
test.innerHTML='Hello, world!';
test.style.backgroundColor='#ffab00';
test2.value='123';
</script>
```

The "style" object of a node offers JavaScript an interface to alter the node's CSS programmatically. The following chart should present a noticeable pattern:

CSS	JavaScript (*.style.)
width: 100px;	width='100px';
color: #ff0000;	color='#ff0000';
opacity: 0.5;	opacity=0.5;
background-color: #cdcdcd;	backgroundColor='#cdcdcd';
transition-duration: 50ms;	transitionDuration='50ms';
-webkit-opacity: 1;	WebkitOpacity=1;

For most of the CSS attributes, their JavaScript counterpart are spelled the same way. If there's a dash in the attribute name, the dash is omitted but the letter after the dash is capitalized. Remember there are exceptions to this rule. You will know it when you see it.

It's important to know that certain attributes are more reliable to write to than to read from. The style object is a good example:

```
<style>
#test{
    width:100px; height:100px;
    position:absolute; top:100px; left:100px;
```

```
  border: solid 1px;
}
</style>
<div id="test"></div>
<script>
var obj=document.getElementById('test');
var x=test.style.left;
console.log(x);
test.style.left='200px';
</script>
```

In the above code, test.style.left is read as an empty string. The position of the test node is updated when *style.left* is assigned with an explicit value. After assigning the value, test.style.left will read as "200px".

In later parts of this chapter we will see techniques that do not rely on directly reading style attributes.

Getting an element by its ID is only one way to obtain a node's handle. The following example uses another method: getElementsByTagName. Note the plural "s" in the command, as it returns an array of objects:

```
<div id="test">
  <span class="asdf">A</span>
  <span class="asdf">S</span>
  <span class="xy">X</span>
  <span class="asdf">D</span>
  <span class="xy">Y</span>
  <span class="asdf">F</span>
</div>
<script>
var test=document.getElementById('test');
var objs=test.getElementsByTagName('span');
for (var i=0; i<objs.length; i++){
  if (objs[i].className!='asdf') continue;
  objs[i].style.color='#ff0000';
}
</script>
```

The above example changes all the "asdf" class span elements to red. The getElementsByTagName method can be invoked by a containing node instead of "document", the entire document. The function returns all the nodes with the specified tag name. If we need to match a specific class name we'll have to loop through each item in the array.

The above code uses a ejective style to increase code readability. Instead of this:

```
for (var i=0; i<objs.length; i++){
  if (objs[i].className=='asdf'){
    objs[i].style.color='#ff0000';
  }
}
```

, the code is written to reduce indentation level:

```
for (var i=0; i<objs.length; i++){
  if (objs[i].className!='asdf') continue;
  objs[i].style.color='#ff0000';
}
```

Similarly, you could use document.getElementsByName to target multiple objects. However, make sure the name attribute does not collide with any IDs, or it'll be included in the node list in Internet Explorer.

Sometimes we need to dynamically create new elements other than changing existing DOM nodes. This is done by *document.createElement*:

```
<div id="test"></div>
<script>
var div=document.getElementById('test');
var span=document.createElement('span');
span.innerHTML='test';
span.style.color='#ff0000';
div.appendChild(span);
</script>
```

After running the above code, the browser sees the document as following:

```
<div id="test">
  <span>test</span>
</div>
```

Remember to append the newly created node to a container. Otherwise it's only accessible to JavaScript but invisible to the DOM.

The above example is contrived. It could be written with innerHTML:

```
var div=document.getElementById('test');
div.innerHTML='<span>test</span>';
```

Adding elements via changing innerHTML or element creating are fundamentally different processes. When we describe an HTML object in a string that's assigned to innerHTML, the browser parses the string and creates the objects. Sometimes we need a physical object to attach events to. There are also cases when we have to create a container to the bottom of the document (e.g. creating an overlay), and we attach the created element to the body:

```
var mask=document.createElement('div');
// ...
document.body.appendChild(mask);
```

It would be too much overhead to change the innerHTML of the entire document.

There are also elements that cannot be created by assigning innerHTML. For example, a dropdown list ("select" tag) cannot be directly populated in IE without the creation of each "option" element:

```
<select id="list">
  <option value="a">A</option>
  <option value="b">B</option>
</select>
<script>
var list=document.getElementById('list');

//the following line does not working in IE:
//list.innerHTML+='<option value="c">C</option>';

var opt=document.createElement('option');
opt.setAttribute('value','c');
opt.innerHTML='C';
```

```
list.appendChild(opt);
</script>
```

DOM node creation is also useful for creating script blocks and dynamically loading JavaScript files from external sites. It is also used for loading CSS files at run-time:

```
var css=document.createElement('link');
css.setAttribute('rel','stylesheet');
css.setAttribute('type','text/css');
css.setAttribute('href','http://othersite.com/test.css');
document.getElementsById('head').item(0).appendChild(css);
```

The above code effectively adds the following line to the document head:

```
<head>
<link rel="stylesheet" type="text/css" href="..." />
</head>
```

8.3 Handling Basic Events

When the user interacts with a web page, the HTML document generates various events. JavaScript can react to these events and subsequently provide richer functionality and user experience.

Some common HTML events are *onclick*, *onmouseover*, *onmouseout*, *onkeyup*, *onfocus*, *onchange*, etc.

An event can be attached to a node through inline declaration:

```
<button onclick="alert('Hi');">Test</button>

<input onfocus="this.style.background='red';"
    onblur="this.style.background='green';">
```

In practice, inline event handlers invoke functions:

```
<a onclick="showmore();">Read more...</a>

<script>
function showmore(){
...
}
</script>
```

Another method to attach an event to a node is by assigning a function reference to a node's event attribute:

```
<button id="test">Test</button>
<script>
function hello(){alert('Hi');}

var button=document.getElementById('test');
button.onclick=hello;
</script>
```

The above code is functionally equivalent to the following:

```
<button id="test" onclick="hello();">Test</button>
<script>
function hello(){alert('Hi');}
</script>
```

However, the following code is incorrect:

```
<script>
var button=document.getElementById('test');
button.onclick=hello(); //INCORRECT
</script>
```

Remember, the "onclick" attribute in the JavaScript object is a pointer to a function. Its value should be only assigned a function, not a result of a function.

The above incorrect code will trigger an alert dialog the moment the page is loaded. Since the "hello" function returns no values, no function is linked to the onclick attribute of the button. Therefore, when the button is clicked, nothing happens.

What if we need to pass in a parameter to the function? Consider the following example:

```
<button id="alice" onclick="hi('Alice');">Hi Alice</button>
<button id="bob" onclick="hi('Bob');">Hi Bob</button>
<script>
function hi(name){alert('Hi '+name);}
</script>
```

Now we attach the events without using the inline notation:

```
<script>
var alice=document.getElementById('alice');
var bob=document.getElementById('bob');

alice.onclick=function(){hi('Alice');}
bob.onclick=function(){hi('Bob');}
</script>
```

Alternatively we can rewrite the "hi" function itself, so that it returns a function:

```
<script>
function hi(name){
    return function(){
        alert('Hi '+name);
    }
}
...
alice.onclick=hi('Alice');
bob.onclick=hi('Bob');
</script>
```

Note that the above event assignment is correct because even though "hi" is called the moment the script is parsed, the inner function isn't executed. Instead, the _definition_ of the function, i.e. a proper function, is returned to the onclick attribute of the object.

By now, you probably have a few questions:

- Why can't we always inline events?
- What's the difference between the two "function shells"?
- How do these no-name functions work?

While it's still too early in the chapter to answer these questions, let me just point out that we should always use inline event handling whenever possible. This is because it makes code maintenance a lot easier.

Imagine there's a bug in a web calculator, and here's the inline event:

```
<button onclick="calculate();">Go</button>
```

versus post-attachment:

```
<button id="calc">Go</button>
...
...
...
<script>
...
...
function calculate(){...}
var calc=document.getElementById('calc');
calc.onclick=calculate;
</script>
```

In the latter case you'll have to hunt for the event handler.

Unfortunately, and quite mindboggling so, the event handling examples you have seen so far do not represent the "contemporary" coding methods. There is a school of thought that strongly advocates the use of event listeners:

```
calc.addEventListener('click', calculate);
```
Or in jQuery:

```
$('#calc').on('click', calculate);
```

The main functional difference between assigning *onclick* and using *addEventListener* is that the latter can link up multiple handlers:

```
calc.addEventListener('click',calculate2);
calc.addEventListener('click',calculate3);
```

This is useful if you want multiple things to happen when one button is clicked.

A more realistic use case would be: there's a web application with a few buttons, and you, the maintenance programmer, want to *extend* the functionality of a button while preserving its existing behavior. In other words, you are hacking the code and making it less maintainable. Chances are, the code is probably built in such way that it's riddled with event listeners.

8.4 Function Closures

What is a JavaScript function closure? By reading its definition you might just lose your chance of understanding how a closure works. Believe it or not, I have used closures throughout my projects long before I realized that I was using closures.

Let's learn by code example instead. We have seen the following code already:

```
function hi(name){
    return function(){
        alert('Hi '+name);
    }
}

var alice=document.getElementById('alice');
alice.onclick=hi('Alice');
```

The above code works because the "hi" function returns a function, which is further assigned to the "onclick" attribute of the "alice" node.

The inner function of "hi" has access to every local variable that "hi" has access to, including the "name" variable that's passed to its call stack. Such variable visibility is achieved by using the nested function structure, or "closure".

Earlier we asked, when can we not just use inline events? An example would be a mouse or keyboard event. In a non-IE browser, the event handling function is given an implicit event object:

```
<input id="search">
<script>
var search=document.getElementById('search');
search.onkeyup=function(e){
        console.log(e.which);
}
</script>
```

If we want to attach two search fields to the same function, we can do this:

```
<input id="search1"> <input id="search2">
<script>
function search(e){
    console.log(e.which);
}

var s1=document.getElementById('s1');
var s2=document.getElementById('s2');

s1.onkeyup=search;
s2.onkeyup=search;
</script>
```

So far so good. What if we want to parameterize the function so that for the first search box it says "searching ###" and the second "looking up ###"?

First attempt:

```
function search(phrase){return function(){
        console.log(phrase+' '+e.which);
}}
s1.onkeyup=search('searching ');
s2.onkeyup=search('looking up');
```

The above code almost works. One question remains: how does the browser pass in the event object? The key is the inner function:

```
function search(phrase){return function(e){
    console.log(phrase+' '+e.which);
}}
```

Yes, it is that simple.

Keep in mind that Internet Explorer uses a different mechanism to describe event details. The *window.event* object, shorthanded as *event*, is globally accessible. The search function can be written to support both browsers:

```
function search(phrase){return function(e){
    var code;
    if (e) code=e.which; else code=event.keyCode;
    console.log(code);
}}
```

8.5 State Keeping & Self-Referencing

The following code shows and hides a container:

```
<a onclick="showhide('test');">Show/Hide</a>
<div id="test" style="display:none;">
    More information
</div>
<script>
function showhide(id){
    var container=document.getElementById(id);
    if (!container.showing){
      container.style.display='block';
      container.showing=true;
    } else {
      container.style.display='none';
      container.showing=null;
    }
}
</script>
```

Earlier in this chapter we mentioned JavaScript's ability to dynamically create attributes. In the above example, "showing" is a made-up attribute. When the show/hide link is first clicked, the "showing" flag is not set. The showhide function sets the container to visible while placing the marker. When the link is clicked a second time, the "showing" marker is already there. The function then clears the flag and hides the container.

It's very important not to rely on the CSS attributes of the container. The following code wouldn't work as well:

```
if (container.style.display=='none'){
    ...
} else {
    ...
}
```

Depend on the browser, the "display" value of the container could be read as a blank string, or "NONE", or "none". Using the synthesized "showing" attribute works more reliably.

The next example counts how many time each block has been clicked on:

```
<div id="c1" onclick="count('c1');">0</div>
<div id="c2" onclick="count('c2');">0</div>
<script>
function count(id){
    var container=document.getElementById(id);
    if (container.count==null) container.count=0;
    container.count++;
    container.innerHTML=container.count;
}
</script>
```

Again, we initialize a custom attribute, "count" instead of reading and parsing the existing innerHTML value. Just like .style, .innerHTML is used for output only.

By now you should see the benefits of this coding technique. The state variables are self contained and easy to debug. The state of each container can be easily inspected.

We can write even more compact, and portable code by using self referencing pointers. The above code is rewritten as the following:

```
<div onclick="count(this);">0</div>
<div onclick="count(this);">0</div>
<script>
function count(d){
    if (d.count==null) d.count=0;
    d.count++;
    d.innerHTML=d.count;
}
</script>
```

The "this" keyword in the inline event declaration refers to the node itself. By passing "this" to the function, the handle to the object is bound to the "d" variable. This saves us the hassle of setting IDs and getting elements by their IDs.

8.6 Timeouts and Intervals

Sometimes we want to have a delayed response to an event. The following code shows a dialog after 2 seconds:

```
<a onclick="show_hi();">Hi</a>
<script>
function show_hi(){
  setTimeout(function(){alert('Hi');},2000);
}
</script>
```

The setTimeout function takes two parameters. The first is a function, the second is the duration of the delay, in milliseconds.

setTimeout also returns a handle for cancelling the timer. It works like the kill switch of a self-destruct sequence:

```
<a onclick="destruct(this);">Self Destruct in 10 seconds</a>
<script>
function destruct(d){
  if (d.timer){
```

```
      clearTimeout(d.timer);
      d.innerHTML='Stopped';
    } else {
      d.timer=setTimeout(function(){
        d.innerHTML='BOOM';
        }, 10000);
      d.innerHTML='Click to abort';
  }
}
</script>
```

Now test the above code and be a hero who saves the planet!

The above code is a good example of the state keeping techniques we discussed in the previous chapter.

Learning the syntax of setTimeout is easy. Building solutions with timeouts requires a bit more experience. Next we'll see a few tactics that use timeouts.

Classic Timeout Pattern - "Rescheduling":

Suppose we are creating a button that behaves differently if it's clicked once, twice, three times and so forth. Sure this is a bad UI decision but this exercise shows a powerful code pattern using timeouts:

```
<a onclick="countclick(this);">click me</a>
<script>
function countclick(d){
      if (d.count==null) d.count=0;
      d.count++;
      if (d.timer) clearTimeout(d.timer);

      d.timer=setTimeout(function(){
            alert('Clicked '+d.count+' times');
            d.timer=null;
            d.count=0;
      },500);
}
</script>
```

The two bolded lines are the heart of this pattern. One line checks if a timeout handler is previously scheduled; if so, the timeout is canceled. The function then schedules a new handler.

The program waits 500 milliseconds for the user action to "settle". If another click comes in, the program waits another 500 milliseconds. In practice this settlement window can be reduced to reflect the average click rate.

There are times when we have to make sure that certain function is called only once within a given timeframe. When working with badly engineered code, for example, maintaining someone else's convoluted code, it can be unclear why a certain function is called multiple times. If such function is not an idempotent operation, or that the function consumes resource, it is essential that the function guards its invocation itself:

```
function call_once(){
      if (document.callonce)
        clearTimeout(document.callonce);

      document.callonce=setTimeout(function(){
        //do your business here
      },50);
}
```

The above two examples use the same code pattern and therefore work the same way. Repeated function calls are discarded; only the last call delivers the payload, once.

It's important to recognize that we can't always throw away events. For example, if each time the function is called, the user sends $5.00, then 5 clicks should register $25.00. In such case we should not use call_once to ignore the previous 4 clicks. Ironically, however, we could use call_once to filter out accidental double-clicks when the user means to hit the button once.

Other operations are immune to how many times they are performed. For example, the command to "switch on the light" can be issued many times, and there is no harm to over-execute the command. These operations are called **idempotent**.

The *setInterval* function works the same way, except that the function is repeatedly called, spaced by the interval specified in the second parameter, in milliseconds.

The following code appends a new line to a test container each second:

```
<div id="test"></div>
<script>
setInterval(function(){
  var test=document.getElementById('test');
  test.innerHTML+='<br>test';
},1000);
</script>
```

Just like *setTimeout*, you can call off an interval by clearing the interval handle. But you have to remember to "keep the receipt" when the interval is set. This is probably more important than keeping the timeout handle, as there is no other way to stop the ever recurring function call if needed to. Remember to use a persistent variable to store the handle:

```
//start an interval:
document.myrepeater=setInterval(...);

//stop the interval:
clearInterval(document.myrepeater);
```

Classic Interval Pattern - "Key Frame Animation"

In theory, every use of interval can be converted to a timeout. For example, instead of calling the same function X every second, we could call X, and make X call itself after a second of timeout. If the condition for stopping the interval is met, the same condition can be used to Not to call the next round of timeout.

Although browsers time these two functions differently, especially when the interval parameter is pushing the hardware limit, the choice of timeout vs. interval really comes down to programming style. That, and the fact that interval heartbeats are more resilient. A JavaScript run-time error will disrupt the timeout chain, but not for an interval.

The call pattern of *setInterval* makes it suitable for implementing key frame animations. The next code snippet animates the size of a container:

```
<style>
#test{width:50px;height:50px;background:#dedede;}
</style>
<div id="test"></div>
<script>
function anim(d){
        var seq=[80,100,90,60,50];
        if (d.anim) return;

        d.anim=setInterval(function(){
                if (!d.animidx) d.animidx=0;

                if (d.animidx>seq.length-1){
                        clearInterval(d.anim);
                        d.animidx=0;
                        d.anim=null;
                }

                var size=seq[d.animidx];
                d.style.width=size+'px';
                d.style.height=size+'px';
                d.animidx++;
        },100);
}

anim(document.getElementById('test'));
</script>
```

The key components in the above code are marked bold, namely, an iterator (animidx), the iteration engine (the interval routine), an array of key frame values (the "seq") and an exit condition, for terminating the animation.

The above code employs a few techniques we've learned so far. It uses a DOM node to store the frame position (animidx). The same node is also used to keep the interval handle for later termination.

The animation key frame array (seq) is defined outside of the interval function. The array, along with the self-referencing parameter "d", is accessible to the interval function. This is an example of closure, as we've explained earlier.

As a practice, before reading on, try to rewrite the above function using a timeout.

Rewriting an interval routing with a timeout in most cases can be quite straight forward. If the interval function doesn't have a name, assign it a name so that it can be called from within itself. The function doesn't have to be in the global scope.

Since the call to setInterval is converted to a function definition, we'll have to manually call setTimeout just once. This is called a "bootstrapping call".

The handling of the exit condition is also inverted. In an interval function, we explicitly clears the interval. In a timeout function, we simply stop calling the next frame.

```
function anim(d){
     var seq=[80,100,90,60,50];

     var nextframe=function(){
          if (!d.animidx) d.animidx=0;

          if (d.animidx>seq.length-1){
               d.animidx=0;
          } else {
               setTimeout(nextframe,100);
          }

          var size=seq[d.animidx];
          d.style.width=size+'px';
          d.style.height=size+'px';
          d.animidx++;
     };

     setTimeout(nextframe,100);
}
```

We are only half way through the Timeout and Interval section. But you can take a break and appreciate the fact that you just wrote (or typed) the world's most compact animation engine, in plain JavaScript, without using a library, without using CSS 3 animation features. If you want this animation routine to behave differently, or interact with user events, you have total control!

Being able to implement a tweening animation is a major milestone in JavaScript programming, as it requires a close understanding of how DOM and JavaScript behave, as well as problem solving skills that put the moving parts into a concerted piece.

We just mentioned the word "tweening animation". A tween is a transition between two states. Since we know the start and end frame, and the duration of the animation, we can pre-define the value of each frame, as we've seen in the previous examples. We can also dynamically determine whether there is the next step, and what that step will be. The key to an interval/timeout function is not to jump to the final frame, but to take smaller steps.

The next example builds a block that follows the mouse cursor. It shows how a timeout handler computes the step each time and access the situation dynamically.

```
<style>
#test{
position:absolute;top:0;left:0;
width:50px;height:50px;background:#dedede;
}
</style>
<div id="test"></div>
<script>
document.onmousemove=function(e){
        if (e){
                document.mousex=e.clientX;
                document.mousey=e.clientY;
        } else {
                document.mousex=event.clientX;
                document.mousey=event.clientY;
        }
}

function catcher(){
        if (document.mousex==null) {
                document.mousex=0;
```

```
                document.mousey=0;
        }
        var obj=document.getElementById('test');
        if (!obj.myx){
                obj.myx=0;
                obj.myy=0;
        }

        if (Math.abs(obj.myx-document.mousex)>10||
          Math.abs(obj.myy-document.mousey)>10){
                var stepx=(document.mousex-obj.myx)/10;
                var stepy=(document.mousey-obj.myy)/10;
                obj.myx+=stepx; obj.myy+=stepy;
                obj.style.left=obj.myx+'px';
                obj.style.top=obj.myy+'px';

        }

        setTimeout(catcher,30);
}

setTimeout(catcher,30);
</script>
```

As an exercise, rewrite the above function using *setInterval*.
(Hint: remove two lines and add a new line.)

Deferred-Binding

The last timeout related topic is deferred-binding - something a seasoned
JavaScript programmer can get wrong from time to time.

Compare the following codes:

```
for (var i=0;i<10;i++){
  setTimeout(function(){
    console.log(i);
  },(i+1)*100;
}
```

Alternative code:

```
var f=function(idx){
    return function(){
        setTimeout(function(){
            console.log(idx);
        }, (idx+1)*100;
    }
}
```

```
for (var i=0;i<10;i++) f(i);
```

The output of the first code snippet is:

```
10 10 10 10 10 10 10 10 10 10
```

And the second snippet outputs:

```
0 1 2 3 4 5 6 7 8 9
```

Why is that?

The two examples differ in *when* the parameter is passed into *console.log*. In the first code, the value of *i* is retrieved long after the loop is finished. We see a terminating value 10 being used for each timeout call.

In the second code, values of *i* are instantly passed to a function that returns a function. Because of closure, parameter values are preserved. The timeout function has access to the parameter value *at the time of invocation* rather than *time of execution*. And therefore, the second code produces the correct result.

You may wonder, why would you ever write a function like this? Well, deferred-binding happens not only to timeout functions, but also callback functions. If the callback function is called after the next loop iteration it is fed the incorrect value. And let's face it, which callback function can run faster than a for-loop? The whole point of being a callback function is that it runs delayed - just like a timeout handler.

When integrating with another site using JavaScript, callback functions are common because transactions tend to take long, and callbacks do not block script execution. The Google Maps API is a good example.

9.0 What's this AJAX Thingy Anyway?

As the title of this book suggests, there really is no such thing as "AJAX". But you might have heard it somewhere before, in various contexts.

AJAX stands for "Asynchronous JavaScript and XML". It was a marketing term coined to push a new breed of web applications - ones that behave more like traditional desktop applications. One of the earliest, publicly known AJAX apps are Google Maps and Gmail.

The technologies that are required to make an AJAX app were ready long before the introduction of the term. As the hype of AJAX wears off, the phrase is often used in a technical context. A typical example would be "do we make an AJAX call or load a new page?"

The above question captures the characteristics of an "AJAX action", that is, the ability to update a portion of a web page without reloading the entire page.

We have seen in previous chapters that user inputs are transmitted either as URL query parameters (GET) or form submit (POST). Both cases result in a page reload. Remember that HTTP is stateless, but a web application has to remember user states. This means every page refresh should forward the current UI state, and the server should persist the changes and loop back to the client. All in all, there's tremendous overhead and complexity.

A so-called AJAX application uses a JavaScript object to communicate with the web server behind the scenes. The server response is then used to update the content of a specific portion of the page. Comparing to the traditional page refresh model, an AJAX call is a lot simpler. The UI state of a web app is, for the most part, transient. Once the user is done using the app, it can start over for the next session. The kind of information that needs persisting is submitted via the AJAX call and stored on an SQL database.

9.1 XML HTTP Request Object

The XML HTTP Request Object (XHR) is *the* AJAX object. It is supported by all modern browsers. Open a web page on your local host, and open the firebug console. Enter the following lines:

```
rq = new XMLHttpRequest();
rq.open('GET', 'test.php', false);
rq.send(null);

console.log(rq.responseText);
```

The first three lines make an HTTP request without navigating away from the current page. The last line shows that we have access to the server response.

If you don't have test.php on your local server, prepare one as such:

```
<?php echo date('h:i:s');
```

Each time you make a new request, the server returns the current time.

The XMLHttpRequest object is not natively supported in older versions of IE, even though it was Microsoft that pioneered the concept of XHR. By using ActiveX, a now outdated Microsoft proprietary extension, XHR has been supported since IE 5.0!

The following function serves as a wrapper to always return a XHR object, regardless of browser versions:

```
function xmlHTTPRequestObject() {
    var obj = false;
    var objs = ["Microsoft.XMLHTTP","Msxml2.XMLHTTP",
                "MSXML2.XMLHTTP.3.0","MSXML2.XMLHTTP.4.0"];
    var success = false;
    for (var i=0; !success && i < objs.length; i++) {
        try {
            obj = new ActiveXObject(objs[i]);
            success = true;
        } catch (e) { obj = false; }
    }

    if (!obj) obj = new XMLHttpRequest();
    return obj;
}
```

9.1.1 Synchronous Mode

Let's expand the previous example and give it more context:

```
<html>
<body>
<button onclick="gettime();">Server Time</button>
<div id="servertime"></div>
<script>
function xmlHTTPRequestObject(){...} //copy above

function gettime(){
  var rq=xmlHTTPRequestObject();
  rq.open('GET', 'servertime.php', false);
  rq.send(null);
  var res=rq.responseText;
  document.getElementById('servertime').innerHTML=res;
}
</script>
</body>
</html>
```

And servertime.php:

```
<?php
echo date('F j, Y h:i:s');
```

Each time the "Server Time" button is clicked, the browser sends an HTTP request without leaving the current page. The server handles the request just like any other requests. The response is retrieved by the responseText attribute of the XHR object. The JavaScript function then replaces the content of the "servertime" container with the server response.

Now take a close look at *rq.open*. The function takes 3 parameters: the request method, request URL, and whether the call is made asynchronously.

We pointed out in Chapter 7.3 that a POST is a special kind of GET. A POST AJAX call can send much larger amount of data than a URL query string:

```
var text="this is a very long string...";
```

```
rq.open('POST','test.php',false);
rq.send(text);
```

Some browsers don't handle the POST data correctly unless the encoding is set:

```
rq.open('POST', 'test.php', false);
rq.setRequestHeader('Content-Type',
                    'text/plain; charset=utf-8');
```

The POST data can be accessed via the *php://input* wrapper in PHP:

```
$text = file_get_contents('php://input');
```

In previous editions of the book, a special global variable was used: *$HTTP_RAW_POST_DATA*. This feature is deprecated as of PHP 5.6.0. Using *php://input* is recommended.

The XHR request isn't sent until the *send* function is called. The send call can be easily forgotten especially when using the GET method.

The second parameter of the *open* function is the URL of the page. For security reasons XHR can only load pages on the same domain. This is called the "Same Domain Policy". The URL is usually appended a timestamp, so that each XHR call is different. This effectively prevents unwanted caching:

```
var now = new Date();
var heartbeat = now.getTime();
...
rq.open('POST','test.php?hb='+heartbeat,false);
```

Another URL treatment is to escape special characters in the query string. For example, the following call creates a user profile:

```
rq.open('POST', 'adduser.php?name=Brian', false);
```

So far so good. But what if the name is John & Co.? The query becomes:

```
rq.open('POST', 'adduser.php?name=John&Co', false);
```

The server-side script will see the value for "name" is John, and the value for "Co" is empty.

To prevent such confusion, the link is encoded as following:

```
adduser.php?name=John%26Co
```

Antradar's Nano AJAX Library has the encoding function, as well as the XHR wrapper and heartbeat function implemented in the tiny nano.js file:

http://www.antradar.com/docs-nano-ajax-manual

The third parameter of the *open* function indicates whether the XHR request is sent asynchronously. When it's set to false, the browser waits for the server to respond. If the server takes 10 seconds, the browser will freeze for 10 seconds.

As an exercise, add the following delay to servertime.php:

```php
<?php
sleep(10);
echo date('F j, Y h:i:s');
```

Then create an interval that updates the content of a container every second. Click on the "Server Time" button and observe how your timer stops.

When the asynchronous parameter is set to false, the request is sent "synchronously". The call is said to be "blocking".

9.1.2 Asynchronous Mode

The XHR request can also be made asynchronously, or in a "non-blocking" manner. Consider the following code:

```html
<html>
<body>
<button onclick="gettime();">Server Time</button>
<div id="servertime">n/a</div>
<script>
function xmlHTTPRequestObject(){...} //copy above
```

```
function gettime(){
  var rq=xmlHTTPRequestObject();
  rq.open('GET', 'servertime.php', true);
  rq.send(null);
  var res=rq.responseText;
  document.getElementById('servertime').innerHTML=res;
}
</script>
</body>
</html>
```

We've made two modifications. They're marked bold.

Click on "Server Time", and the *servertime* container is instantly wiped out instead of being filled with the server response. Some browsers will even issue a JavaScript error, complaining that the value of *responseText* is accessed too early.

Come to think of it, it makes sense. We called rq.responseText right after the XHR request is sent. Yet the server won't respond for another 10 seconds.

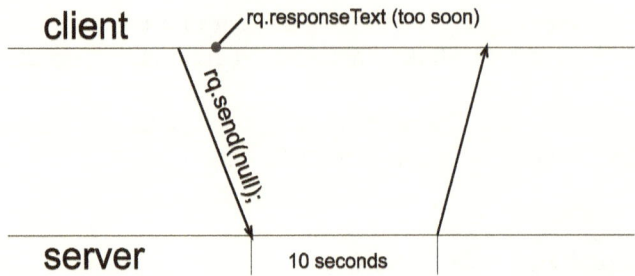

To prove a point, let's wait 12 seconds before getting the content:

```
var rq=xmlHTTPRequestObject();
rq.open('GET', 'servertime.php', true);
rq.send(null);

setTimeout(function(){
  var res=rq.responseText;
  document.getElementById('servertime').innerHTML=res;
```

}, 12000);

This time the program works correctly (but inefficiently):

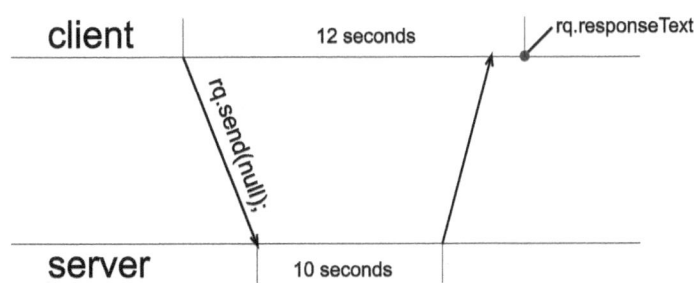

A realistic server response may take much shorter than 10 seconds, in which case a 12-second wait is wasteful; it could potentially take longer than 10 seconds, in which case 12-second is not enough.

The XHR object offers a more sophisticated mechanism to deal with the unknown time it takes for the server to respond - a callback function.

```
rq.open('GET', 'servertime.php', true);
rq.onreadystatechange=function(){
  if (rq.readyState==4){
    var res=rq.responseText;
    document.getElementById('servertime').innerHTML=res;
  }
}
rq.send(null);
```

The above function is called each time the *readyState* property of the XHR object is updated. Each request goes through 5 states:

- 0 - uninitialized
- 1 - request set up
- 2 - request sent
- 3 - request in process
- 4 - request complete

9.0 What's this AJAX Thingy Anyway?   327

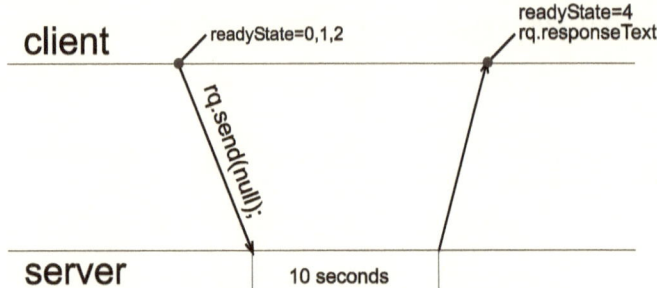

In most cases, testing readyState equals 4 is sufficient. Keep in mind, however, that a server response may not be successful. The HTTP status code could be anything other than 200. If the page is missing, the status code is 404. If there's an internal server error, the status code is 500.

In PHP, we can override the status code of a response:

```php
<?php
header('HTTP/1.0 403 Forbidden');
```

Then in our XHR callback function, we can check the status code:

```
rq.onreadystatechange=function(){
  if (rq.readyState==4){
    if (rq.status==304) alert('Access denied');
    else {
      var res=rq.responseText;
      document.getElementById('servertime').innerHTML=res;
    } //status
  }//readyState
}//readystatechange
```

In addition to status code, the server can communicate with the client using custom HTTP headers:

```php
<?php
header('myerror: Custom error message');
```

In XHR callback:

```
rq.onreadystatechange=function(){
  if (rq.readyState==4){
    var myerror=rq.getResponseHeader('myerror');
    if (myerror!=null&&myerror!=''){
      alert('Error: '+myerror);
    } else {
      //...
    }//header
  }//readyState
}
```

Be sure to compare the header with both null and empty string for maximum
browser compatibility.

Aborting XHR Requests

The XHR object has another function that cancels an in-flight request:

```
<button onclick="gettime();">Server Time</button>
<button onclick="canceltime();">Cancel</button>
<script>
function gettime(){
  var rq=xmlHTTPRequestObject();
  rq.open('GET', 'wait.php', true);
  rq.onreadystatechange=function(){
    if (rq.readyState==4){
      document.rqobj=null;
      var res=rq.responseText;
      document.getElementById('servertime').innerHTML=res;
    }
  }

  document.rqobj=rq;
  rq.send(null);
}

function canceltime(){
  if (document.rqobj) document.rqobj.abort();
}
</script>
```

The cancelation of an XHR call is similar to clearing a timeout. When *setTimeout* is called, the function returns a handle. We use *clearTimeout* on the same handle to cancel a previous scheduled event.

In the case of XHR, the XHR object itself is the handle. The above code uses the *document* namespace to store the object. In practice, a more specific DOM node can be picked to keep this object.

It's important to know that once *abort* is called on an XHR object, the object's callback function will never be called. The abort call will fail if there is no in-flight request either because the request hasn't been sent or is already completed. The above code also guards against these scenarios by setting and clearing the XHR object handle.

It's also important to understand that canceling an XHR request does not prevent it from reaching the server. If a lengthy request for indexing the database is sent, and the server is busy processing the request for the next 2 minutes, aborting the request only ignores the server call back notification. The server will respond to the request regardless.

In the JavaScript Timeout section we talked about idempotent operations. The same principles apply to XHR calls.

9.2 AJAX Patterns

So far we have seen some raw capabilities of the XHR object. There are several ways to incorporate XHR's communication channel (also called an "AJAX Transport") with the rest of the JavaScript code.

This chapter explores different ways, or "patterns" to use XHR to partially update a web page.

Suppose we create a web application as following:

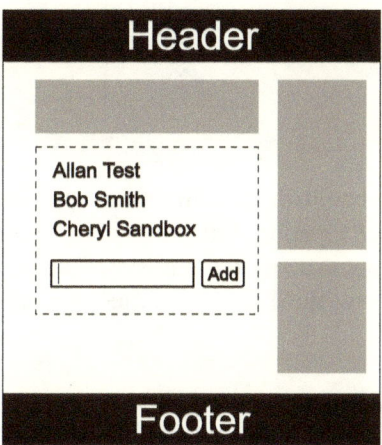

The content outside the dashed box should be unchanged. Inside the box is a list of names. As the user enters a new name, the updated list should show without reloading the entire page.

In Chapter 6.5 we learned how to print a list from a database table:

```
...
<div id="contacts">
    <div id="contactlist">
    <?php
    $query="select * from contacts order by fname";
    $rs=mysql_query($query,$db);
    while ($myrow=mysql_fetch_assoc($rs)){
        $name=$myrow['fname'].' '.$myrow['lname'];
    ?>
    <div><?echo $name;?></div>
    <?
    }//while
    </div><!-- contactlist -->
    <input id="newname">
    <button onclick="addcontact();">Add</button>
</div><!-- contacts -->
...
<script src="nano.js"></script>
<script>
function addcontact(){
   var name=encodeHTML(gid('newname').value);
```

```
    var rq=xmlHTTPRequestObject();
    // ...
}
</script>
```

The rest of this chapter will discuss different approaches for implementing not only the *addcontact* function, but the overall data flow. The goal of this exercise is not about memorizing the patterns. Rather, it illustrates the flaws of each pattern, and how the LCHH architecture, as discussed in the next chapter, came to be.

Pattern 1 - Block and Inject

The first strategy is the most straightforward - make a blocking call to update the database, then make another call to display the updated list. Clear the input box for the next entry.

```
rq=xmlHTTPRequestObject();
rq.open('GET', 'addcontact.php?name='+name, false);
rq.send(null);

rq=xmlHTTPRequestObject();
rq.open('GET','listcontacts.php',false);
rq.send(null);
gid('contactlist').innerHTML=rq.responseText;
gid('newname').value='';
```

And listcontacts.php is the same as the listing on the main page:

```
<?php
$query="select * from contacts order by name";
$rs=mysql_query($query,$db);
while ($myrow=mysql_fetch_assoc($rs)){
    $name=$myrow['name'];
?>
<div><?echo $name;?></div>
<?
}//while
```

The record adder, addcontact.php, is also simple:

```php
<?php
$name=$_GET['name'];
$name=str_replace("\'","'",$name);
$name=str_replace("'","\'",$name);
include 'connect.php'; //get a DB handle

$query="insert into contacts(name) values ('$name')";
mysql_query($query,$db);
```

Of course you may write the above XHR requests in a non-blocking manner. Make sure the second request is sent in the callback function of the first XHR object. Two levels of nested callbacks can look messy.

The main issues with this pattern are duplicate code and excess connection. The query-bind-render routine is written in both the main page and listcontacts.php. Adding a record also takes 2 XHR requests.

We'll address these issues later.

Pattern 2 - JavaScript Rendering

The second pattern is not an improvement of the first one. But you will see this pattern in other programmers' code. The basic idea is to transmit "pure data" and synthesize the HTML code using JavaScript.

First let's rewrite listcontacts.php to print a JSON object:

```php
$recs=array();
$query="select * from contacts order by name";
$rs=mysql_query($query,$db);
while ($myrow=mysql_fetch_array($rs)){
  array_push($recs, $myrow['name']);
}
echo json_encode($recs);
```

Alternatively you can build a JSON string manually:

```php
$str='';
$query="select * from contacts order by name";
$rs=mysql_query($query,$db);
while ($myrow=mysql_fetch_array($rs)){
```

```php
    $str.=",'". $myrow['name'])."'";
}
$str=trim($str,',');

echo "[$str]";
```

Since it's a simple array we're encoding, the output looks like this:

```
['Allen Test', 'Bob Smith', 'Cheryl Sandbox']
```

Instead of injecting the above array directly into a DIV container, we convert the string to a JavaScript array, then build an HTML string before injection:

```javascript
rq.onreadystatechange=function(){
  if (rq.readyState==4){
    var res=rq.responseText;
    var recs=eval(res); //recs is now an array
    var html='';
    for (var i=0;i<recs.length;i++){
      html.push('<div>'+recs[i]+'</div>');
    }//for
    gid('contactlist').innerHTML=html.join('');
    gid('newname').value='';
  }//readyState
}//onreadystatechange
```

The rationale behind this pattern is to separate presentation from data. It is also efficient in terms of data transfer. When your JavaScript logic needs to communicate with the server about raw data objects, this is a suitable pattern.

Most of the partial page updates are, however, simple content injections. There is no benefit of data and presentation separation in this case. Making HTML string is also slower in JavaScript than in PHP.

Another issue with this pattern is that the rendering routing has to be written twice. Once in PHP, for the initial display on the main page; then in JavaScript for AJAX load. Having two pieces of code doing the same thing is bad engineering. Basically there are two sets of code to maintain, and making a change in one doesn't change the behavior of the other, resulting in code inconsistency.

To work around this "double rendering" problem, many programmers cut corner by leaving the initial container (*contactlist*) empty. A extra XHR request is sent to bootstrap the screen:

```
<div id="contactlist"></div>
...
<script>
ajxpgn('contactlist','contactlist.php');
</script>
```

There are two problems with this. One is too many XHR requests. Imagine a web application that has 8 such widgets. Since the user can interact with one of them at any time, we won't always send too many XHR requests in parallel. The initial screen load, however, will send all 8 requests, plus the main page load.

The second problem is search engine visibility. Search bots do not typically support JavaScript. Instead of seeing a list of contacts it sees an empty container.

Pattern 3 - JavaScript Callback

This pattern is a variation of Patter 2. Instead of returning the string presentation of a JSON object, the server response calls a function. The sample output in the last pattern now becomes this:

```
listcontacts_callback(
    ['Allen Test', 'Bob Smith', 'Cheryl Sandbox']
);
```

On the receiving end, the XHR callback function sees the response as a string. We use "eval" to bring meaning to this string:

```
...
var res=rq.responseText;
eval(res);
...
```

This will call a function *listcontacts_callback*, which is defined as following:

```
function listcontacts_callback(recs){
```

```
    var html='';
    for (var i=0;i<recs.length;i++){
      html.push('<div>'+recs[i]+'</div>');
    }//for
    gid('contactlist').innerHTML=html.join('');
    gid('newname').value='';
}
```

This pattern is essentially a restructure of Pattern 2. Instead of returning a JSON object, it calls a function that takes the very object as a parameter.

This pattern has an official name - JSONP, or "JSON with padding".

So what's the big deal with JSONP? Can it do anything that the JSON pattern cannot do?

The answer is yes. JSONP allows us to perform an AJAX call to a different domain - something that XHR cannot do because of the same-origin policy.

When a string containing a script block is added to the DOM tree, the script is executed. Also, when a string that presents a JavaScript function call is added as a script block, the function call is executed.

We already know that if we have the following test.js:

```
alert('hello!');
```

And include the file as a script:

```
<script src="test.js"></script>
```

The page will prompt "hello", as instructed by test.js.

In Chapter 8.2 we discussed the dynamic creation of DOM elements. Here we create a script block on the fly:

```
var script=document.createElement('script');
script.setAttribute('src','listcontacts.php');
document.body.appendChild(script);
```

The above code will execute the server response and subsequently call the *listcontacts_callback* function. Since the script source can be hosted on any domain, the above code effectively makes a cross-domain AJAX call.

Pattern 4 - Content Piggyback

The patterns we've seen so far have the same data flow. A first XHR request updates the database; a second request updates the view. Pattern 2 and 3 use different techniques to load and display the view. But we are still sending two requests.

What if we combine addcontact.php and listcontacts.php and use one round-trip to both update the database and retrieve the latest contact list?

```php
<?php //addcontact.php

$name=$_GET['name'];
$name=str_replace("\'","'",$name);
$name=str_replace("'","\'",$name);
include 'connect.php'; //get a DB handle

$query="insert into contacts(name) values ('$name')";
mysql_query($query,$db);

include 'listcontacts.php';
```

The server-side include allows us to reuse the rendering code. The same *listcontacts.php* can be included in the main page. This solves the "double-rendering" problem.

The client side function can now be written more efficiently:

```
function addcontact(){
  var name=encodeHTML(gid('newname').value);
  var rq=xmlHTTPRequestObject();
  rq.open('GET', 'addcontact.php?name='+name,true);
  rq.onreadystatechange=function(){
    if (rq.readyState==4){
      gid('contactlist').innerHTML=rq.responseText;
      gid('newname').value='';
```

```
  }
 }
 rq.send(null);
}
```

We can take a step further by moving the "new name" input field into *listcontacts.php*. Then instead of reloading the *contactlist* container, we reload the *contacts* container altogether. Since the new input field has no initial value, this reload removes the need to manually clear the input field.

In fact the entire function can be written using the *ajxpgn* function in Antradar's *nano.js* library:

```
ajxpgn('contacts',
    'addcontact.php?name='+encodeHTML(gid('newname').value));
```

And yes, that's a one-liner.

9.3 The LCHH Architecture

I created the LCHH architecture to take full advantage of the XHR data flow, as showing in AJAX Pattern 4 in the previous chapter. The architecture allows quick development, easy maintenance, efficient execution and low resource consumption.

LCHH, pronounced as L-C-H (second H is silent), stands for Loader, Content, client-side Handler and server-side Handler. The following diagram shows how these components fit together:

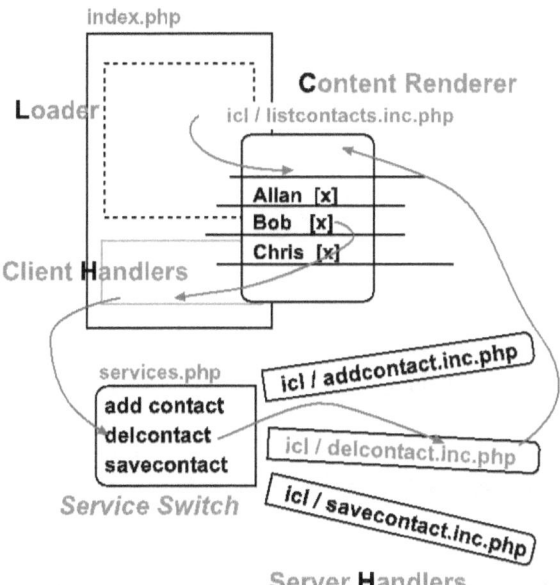

index.php

Loader

Content Renderer

icl / listcontacts.inc.php

Allan [x]

Bob [x]

Chris [x]

Client Handlers

services.php

icl / addcontact.inc.php

add contact

delcontact

savecontact

icl / delcontact.inc.php

Service Switch

icl / savecontact.inc.php

Server Handlers

The Pattern 4 code we wrote in the previous chapter can be easily transformed to LCHH.

First, move listcontacts.php to a sub folder "icl". Rename the file to listcontacts.inc.php.

Then we put the code in listcontacts.inc.php in a function:

```php
<?php
function listcontacts(){
  global $db;

  $query="select * from contacts order by name";
  $rs=mysql_query($query,$db);

  while ($myrow=mysql_fetch_assoc($rs)){
      $name=$myrow['name'];
      $contactid=$myrow['contactid'];
  ?>
  <div>
      <?echo $name;?>
      <a onclick="delcontact('<?echo $contactid;?>');">[x]</a>
  </div>
```

```
<?
}//while
?>
<div>
<input id="newname">
<button onclick="addcontact();">Add</button>
</div>
<?
}//function
```

Note that including listcontacts.inc.php doesn't automatically print the contact list. The function has to be called. This arrangement allows better code reuse.

The main file, index.php, loads the list in the loading container:

```
<?php
include 'icl/listcontacts.inc.php';
?>
...
<div id="contacts">
<? listcontacts(); ?>
</div>
```

Now load index.php in a browser. You should see a list of contacts. Next to each context there's a [x] symbol to remove the contact, and an "Add" button for inserting a new contact.

The deletion and insertion links call the JavaScript functions, or client-side handlers *delcontact* and *addcontact* respectively. This functions are defined at the bottom of index.php:

```
<script>
function delcontact(contactid){
  if (!confirm('Are you sure you want to delete this
contact?')) return;
  ajxpgn('contacts','delcontact.php?contactid='+contactid);
}

function addcontact(){
  var name=encodeHTML(gid('newname').value);
```

```
  if (name=='') return;
  ajxpgn('contacts','addcontact.php?name='+name);
}
</script>
```

Both JavaScript functions communicate with the server via XHR, and using AJAX Pattern 4, populate the container with piggy-backed content. For example, delcontact.php is written as following:

```
<?php
include 'icl/listcontacts.inc.php';
include 'connect.php'; //get DB handle

$contactid=$_GET['contactid']+0;
$query="delete from contacts where contactid=$contactid";
mysql_query($query,$db);

listcontacts();
```

And addcontact.php follows the same pattern:

```
<?php
include 'icl/listcontacts.inc.php';
include 'connect.php'; //get DB handle
$name=$_GET['name'];
$name=str_replace("'",'',$name);
$query="insert into contacts(name) values('$name')";
mysql_query($query,$db);

listcontacts();
```

The above two PHP scripts are server-side handlers. The output of these functions are directly injected into the Loaders as the new Content. This completes an LCHH cycle.

Let's quickly walk through the implementation process again. Note how each component is built in the same order as code execution. For example, the container DIV tag is declared, and thus rendered first. The content file, *listcontacts.php* is loaded next. The content contains links and buttons to click, which subsequently invoke client-side handlers, which further call server-side handlers, which, in turn, returns the updated content after some database work.

Since the files are organized along the execution path, stepping through an LCHH program is straight forward.

An actual LCHH setup would put both *delcontact.php* and *addcontact.php* in the *icl* sub folder, and factor out the common include files such as the database connection. Introducing the "big fork", services.php:

```php
<?php
include 'connect.php';

$cmd=$_GET['cmd'];
switch ($cmd){
    case 'addcontact':
        include 'icl/addcontact.inc.php';
        addcontact();
    break;
    case 'delcontact':
        include 'icl/delcontact.inc.php';
        delcontact();
    break;
}
```

The URL parameter in the XHR call needs some modification:

```
ajxpgn('contacts',
    'services.php?cmd=delcontact&contactid='+contactid);
```

Now it's a lot easier to manage all the server-side handlers. With a single point of entry, we can add user authentication, helper functions and other shared features by changing just one file.

You may have noticed that the server-side handlers are included inside the switch condition. This makes the script both memory efficient and less prone to syntax error related down time. If all the functions are defined in the same file, or all the handlers are included in the same file, any syntax error in any module will bring down the entire fork. Including the files separately makes the script more robust.

As an interpretive language, PHP builds an internal presentation of the code (in the form of a tree). The amount of memory required is often proportional to the script length. This is even true with accelerated and JIT-compiled PHP environments. By segmenting the functions into individual files, we keep memory consumption minimum.

Thank you for having read this far. It has been an honour to write for you. Believe it or not, this is not the final chapter of this book. As I refine both my coding and teaching techniques I will update and add chapters to revisions of the book. For those who have worked with me, or are still working with me, you understand that the last chapter of this revision, LCHH, is the mere beginning of endless possibilities.

Acknowledgement

Throughout the course of my professional development I've had the luck of working with some extremely bright minds. The following friends and co-workers have contributed tremendously to the knowledge system I have today. Thank you!

Matei Zaharia, *University of Waterloo*
Nicholas Engelking, *Scotiabank*
Steve Fredette, *Endeca Technologies*
Chris Roby, *Endeca Technologies*

* the organizations in the above list are where these friends worked at the time that we collaborated; many of them are now working at different positions or companies.

I'm also grateful of the facilities and learning environment the following organizations have made available to me. In an effort to sustain the educational capability of these organizations, so that they can nurture new generations of developers, part of the sales from this book, as well as copies of the book are donated as training material or technical reference.

The Toronto Public Library
Office of Research, University of Waterloo
Innovate Inc. [1], University of Waterloo
Test Automation Group, Scotiabank
Spec Ops[2], Endeca Technologies
Boston Public Library

---

[1] Now part of University of Waterloo Enterprise Co-op Education
[2] Dissolved; Endeca is now part of Oracle.

www.ingramcontent.com/pod-product-compliance
Lightning Source LLC
Chambersburg PA
CBHW031819170526
45157CB00001B/116